Letter from America

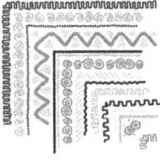

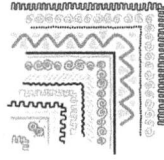

Letter from America

Memoir of an Adopted Child

Gil Ndi-Shang

Spears Media Press
DENVER, COLORADO

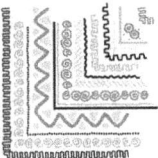

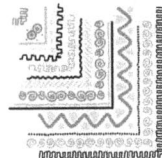

Spears Media Press LLC
DENVER
7830 W. Alameda Ave, Suite 103-247 Denver, CO 80226
United States of America

First Published in 2019 by Spears Media Press
www.spearsmedia.com
info@spearsmedia.com
Information on this title: www.spearsmedia.com/shop/letter-from-america

Library of Congress Control Number: 2019954919

ISBN: 9781942876489 (Paperback)
ISBN: 9781942876496 (eBook)

Also available in Kindle

Spears Media Press has no responsibility for the persistence or accuracy of urls for external or
third-party internet websites referred to in this publication, and does not guarantee that any
content on such websites is, or will remain, accurate or appropriate.

Book Design by Spears Media Press
Cover Design by Doh Kambem

To all those for whom the face of the other is a passion

Contents

Superiority? Inferiority? Why not the quite simple attempt to touch the other, to feel the other, to explain the other to myself? Was my freedom not given to me then in order to build the world of the You?

Frantz Fanon, *Black Skin, White Masks*, 1952.

Prologue

Letter from America
In memory of Sir Alistair Cooke

Upon arriving in Peru, I wrote to a friend of mine residing in the UK on Facebook telling him that I was in America. He asked me in which State I was. I told him I did not mean "USA" but rather "America". Once I made plain to him that I was actually in Peru, I could sense the prestige I earlier aroused in him turn into disappointment and even a slight sense of mockery. After dabbling with the location of Peru on the world map, he said: "If you meant the other America, you should have specified "South America" and not just say "America". Now, like my friend you may blame me for being imprecise; the truth, however, is that our exchange revealed a deeply entrenched tendency (not to say fallacy) in almost all of us. I am always intrigued each time I read news reports in the Spanish daily El País concerning the United States of America. They have the habit of using the Spanish "norte americano" for the attribute "American", whereas the Spanish version rather means "North American" in English. To me, this seemed slightly odd. Why couldn't they just say "Americano", the direct Spanish rendition of "American"?

This took me back to one of the greatest contemporary icons in the field of radio broadcasting: Sir Alistair Cooke (1908-2004) who presented the BBC World Service Radio programme "Letter from America" for more than half a century. A Briton by birth but naturalised American, Cooke presented various faces, phases, events and processes of US (American) history to a Great British (i.e. global) audience. In his usually playful but insightful style, Sir Cooke asks in one of his letters: "Who was the First Whiteman to discover America?" He goes further to state that America "was accidentally named after the Florentine business-man and promoter, Amerigo Vespucci, who promoted himself so well that he got his name attached first to South America, and then to the whole continent, though he took no part in the early voyages. But the first? We simply do not know." Amerigo was a good promoter, the first American, a perfect one for that matter whose disputable letters from America almost sought to displace the legacy of Christopher Columbus. Columbus discovered America, Vespucci sold it.

Secondly, it would come as a surprise to many today that Vespucci's "America" initially referred to "South America". However, by a gradual process of history, a complex interplay of soft and hard power, the entitling dimension of the name "America" has come to represent the United States of America. From the Monroe Doctrine of 1823 through Andrew Jackson's Manifest Destiny of 1845, to the Cold War interventions, contemporary gold rush and neoliberal "coca-colonisation", the South has had to struggle with its rather bossy Northern neighbour. (If European housewives' obsession for Indian spices led their husbands to war in India in the 17th century, the hunt for South American natural resources in the current century still reaps strips of land bear, creating new Potosis and triggering immense social tensions in a town like Cajamarca, Peru, where the Peruvian jamboree all started in the 16th century. The Monroe Doctrine, in particular, is "commemorated" in these parts as the official transition from Spanish and Portuguese hegemony to the avuncular influence of Uncle Sam. The supremacist tendencies in the North were so rife that even a foolhardy mercenary like William Walker could organise private military expeditions to establish colonies in Mexico and Central America. Of course, Walker met his death in Honduras, defeated and executed in 1860 by the government of that country, after having usurped Nicaraguan presidential powers from 1856-57. There was no doubt that his filibustering could have continued further South. Following the footsteps of his ancestors, Walker wanted to "do America", not from Europe this time around, rather from America. Considered by some of his compatriots as a patriot and by others as a pirate, General Walker's dreams were far-reaching, even more than those of that true son of British Empire, Cecile Rhodes, whose aim was to offer Queen Victoria the African territory that stretched from Cape to Cairo as a gift.

What happened that modernity's first son had to constantly grapple with its overruling sibling from the north? Let us turn to history. The historical destinies of the two American poles are like ships that crossed at night. While the New England colonies found a formula to yoke together into a confederation after defeating the English King George III's forces, New Spain, however, knew a different fate. In spite of the fervent attempts at unification by the continent's most illustrious son Simon Bolivar (claimed by some historians to be partially of African descent[1]) and his lieutenant San Martin, the continent ended up being balkanised by particularistic nationalisms. The cracks were already evident during the central authority of viceregal Lima, "the City of Kings" and the eventual decentralisation of power through the creation of the viceroyalties of Nueva Grenada (1717) and Rio de la Plata (1776). At the time of independence, the continent got parcelled out almost strictly along the lines of its influential trading ports controlled by both peninsular Spanish and Creole merchants, battling for commercial supremacy. But what if Bolivar's union plan had succeeded? What would have been the consequence on the balance of power in world history? Well, the great wizard of the Second World War History, A J P Taylor once wondered: "How can we decide about something that did not happen? Heaven knows, we have difficulty enough in deciding what did happen." But it is in the very nature of man to figure out the possibilities of history beyond what actually happened. In spite of his prior admiration for the United States of America, some may consider premonitory his statement that that nation's "tale of liberty will end in a plague for us all…the United States, which seems destined by Providence to plague America with miseries in the name of liberty."

Bolivar had much in common with the American Fabius, George Washington. Both were key masonic members, even Masters. Washington was Grand Master of the Grand Lodge of the American Free Masons. Bolivar was a Master Mason, who was initiated in Cadiz but frequented many Masonic Lodges in European capitals during his time in Europe in the first quarter of the 19th century. Both were valiant soldiers and seasoned strategists. Last but not least, both men owned slaves in spite of their libertarian creeds. In some sense, they were men of their time. But the Grand Architect of guerra a muerte (war to death) did not share the strong republican values and the anecdotic humility of Washington, who despite his immense popularity, denied calls for a third term of office and purported proposals to be crowned George I of America in replacement of George III of England. Bolivar's dictatorial tendencies in Gran Colombia (present-day Colombia, Ecuador, Venezuela, Panama,

---

1   According to Gene H. Bell-Villada, "in his vein there coursed some African blood, result of an illicit liaison between a remote peninsular ancestor and a black slave" in *Garcia Marquez: The Man and his Work* (2010).

a small part of Peru, northwest Brazil and a small portion of Guyana) were soon manifest in his parliamentary arm-twisting to enable him to concentrate power on the executive, i.e, on himself. One of the casualties of Bolivar's inclinations for absolute loyalty would be his hitherto henchman, the black General Jose Prudencio Padilla, nicknamed "the Black Nelson" thanks to his valour in the Spanish Army in the Battle of Trafalgar (1805) against Lord Nelson's forces and his tremendous sacrifice for the Bolivarian battles for independence. In a spurious court case, he was hanged on 26 May 1828 for planning a black revolt against Simon Bolivar. Colombian blacks, including Padilla, had insisted that Bolivar comply with the treaty signed with Haitian President Alexandre Pétion who virtually sponsored Bolivar's wars in men, ammunition and money. In fact, Pétion psychologically resuscitated the deeply depressed Bolivar, almost on the brink of suicide after a disastrous first round of independence battles. Paradoxically, as almost everything American, Haiti was not invited (even as an observer) to the Panama Congress of 1826, aimed at charting a unifying ground future for the continent. The sidelining of Haiti coincided with the relegation of Blacks in Bolivar's continent in spite of their being used as cannon fodder in the independence battles, first by royalists, but later on mostly by patriotic forces. From Cartagena to Titicaca, from Chacabuco to Ayacucho, the story was the same. The story in Washington's land was no better. Anyway, that is another story.

Bolivar's attempt to bring Peru and Bolivia into a union in order to eventually include them in a grand confederation with Grand Colombia was short-lived. Bolivia and Peru preferred good neighbourliness, though not always as good, to building political capital out of their shared Inca lineage. Anyway, though not ready for the deal, the Bolivian Congress compensated Bolivar by naming their new country after him: Bolivar. But as he turned his back to La Paz, the "Bolivarian" Congress inserted an "i" between the "v" and "a" and did away with the "r". When Bolivar reached Bogota, he had to cope with the subtle rejection. The story ended. In his core constituencies of Colombia, Venezuela, Panama and Ecuador, Bolivar's project also shattered. As I am writing this section, today 7 December 2015, Bolivar's compatriot Nicolás Maduro is making a speech (full of superlatives) after losing elections in yesterday's historic parliamentary elections. Not only is his stature overshadowed by the watchful eyes of El Libertador Bolivar and El Comandante Chavez on the wall behind him, he can't afford to make a statement without quoting these two figures. Bolivar is in the room, Chavez is watching. We may lose a battle, but like Bolivar, we will win the war.

When I visited the stand of the Venezuelan Embassy during the Lima Book Fair in July 2015, the lady in charge subjected me to a long historical treatise on her country, and by some implication, that of the continent. After a profuse use of the word El Comandante in a way that I previously thought was more typical of Che Guevara whereas she meant Chavez, she handed me three things: the Venezuelan Constitution, brief biographies of Simon Bolivar and Hugo Chavez and a handbook of "gift" projects that Venezuela has sponsored in almost the whole continent, including Haiti and Peru. I felt like Barack Obama, receiving a gift from El Comandante Chavez: Eduardo Galeano's The Open Wounds of Latin America[2]. I do not know how exactly Obama felt, but in my case, the booklets were quite heavy in my hands, but more so in my mind. Coincidentally, Galeano's book was the first-ever gift I received from a South American, a Peruvian Professor based in Hamburg, Germany in 2012. It was the first book I ever read from cover to cover from that continent. After a roundtable presentation organised by the Uruguayan Embassy in Peru during the aforementioned Book Fair, I went up to congratulate the ambassador for his wonderful endeavour. After confessing to him that Galeano is one of my favourite authors for his ability to look at history from contrapuntal perspectives, with much insightful reference to African history, I won't forget the embrace I received from him, far beyond the diplomatic code of conduct most often based on reservation and restraint.

Let us turn to the North again, not to meet Obama, but rather to listen to vintage Sir Alistair Cooke. In one of his letters on the continuous subtle disregard for Americans by the British, he states that: "A small but telling sign has been that many Englishmen, beneath the surface admission that Americans have developed their own civilization, still think of Americans as Englishmen gone wrong." I guess he means the United States here but it would be interesting to then know what Englishmen think of South Americans, though it won't matter as much. Anyway, no people are better placed to pass such a judgment than Englishmen, the only people, and I say this without any fear of contradiction, who

---

2   First published in 1971, it details the colonial empire in Latin America from an economic perspective. In theme and tone, it is somewhat the Latin American version of Walter Rodney's *How Europe Underdeveloped Africa* (1972)

throughout history have always done the right thing at the right time. As Bernard Shaw once said, one thing admirable about Englishmen is that they do everything out of principles. They crown a King out of principle and later on kill him on principles. They know when to start but perhaps, more importantly, when to end something. And when the time for ending comes, they summon their friends and even coerce them to do same. Trade in spices. You name the rest. Had Bernard Shaw lived longer, perhaps he would have admired to some extent, the same quality in the Englishmen gone wrong, the Americans. Anyway, the Nobel laureate passed away in 1950 when America began applying principles more strictly.

Coming back to the South, I wish to present my diary on Peru. In a postcolonial age where our colonialist epistemologies have taken refuge in lexicons baked in political correctness, I know it is a dangerous endeavour to write about a country/continent without being blamed for stereotypical othering. I agree. But I bet you we might also agree that Sir Alistair Cooke, one of the many Englishmen in "foreign service" who truly deserve their knighthood, did this with a masterly hand. It is this great man whose footsteps I wish to follow, for are we not in some sense aspirants of the Anglo-American tradition? Being adopted in Peru just within a very short time upon my arrival, I felt I should report to my friends "back home" in response to their curiosities about life in Peru, America. Therefore, I chose the memoir form, in pursuit of Alistair Cooke's style but even more so of the conquistadors who reported back home to friends and relatives on their experiences in and impressions of the New World through letters and memoir entries. Five hundred years after, popular opinions about the continent are still to some extent shaped by these diaries. The trip to America was a journey into myself, my memories, those of my race, my continent. The people I met, the places I visited, the mutual gazes, my hopes and fears, the happy moments as well as dour occasions make up my travel memoir. I write to represent the tracks and traces of my memory, perhaps also part of your memory, deeply convinced that there is America in you and me, and lastly, that America is human. I feel the impulse to write because no one visits America without having a slight and almost illusory sense of having made a discovery.

Gil Ndi-Shang
7 December 2015, Bayreuth, Germany

Acknowledgments

I am deeply beholden to my colleagues Serawit Bekele, Nsah Mala, Jimam Lar, Simon Nganga, Nsaibirni Warren and Ndi Derrick Nganji for going through the manuscript at various stages and making invaluable and critical suggestions. I have come to regard the gesture of reading the early versions of a colleague's manuscript as true love hard-earned! My humble gratitude also goes to my literati mentors Eunice Ngongkum and Christopher Joseph Odhiambo with whom I shared many of the stories recounted here. Their creative (mis)readings of some of the episodes often compelled me to look at them through different lenses. I am profoundly indebted to the venerated African writer, Ngũgĩ wa Thiong'o for finding time out of his busy schedule to read the manuscript and to let me know his take on both the style and content. It is through the works of pillars like Ngũgĩ that I have come to value the power of (re) telling and the connections that narratives (re)build.

CHAPTER 1

Beginnings

From my German hometown Bayreuth, I arrived in Frankfurt on the eve of my flight to Lima through Atlanta, USA. However, I had to cancel the flight to Atlanta because I could not obtain a United States transit visa at the Frankfurt airport as I hoped. I had called the American Airlines agent to inquire before and she assured me it was possible. She thought I was German. Only citizens of specific countries like Germany could do that. As a Cameroonian, I needed to go through a complete visa application process. That would take more than a month. Just to get an embassy appointment was not possible within three weeks. It was a lost battle. Luckily enough, I had a rather narrow escape - I cancelled my ticket just in time to get a full reimbursement and be able to search for an alternative flight from Frankfurt to Lima without transiting through a US airport. With the help of a very kind American Airlines travel agent, I got an Air France flight that would take me to Lima through Paris' Charles de Gaulle airport. That flight was at 4 A.M. the next morning after my scheduled flight! I could not even think of spending the night in a hotel or hostel.

The other inconvenient detail about the new flight: I was only allowed one full luggage and one hand luggage. I had brought two half-full bags along. From the very start, arranging my bags for this trip was a puzzle. What should I take along? Apart from my host whom I knew through Facebook, I could not imagine the kind of friends I would make in Peru. What would be their tastes? What would they expect from a friend travelling from Germany? Another reason for the two bags was in expectation of what I might bring home from Peru. Perhaps some foodstuffs like those in Cameroon, perhaps something different but beautiful. Now I had to prioritize and possibly leave certain things at the airport. Therefore, I squeezed my luggage, leaving out some of the few clothes that I could dispose of if necessary. I also left out three bottles of Dornfelder wine which I had bought for my yet-unknown-friends in Lima. I then

1

took the bag to the check-in desk to be weighed. This was just so that the following day (the day of my flight) I should not have anything to worry about. The lady told me the weight had an excess of 1 kilogramme. 'That is ok, don't bother, it is not much', she told me. I tried to inquire how much it would cost me to keep the bag at the reserve luggage store for the one month I would be in Peru. For the empty bag, it would be €5 a day. Multiply it by the number of days you would be away. I just didn't want to get the result of the arithmetics. I had bought that bag for €20. I carefully took the empty bag to the information desk to inquire where I could dispose of it. The lady directed me to the corner where I could leave it, near other bags and objects of a similar fate. It was painful throwing away the bag but I had no choice; I had no acquaintance in Frankfurt whom I could call to pick it up.

As for the bottles of wine, I had to find a way of consuming them at the airport! I took a seat in front of a restaurant, three bottles of wine in my hand luggage. I tried to talk to a young guy sitting close by. He was quite friendly. I told him I had some wine and I needed some company for a drink. I explained the situation to him. He told me he just freshly arrived from Australia and was waiting for his grandparents to pick him up to Munich. He was quite enthusiastic about sharing some wine with me and dashed into the nearby shop to get some plastic cups. He told me he was of Russian origin but was living in Germany, with a German passport, which he accidentally washed in his trouser pockets. He showed me the quasi-passport, totally battered. He had had to get a supporting document from the German Embassy in Australia to be able to get back home. Fortunately, he got no problems on the way. He had been doing what is known as travel-and-work programme whereby he could visit several South-East Asian countries while earning money through short-term employment contracts. It was a form of tourism, he told me. "I just enjoy travelling", he confessed. "Me too," I told him.

He was an incredibly easy-going guy, with great ability to develop familiarity with a stranger at a very short interval. He later introduced me to some Russian friends, a man and lady, whom I quickly guessed were a couple. Yes, they were. I was surprised by the air of familiarity between them and my newly begotten friend. I thought they had been travelling together. No, they had just met at the airport some few minutes before, my friend explained to me. The lady had to visit the toilet and could not find her way. She had come up to him to inquire and he immediately noticed that she spoke English with difficulty. From her

accent, he had guessed she could be Russian and had responded immediately in Russian. She was pleasantly surprised at that. So the bond was
created. When she had come back from the toilet, she had thanked him
and had gone ahead to introduce him to her husband who was standing
near the restaurant with their luggage.

The lady was very communicative. Her husband, on the contrary,
was rather a man of few words. Whenever she had difficulties express-
ing herself in English, my friend and I helped her along by filling in the
gaps. We talked about life in Germany, Russia, Cameroon and the Asian
countries my traveller-friend had visited. It was such a nice meeting of
people brought together by circumstances. After drinking about two
glasses of wine each, the Russian couple thanked us and left.

My friend told me his battery was low and risked getting flat before
his grandparents arrived. I located a socket at the corner behind where
we were sitting. I also needed to recharge my laptop. We decided to relo-
cate our bottle of wine and our entire luggage to a small corner, beside a
glittering jaguar car on exhibition. We just sat there on the floor, sipping
our wine and chatting as a stream of passengers passed by, arriving in
their numbers as the flight agents announced arrivals from Minneapolis,
Athens, Barcelona, Bogota, New Delhi, Cairo, etc. The airport is a space
of absolute freedom under the auspices of the camera. The gaze of the
passing police officer is both incisive and relaxed, disinterestedly interested. One of them passed by us, grinned very snappily, a rather legal
smile. Later, he passed by again, this time with his colleague. He came
closer and greeted us while his friend stood, watching.

"Is everything ok?"

"Yes, we are fine", we answered, almost in a chorus. He tried to be as
friendly as a security officer can be. I felt as if that question ought to be
kindly thrown back at him. We had just no problem. He went back to
his friend and they continued without exchanging a single word. Well,
for the airport police officer, words do not count for much. Looks alone
contain many pages. But from the *look* of things, he was convinced we
were just having a nice time with wine. Nothing to bother about. The
port security officer is law and order incarnated. Even his body movements, his steps and facial expressions respond to the edicts of the rules.
The geometry of their movement is usually quite curious. They walk by
the book.

Later on, my friend's grandparents came to pick him up. He noticed
them from far; one could say he scented their presence.

"Hey my friend, see you again." He said as he hugged me.

"Ok. Thank you so much for your company, see you next time." I replied.

I exchanged only eye contacts with his grandparents who stood by while he packed his accessories into his backpack. I was left alone and there was still half a bottle to finish. It was getting to 10 P.M. This means I still had twelve hours to go. I moved close to the bare bench where I had to spend the night. Then I discovered I had not even exchanged contacts with my friend that just left. Not even Facebook. We did not even ask for each other's names!

The airport was getting a bit dry but flight arrivals were announced: Madrid and Munich. A smartly dressed guy was sitting on the edge of the bench. He came closer to me and introduced himself in very exquisite German. He was Ahmet, from Morocco. He had lived in Germany for the past 12 years and had the habit of going home every year for Ramadan. Ramadan was in less than a week. Ahmet was such a chatty guy and we literally killed the night by just talking. We talked about life in Germany, our professions and terrorism. I will never forget the energy with which Ahmet condemned those who commit suicide bombing in the name of Islam. "They are just bastards, these guys." He told me. I almost asked him to reduce his pitch so we do not attract any kind of attention.

We both spent the night on the bench. At 5 A.M. Ahmet woke me up to bid me farewell. He hugged me and said: "You will travel safe, Inshallah." After that, I continued on the bench but I doubt if I slept again. The airport was already like a beehive. I was in-between day-dreaming, wakefulness and sleep. I finally stood up at some few minutes past 6 A.M. I lingered around and went to the washroom to clean up. I checked in at almost 8:30 A.M. for the flight to Paris. At the check-in point, I was distracted by a family; seemingly American from the accent, laughing out their lungs, casting out veiled glances at a group of Chinese gathered around the corner. Their pitch was quite high and almost everyone's attention was drawn towards them. It became even more interesting when the Chinese group leader started reading out the names from the attendance list. The two boys were shivering with laughter, resting their chin on their mother's laps. She tried to hush them down to no avail. Their dad just kept a tight face as if the kids were not his. After restraining the giggling kids in vain, the lady helplessly joined in the fray, basically choking.

We passed through the security checks and proceeded to the boarding.

It was a hitch-free flight from Frankfurt to Paris. Roughly fifty-five minutes. I had close to two hours of transit time in Paris. Boarded the flight to Lima at 1.30 P.M. but the airliner effectively took off at 2.40 P.M., with nearly 30 minutes delay. Duration - 11 hours 50 minutes, says the screen. Excited but uncertain about what awaited me in Peru.

I was set for the journey to the New World, to discover South America. I felt like a new Columbus, a black Pizarro, with all the ambition and uncertainty that go with it. Perhaps, armed with the Bible, these five-hundred-year-old precursors had a more promising and self-assuring mission. What awaited me in my adventure? What kind of people was I going to meet there? How would they relate to me? All kinds of projections flooded my mind. History connected me to South America. Certainly, one of my forefathers crossed to this continent under very different conditions, centuries ago. Connection through chains, of human goods, connection by separation. The two continents have remained somewhat strange to one another since then, both looking to the northern rays for salvation. The North wounds, the North heals, perhaps.

CHAPTER 2

Bienvenido a Lima

15 July 2015

I arrived in Lima at 7:36 P.M., almost thirty minutes later than the estimated time. Of course, with the delay in Paris, this was foreseeable. After luggage claim, I moved on to the currency exchange kiosk to convert the euros I had on me into Peruvian *nuevos soles*. Since some money exchange booth operators all over the world are short-change artists, I made sure I counted my banknotes meticulously, weighing them carefully against the exchange rates. I then proceeded like all other passengers to the customs. My luggage passed through the security machine and I collected it at the other end. The lady behind the control machine was quite friendly, nothing of the stern and rather astute countenance of a standard airport security officer. *Bienvenido a Lima,* came the sound of her voice, accompanied by an enchanting smile. What a cosy way of receiving a stranger to a city, to a country, to a continent. LATIN AMERICA. How did the name move from Spanish America to Latin America? I wondered. There was certainly some politics of naming that I shall need to examine closely.

As I moved out of the airport, the historical knowledge in my mind touched the ground. Latin America, there is that sense of meeting something strange and familiar. I might have read several books, conversed severally with Peruvian and Latin American friends, but approaching it from the historical point of it being the historical first son of the enlightenment project, there was something special about setting foot on that continent, on its hitherto capital Lima, *la ciudad de los reyes*, "the City of the Kings", The Rome of Latin America. So much buried under the ground, almost literally, a place where fiction meets reality in a continuum.

Outside, roughly ten metres from the exit door, there was a multitude waiting for their loved ones, family members, business partners and, perhaps, customers. Many carried different forms of placards with names of persons they were looking out for. *Señora*¹ Milli Sanchez, my host's friend, had promised to pick me up from the airport in her car. I had written to her earlier on to inform her of the delay at Frankfurt airport. By the time I was leaving, she had not yet responded. I craned around once more but saw nothing similar to my name. I also scanned through the crowd to see if someone looked like Milli. I had only seen her picture on Facebook and hoped she was not too different. All in vain.

One man, well-kempt, in sleeve pleated shirt, looking relatively old, having noticed me trying to peer helplessly at the raised nametags, came and inquired which direction I wanted to take.

"Don't bother, *Señor*², certainly the person has not come. It happens very often. I am willing to take you to your destination," he said, brandishing his taxi-driving card to me. I told him I had to call my host to know exactly what happened to the arrangement with Milli Sanchez. He offered to call for me, saving me the trouble of looking for a phone booth around that area. He then dialled the number and gave me the handset to converse with Elena Alvarez, my host.

"Hi Elena, it's Gil."

"Hi, Gil. I hope you arrived safely."

"Yes Elena, but I can't see Milli anywhere here. Is there anything amiss?"

"Oh! Perhaps you did not see her last message to you. She called me yesterday saying her cousin fell sick and she is with her in the hospital tonight. Just take any taxi and it will bring you here, *Jirón Soledad 565, Cuadra 26 de Avenida Petit-Thouars*. It will cost you about S/60."

"Ok Elena. No problem. See you soon."

The taxi driver followed our discussion anxiously and was finally happy for getting a customer. He agreed to the price and so we went out to his vehicle, a Toyota corolla in perfect shape. He was quite a lovely old man. On our way, we discussed life in Lima, a city of about 10 million inhabitants, almost 1/3 of the total population of Peru. He asked me about the political situation in Cameroon.

"It is a democracy, *mas o menos*."³

"*¿Por qué más o menos?*"⁴

---

1   Spanish word for "Ms."
2   "Sir."
3   "More or less"
4   "Why more or less"

"We have the same president for thirty-two years."

The guy burst into laughter and confessed he now understood why I used that expression. He told me the history of Peru had also been very turbulent until recently. Things are generally stable now. In the middle of the discussion, he insinuated, in a rather benign way, that I was going to pay him S/70 because the distance was QUITE far. And I should not forget his tip, he insisted.

I told him I would pay nothing more or less than what Elena recommended and to which he initially agreed. We argued in a very friendly way. I told him I was a student and did not have the status of the many tourists he was used to carrying.

"Oh, now you have become a student since I raised the fare to S/70!" He exclaimed, laughing.

"Both of us are students; we have been playing master and student on Cameroon and Peru respectively ever since we left the airport!" I retorted in the same jolly mood.

"I thought you have become a student just because of the taxi fare."

"Tell me, you said you were in Paris some days ago, how is Paris? Is it the gateway to heaven as we usually think here?" I smiled and responded. "Of course, it is a very beautiful city but not the gateway to heaven as such. I doubt if any place is! Every place has got its challenges. Life is quite expensive there for an average earner. For example, I went to a kiosk to buy a piece of *döner kebab*[5] and it costs €5.80 whereas in Berlin and most of Germany it is less than €4. However, it depends on what you want in any place in the world, you will always get it."

"Oh! I see, people here have a very high esteem about Paris. They also have good food. Above all, my friend, one thing you will enjoy in Peru is the food. Best in Latin America and even the world, only equal to Paris, but I am not sure."

"Oh, that is great, I have heard so much about Peruvian food. I hope to have a taste of that very soon."

"Sure, you will. And the women too!"

Our discussion was interrupted by an incoming call to which the driver responded with an expression full of slangs. I could hardly get a word. The remaining part of our trip was dedicated to a difficult German crash course.

---

5   Turkish dish consisting of spiced lamb or calf cooked on a spit and served in slices, typically with pitta bread and a variety of spices.

"How do you say good morning in German?"

"Guten Morgen."

"Biken Makene", he repeated after me, with enthusiasm.

"G-u-t-e-n M-o-r-g-e-n."

"P-u-t-i-n M-o-n-i-n-g-e-n."

It took us about ten similar trials to come to something that could be associated with the original German expression. In the end, I congratulated him for being a fast learner, in a bid to avoid him committing an accident for the sake of learning German.

I tried as much as possible to catch a glimpse of the city. When you arrive at a strange and foreign destination at night, it is a psychological torment. You are tormented with a sense of non-arrival, you feel frustrated that much is offered to you in twilight form. You wait impatiently for the light of the day in order to consume the full breadth of the city with your eyes, and since it is Peru we are talking about, with your mouth too. However, I was slightly disconcerted by the heavy trail of smoke that cars emitted as they drove. I always feel nauseated amid petrol scent, be it in Cameroon or Germany. It seemed Lima was not going to make the situation any better. From the cars on the avenues, you could notice the conviviality between American-style dream cars and more modest ones, some of whose slightly dirty linen could be perceived right from the outside.

"Tell me, my friend, since I arrived here I have not seen any signs of a black man. From the airport to where we are. Am I the black Columbus, coming to re-discover the new world?"

"Hahahahah! This young man is very funny. Hahahahaha! There are some blacks in Lima. But not many. Where you can see them in their numbers is in the town of Chincha. They have a big community there."

"Is it far from here? I would like to go there."

"Not very far, just about two hours drive. They usually organise cultural festivals and it is a big tourist attraction."

"I really would like to go there if time permits."

"Sure. Sure. You will identify with their dances... We are almost around the street to your destination. In two minutes, we will be there."

We arrived at Jirón Soledad 565 at about 9 P.M. Elena had been standing at the entrance with her friend. After embracing me, they offered to help me carry the bags. I settled the taxi bill as he was about to leave, the taxi driver said to me.

"Goodbye, my *Chinchano*[6] friend, have a nice time in Peru."

I answered: "Thank you," but Elena was not impressed by the driver's expression.

"Why call him *Chinchano?*"

"Just joking, we were just talking about Chincha some few minutes ago."

"He told me about Chinchano and I would like to go there." It is then that Elena calmed down. Certainly, she had taken offence for the appellation, with the lightheartedness, shown by the taxi driver. We went upstairs with the bags to the flat, the second floor of a green/white painted structure.

"Gil, this is your room."

"Thank you, Elena, it is nice meeting you finally."

"You are welcome."

"Thank you."

She showed me around the house and explained how to manage the main utilities. I took my bath soon after. When I was through, Elena invited me for coffee with pear and some biscuits, to the parlour where she had been drinking with her friend. I relished the combination. After a few minutes of self-presentation between the three of us, I took my leave to recover from the long and tiresome trip. More so, I had to make up for the night spent at the airport in Frankfurt.

---

6   Related to the town of Chincha, Peru.

CHAPTER 3

First Day in Lima

16 July 2015

In the morning, Carmen, Elena's tenant took a stroll around with me to show me a money exchange kiosk, cyber-café, and restaurants where I could eat good food at a relatively modest price range.

Lima is a busy city. I found myself in a situation like Yaoundé or Douala with the exception that the town is well planned. Less noise. Less crowdedness. Much cleaner. Everywhere there were restaurants and the most visible inscriptions by the roadsides are the menus of restaurants. I got into a restaurant and ordered some food. The menu read: *Chaufa con polllo.*[1] *Ceviche.*[2] *Lomo salteado.*[3] *Papa con frijoles*[4], etc. *Chaufa con pollo* was the only dish that was ready since it was a bit early. First, I am served hot soup full of onions and pieces of cassava and sweet potatoes. Then the main plate. Finally, salad was brought in. It was quite a delectable meal, with a measured mixture of a world of spices.

"Quite delicious."

"Thanks, see you next time," she responded, collecting the S/7 I handed to her and then the plates.

I asked my way to an electronics shop to buy a sim card and to unlock my phone to be able to use it in Peru. Most of the streetwalkers were just too busy to respond to any query. I decided to go into a store or a restaurant to ask for directions which they did very kindly. Eventually, I found my way to the technical centre where I got my phone first

---

1   Fried rice dish with chicken, a mixture of Peruvian and Chinese cuisine.

2   Seafood dish popular in Peru and other coastal regions of Ecuador, Colombia, Chile and Perú and other parts of Latin America. The dish is typically made from fresh raw fish cured in citrus juices, such as lemon or lime, and spiced with ají or chilli peppers.

3   A stir fry that typically combines marinated strips of sirloin (or another beef steak) with onions, tomatoes, french fries, and other ingredients; and is typically served with rice.

4   Sweet potatoes and beans.

unlocked and then bought a *claro* card.

From the technical centre, the open market is just a stone throw. I felt very much at home. It is a kind of Douala market on another continent. I could smell the same air, a mixture of all kinds of fruits and vegetables with the exposed chicken and beef. An immense array of fruits, more variety than what one finds in Germany or Cameroon. The inviting smile of market women, luring you to their products with an air of familiarity is extraordinary.

I was amazed by the presence of both private security agents and police officers in every corner of the street. Almost every fenced compound in Lima has got a guard, the G4S security agency is omnipresent in this town. I did not know G4S was so globalized. In front of the banks and especially the forest of American-style casinos that abound in Lima, you see a police officer standing, observing the goings. Strapped to his/her belt, visibly, threateningly, pornographically: a gun and the rim of cartridges, a stark warning to *rateros*[5] and *delincuentes*[6]. I have never touched a gun in my life, but every day I live with the ugly reality of this strange object. I have never summoned enough courage to peer into the dark trunk of its muzzle. Imagine the dreams it shattered, the lives it destroyed, and then the bodies it injured to death. The nothingness it produces. When I told Elena I have never touched a gun in my life, she was astonished.

After just one day, Lima was entering my mindscape with ease. Though slightly out of place, I disbelieved I could easily adapt. In the evening, I told Elena I had not seen a black person during my stroll to the market and the exploration of the junctions around. This was unusual, for a city which in the 18th century was 40% black as I read in one document. She assured me that blacks were few in Lima, generally. She inquired if I was looked upon with a sense of curiosity.

"No, not actually, I didn't think I attracted attention in any way."

"So you think!!" She said, with an air of irony.

5   Pick-pockets
6   Delinquents

CHAPTER 4

Second Day

17 July 2015

I went with Elena to one of the posh districts of Lima, Miraflores. It was a kind of Bastos[1] in Yaoundé. At the Avenida Berlin, we saw a signpost indicating there was an exhibition going on, sponsored by the British High Commission. We got in and perused through the visual representations of the Lima landscape. We proceeded to the front of a chain of bars and nightclubs.

"Why are there so many flags on the rooftops, Elena?"

"You know our national day is on 28 July, in some few days."

"Oh yes, that could be the reason. But it means there must be a compelling order since almost no roof is left without the flag."

"Yes, there was a law under one of the presidents that flags must be raised on the roof of every habitation in July I think it was President Oscar Benavides. And the fine is very high for any renegades."

This was quite interesting. I have never heard such a thing in other countries. Every nation has its policy with flags, I thought. During the evening performances at the Feria del Libro, I was intrigued by the repeated invocations of *Viva el Peru!!* I was not very much used to this phrase.

We went to the beach, an immense sight with several tourists. I heard one gentleman speaking German to his female companion and I greeted them, introduced myself in German and they were so positively surprised to find that someone speaks the same language as them. They said they would have loved to meet me again but they had to leave Lima the following day to Buenos Aires, Argentina. No problem. The kind of mutual joy when you meet someone from the same country in a foreign land with whom you speak the same language.

---

1   An upper-class residential quarter in Yaoundé, the capital city of Cameroon.

After taking some photos on the escarpment of the beach, we began the long march across the shores. Great commercial centres. Dreamlife restaurants with a fantastic view on the Lima shores. We looked at the menu. Cutthroat prices. Those we met around that vicinity looked more like business magnates and top-class financiers.

We took a cab back towards Lince, the district where we were living. No, no, there is an important event here in the district of Jesus Maria. A Book Fair. We paid the driver and alighted. The entrance to the venue was damn full as people struggled to get entry tickets. The attendance was impressive, apparently a very well organised event. The auditoria that hosted the discussions, book presentations and performances were named after Peruvian literary and cultural figures like Blanca Varela, Jose Maria Arguedas, Clorinda Matto, Cesar Vallejo, etc. My mind went back to Cameroon where, unlike what I witnessed here, politics had completely covered all aspects of life, where the image of the politician was everywhere at any time, where the president's photo was omnipresent.

I was grateful to Elena for having brought me to this instructive space. Exactly the kind of events I need so as to know more about the politics, history and culture of Peru. There were several discussions by specialists of every aspect of Peruvian cultural life, an ideal meeting point between the academics and the society. The most prominent publishing houses of Peru are present with books at promotional prices.

In the evening, there was one of the most enchanting performances I have ever witnessed; well-choreographed indigenous folklore music accompanied by poetic recitation in French and Spanish. The half-lit stage was well set with an eerie atmosphere of mythical profundity and the sound of the flute, the drum and the piano conjured a sense of transcendence through music. I have not seen many of such beautiful and artistically profound spectacles before.

Elena and I had to move to a junction to take the bus. Just within that short distance, I saw about two to three university signboards. There seems to be a university in Lima in every corner. I noticed this when I took an adventurous stroll down to Avenida Arenales, the two previous days. Most of them bare names of key Peruvian intellectual figures. Though singling out some few ones, Elena was a bit dismissive of the quality of some of them. She said some liberal laws turned the university into a business institution leading to a lot of "mushroom" institutions whose sole aim was to make money.

CHAPTER 5

Third Day

Earlier on in the day, I looked for the nearest church to experience the worship service in Peru. After asking around, I was directed to a nearby church called La Alianza Cristiana. It is a mega-church capable of hosting thousands of Christians worshipping with a live-stream broadcast on YouTube. The pastor was very insightful and a good orator for that matter, speaking on what it means to trust God for those who believe. The preaching was followed by a praise and worship session. I admired the fluting skills of the traditional musicians and their beautiful attire. I was told these were tunes from the mountainous regions of Peru. And the colourful attires too. What a beautiful combination.

After the service, I met a group of youth and introduced myself to them. I could see the curiosity on their faces when I told them I was originally from Cameroon while I live in Germany.

"Oh, the country of Samuel Eto'o!" One young guy exclaimed.

I had experienced this kind of excitement with football during my first days in Germany. Whenever I mentioned Cameroon, the names that came up were either Samuel Eto'o Fils or Roger Mila, depending on the generation to which the person belonged. Some would go further to comment about the fact that it was a German colonial territory. Though football would enlighten our faces, the talk on colonies sometimes killed the show. In Peru, among the older generation, I was reminded of the game in 1982 between Cameroon and Peru, which Cameroon won. I provoked the young man who introduced himself to me as the organiser of the church youth football team by saying that if there was to be a game between the two sides Cameroon would obviously win.

"Of course, they will. If you are talking about a play station game", he said.

We burst into laughter. I admired the efficiency of his sarcasm. Later on, we exchanged email addresses so that he could inform me on the next game during which we will see who is who, not just Gil Vs Mango, but rather Cameroon Vs Peru.

From the church, I decided to trek to the Book Fair at Jesus Maria. Elena had an appointment with her doctor on that day and was not very sure of attending the fair. I had already mastered the road though the map was still a little bit fussy in my mind. Whenever I had doubts, I asked around and though some were too busy to respond, I once in a while stumbled on some good Samaritans. And again, most of them were shopkeepers and salespersons in nearby stores. I arrived and decided to visit the stands of the various embassies. There were a number of them with lots of publicity materials, flyers marking events organised by the embassies, areas of cooperation between the various countries and Peru, key aspects of tourism in the said countries, etc. In short, just the best that country could offer in terms of image-making. I passed by the Italian Embassy and spoke some Italian to the representative. I could sense his amazement. Even though I was mixing Spanish with Italian, he was just surprised to hear me speak his language. A certain sense of brotherliness developed between us. I tried my best and he fell in love with me for that. I proceeded to the Chilean Embassy stand. I asked the girl standing in front of the stand:

"How is the relationship between Peru and Chile?"

"It's fine, though it has known some slight difficulties, but generally ok."

"Are you from Chile?"

"No, I am Peruvian."

"Oh, a Peruvian but you are representing Chile! That is interesting!!"

The girl smiled and bid me farewell as I continued further to the Chinese, Japanese, and Turkish stands. What was of particular interest to me was the Venezuelan stand. Two ladies stood there, seemingly very eager to respond to the inquiries of the visitors. I noticed their interest in communicating with the guests and engaging them in a brief discussion on their country.

"Why is the Venezuelan Republic officially referred to as "The Bolivarian Republic of Venezuela?"

"It is in tribute to the founder of the nation of Venezuela, El grand Libertador Simon Bolivar. He is a very important figure in our history and El comandante Hugo Chavez has always wanted to reinstate his image."

"Oh yes, I see. So, the comandante Che Guevara is like the new

Bolivar."

"El comandante Hugo Chavez!"

"Oh sorry. Hugo Chavez. El comandante is more associated in my mind with Che, so I easily mix things up. Venezuela is a very important country and I always like to listen to news about this country." I tried to cover up with a good note for the country.

"That is great. Where do you listen to Venezuelan news, which channel?"

Tricky question.

"I watch Telesur."

"That is a very good channel!! It gives real and balanced information on our country." I was happy to have by now fully vitiated the error on "El Comandante." I understood the lady's worry that I might have been fed with information from western media that was mainly negativist about Venezuela. She was not only relieved but impressed when I mentioned Telesur, a creation of Hugo Chavez in partnership with other socialist and putatively anti-American governments of Latin America. After our discussion, the lady proceeded to offer me a series of documents on Venezuela like the constitution, touristic sites, Hugo Chavez's most important speeches, etc.

In my whole review of the embassy stands, I felt a sense of rejection concerning my new Peruvian identity. I had met embassy representations from countries from all continents except one: Africa. No single African country was represented. I proceeded to the stand of the Peruvian Ministry of Culture. Perhaps, that was the right place to raise the issue, in a very friendly way, though.

"I have gone through all the stands, but there is no African country represented. Is there any specific reason for that?"

She felt a bit taken aback by the question and humbly responded.

"Yes, you are right. It's something I can't really explain. It's like Africa is a bit far, but that notwithstanding we have some connections with African countries."

"Too far yet too near", I commented and we both exchanged smiles over it.

After discussing with her on my mission in Peru, she jokingly said to me,

"We need people like you. With the work you are doing, the relation would certainly get better in future."

I concurred with a sense of humility regarding the possible

contribution of individual efforts in the domain of cultural exchange.

"Thanks for your very pertinent remark; it just didn't cross my mind." She said, pensively.

"But you have the French Embassy. It is right around the corner." She said, almost jubilant, like after a redemptive afterthought or brainwave, just when I was about leaving.

"Thank you, but I was already there."

"Ok, bye-bye." she responded, perhaps surprised that I did not share that much in her enthusiasm about the French Embassy.

CHAPTER 6

Fourth Day

20 July 2015

There was a performance in the evening. It was one of the greatest moments of my stay in Peru when I lived Peru's past represented in its culture; the ludic and the tragic; the far past and the present. It was a moment of performing the nation, trying to make meaning of history and to assume it, to accept a history dipped in drama, irony, paradox to the point of humour, but also in sweat and blood.

The tunes moved the pulse of my heart, entrancing rhythms that moved body and mind, the re-enactment of the confrontation between conquistadors and indigenes, marineros and the art of courting. The drums took me very far down memory lane.

At some point in the hall, the lights went off. But I was surprised by the relative calmness of the attendants. Was it so normal for lights to go off in these parts. A kind of a deja vu? But I had not witnessed "delestage" (power cut) ever since I landed here. Or was Peru much like Germany, a country that has made me to get used to the voice of silence? I noticed earlier that Peruvians were from my judgment, quite calm in nature.

On Tuesday morning, I went with Elena to the University of San Marcos. I was much impressed by the images and sculptures of Peruvian fathers of modern letters like José Mária Arguedas, Jose Carlos Mariátegui, Cesar Vallejo, etc. Their aura hung over the entire place, not only in the form of statues but rather very much alive in scientific discourses and discussions.

At the gate, there was a security officer checking incomers for the student card or any form of identity. Notwithstanding, people just thrilled in at the gate, paying scant attention to the security guard. Elena acted the same, leaving me with the impression that I did not get the lady well. I hesitated at the gate but was ushered in even as I was struggling to scamper through my pockets for my passport.

"Isn't she asking us to present our identity cards?"

"Yes, but who cares?"

She later explained to me that there had been some trouble on the campus in the days of the Shining Path and that made security on campus a serious issue. "But then, why are the security measures not respected?"

"Well, I don't know why. People are just too busy getting into campus."

People just ignored the laws so easily here? This was quite different from the Catholic University, the *Pontificia Universidad Católica del Perú* (PUCP). Both universities are close to one another, located at the *Avenida Universitaria*. During my entire stay in Lima, I visited the Catholic University campus only once, to attend a seminar on the memories of violence in Peru. I had planned a second visit, to participate in the poetry class of my friend Victoria Guerreiro but my travel arrangements could not permit me to honour it. As a non-student, to take part in any event on campus, you have to register online in advance. Upon arrival at the gate, you have to present your identity card or passport which is thoroughly verified through the computer security systems. The Catholic University has all the physical properties of a University for the privileged. The modern architectural designs of its buildings, their clean walls and the beauty of the environment with its lush lawns do not say the contrary. Elena told me that the cadres of modern Peru are products of this university that also recruits some of the best staff in the country.

Thus, the two universities are close but worlds apart. Entering San Marcos is like entering the University of Yaoundé 1 campus. There is something paradoxical about public universities. Their worn-out walls and their systematic disorderliness add to their wild beauty. In the middle of the campus, I found a small portion with trees, tree trunks with almost-neglected undergrowth, some sort of wasteland in the middle of this centre of knowledge. Some students sat on the trunks, chatting and discussing. I immediately thought of the *jacaranda tree* above the English Department of the University of Yaoundé 1 or the tiny baobab behind the central library under which we did most of our assignments. The probity and concentration required by those assignments did not, however, prevent us from, now and then, squinting our eyes around and appreciating the endowments of the female students passing by. Before you get distracted, remember this fact: San Marcos was the First University in the New World, opened in 1551 by a royal decree signed by King Charles of the *Holy* Roman Empire. Do not mind the faded letters on the slanting signboard that welcomes you into the campus. Have this history in mind as you move close to these grounds of knowledge.

At the entrance, there are a group of stores and photocopy shops. The area opposite the main entrance has all the features of *Château Ngoa-Ekellé*, in the University of Yaoundé 1. It is a layout for students' necessities: semi-standard restaurants, call boxes, money transfer agencies, photocopy, binding, lamination services, paper stores, and in the case of San Marcos, an informal industry that transforms juices and grains into a thousand forms of fries and chewable.

Elena and I moved to the school restaurant. It is quite small, looking rather like a canteen for the lecturers. We met some professors whom Elena recognised and briefly greeted. They were members of her philosophy workshop, *El Búho Rojo*[1] where I have to do a presentation in some weeks to come. When we came to the Arts Faculty, I was attracted to the flyer announcing a philosophy colloquium in honour of the Argentine philosopher of liberation theology, Enrique Dussel. It was in commemoration of Dussel's 80th birthday. Unfortunately, I could not make it to that colloquium. Professor Emeritus in Mexico's "San Marcos", *Universidad Nacional Autónoma de México*[2] (referred to affectionately as UNAM), Enrique Dussel is one of the few Latin American philosophers who made laudable efforts to integrate African philosophy in interrogating Western epistemological hegemony. I had planned to interview one author on that same day. As we moved out of the faculty building, I saw a group of students checking up marks on the scoreboard opposite the security desk. They were just a handful of them. Most seemed quite serene. Perhaps they were satisfied with their scores. Memories of my last encounter with the scoreboard of the University of Yaoundé 1 and its trauma came to my mind.

Revisiting one's alma mater always arouses some sense of nostalgia, but also ambiguity. Stepping foot on Yaoundé 1 campus years after leaving that campus, one is gripped by the aura of that mythic wall, the scoreboard, *le barbillard*. Anxiety incarnated. Looking at students streaming to that wall to check their end-of-semester marks brought me back to those days. An assailing volley of mixed feelings hit my mind. Those days, those days! Sometimes, before facing that wall, you murmur a confidential prayer, a sign of the cross (even though not a Catholic). You might have written the exams with self-confidence, you might have

---

1   Literally "Red Owl"
2   National Autonomous University of Mexico.

burnt the midnight candle, one truth remained permanent: the wall will have its say. The scoreboard wall was independent, impartial, objective, irrespective of your desires. The wall decided your fate. Sometimes you left the scoreboard with light feet, poised to conquer the world, crossing "Carrefour Condom" and "Parlement" with music in your heart. But most often, the wall's decision converted you into a doppelgänger.

Checking your marks on the board, stretching your neck, disbelieving your eyes in broad daylight, hoping to be mistaken, wishing something could change even in the act and process of looking, pinning your finger on the name, dragging it past the matriculation number, percentage, coefficient and final mark columns. You could not deny your name. It is yours. Self-fragmentation. De-familiarisation. Self-alienation. By your side, someone is jubilating for their (sometimes surprisingly) good results. Resigned to your fate, you look around and wonder like Skater Davies why people around you go on existing, why the birds in the sky go on singing when it is the end of the world, of your world....

There you would stand like a fallen albatross, wings clipped, forced to complain to the merciless Ngoa-Ekelle gods. "*Requêtes*", i.e, an official letter of complaint to the Head of Department, never led anywhere. When I look back, I see a lot of the casualties of that wall who had to go back home for reasons unexplained to them. I can say it made me strong since it did not kill me. I remember, when I stepped on the plane to pursue my studies in Germany on a scholarship award, I waved at my family and my friends who had come to see me off. But I also waved at the wall, in affectionate mockery.

When I came to the Bayreuth University in Germany, I felt something vital was missing on the topography of the university campus: The image of students stretching their necks on the wall, the formation of the imagined community of the university. There you get to know your marks online. It is individual, efficient, confidential.

When Elena and I came close to the gate on our way out, it is then that I had a better glimpse of the women selling school accessories, ice cream and making photocopies. The woman making photocopies made me recall the book I had bought from the *Book Fair: Los Rendidos: El don de perdonar*[3] by Carlos Aguero which narrates the tragedy of his parents, members of the *Sendero Luminoso (Shining Path)* Rebel movement. From the description, she owned a photocopy and binding shop there,

---

3   *The Surrendered: The Gift of Forgiveness*

in which young Carlito assisted her after school hours. She became very close to students, sometimes doing their photocopies on credit and even for free. During those days, the bonds of affection became complicity since many students were Sendero members and sympathisers. After several days of warning, Carlos' mother and her husband were finally arrested by the secret police and brutally murdered in the cells, leaving Carlos and his siblings to face the stigma of *Sendero* parents, with former playmates and neighbours constantly pointing fingers at them as terrorists. A painful memory, one woman was here and is no more. Terrorist, but kind, a mother. Every university student knows what a friendship with someone who runs a photocopy machine on campus meant. It reminded me of my first holiday to Cameroon from Germany. I went to the Yaoundé campus to meet my friend JP, who owned a photocopy shop. I didn't even know his real name. We just called him JP. He was kindness in human form, sometimes photocopying our documents for free during tough times. I had always said to myself, if ever I have the means, I will make a significant gesture of gratitude to JP. Here was I, behind the Faculty of Arts and Letters building where the photocopy shops were relocated. I did not see JP. I asked one other guy whom I could recognize. In those days, his shop was near JP's. He told me he had just returned from JP's funeral the week before!

CHAPTER 7

Tschüss[1]

22 July 2015

I went out in the morning to make a call. On my way back, I passed some few metres in front of an old man who was sweeping. As I approached, he stopped cleaning. I thought it was just to avoid letting the dust fall on me. He rather looked at me with a welcoming smile.

"*Hey my friend, how are you?*"

"*Am fine. Thank you. And you?*"

"*Fine, where are you from?*

"Am from Cameroon but I live in Germany."

"Oh, that's great. *Guten Morgen.*"

"Guten Morgen, you speak German, wow that is wonderful."

"Yes, I lived for some years in Germany."

"That is wonderful. Nice to hear that". I said, both with an air of familiarity but also with the intention to continue my way.

"Wait a minute, let me tell you something." His face grew rather grave. "Here you have everything: good food, touristic sites, beautiful women, etc."

I felt a sense of sensation, not because of the last item on the list, but because, generally, the old man seemed to be validating my honest aspirations during my time in Peru. But his face remained quite calm and serene. And then he continued:

"But you also have one thing…"

I waited anxiously for the next item on the list of niceties every visitor needs to enjoy in Peru, according to the old man. I do not know if it was in descending or ascending order. The pause of the old man's voice meant the order was not rampant. But for some reason, I felt what was to come last would be the most important of all. A veritable last but not least.

---

1   Bye Bye (in German)

"Yes, you have one thing, a problem, actually: The colour of your skin. You are black, and that is the problem."

I was speechless. In the twinkle of an eye, I scanned the old man's face for any inkling of a joke. I needed just a trace or symptom. Perhaps it was my baptism of fire in Peruvian humour. But his face remained serene, unmoved, marked by a complex network of wrinkles. I tried to smile, I tried to speak, I was just confused.

"It hurts but that is the truth. And I tell you this with much respect."

I waited for him to go further, to explain something, to give an instant or just an anecdote.

"Tschüssssss", said the old man in German and resumed sweeping with energy.

The word "Tschüss" was one of my most nice-sounding words in German. But for me, it was also the most hurtful, not in the sense of parting with a loved one. In a quite different way. Go to an office and demand any service, and if for some reason, perhaps because the deadline has passed, your request cannot be met, the officer tells you: "Sorry, I can't do anything to help you. Tschüss", with a smile on the face, the sharp vowel and sibilant unusually overstretched. Irrevocable, your fate is sealed, no further room for negotiation. The word enters your skin like a needle, meandering through the epidermis, distressingly slowly until it meets the crust under the earth of your skin where dreams meet with reality, where aspirations meet frustration, killing you softly. At that point, you don't know who to blame, the officer or your own self, or destiny. Naked, with a renewed consciousness of your fragility.

I walked back to the house, lost in thoughts. So direct, so violent, so categorical.

I left, hard-pressed. Should I blame the old man, the Peruvian society or my race? I could not even blame Peru because I had not met the reality yet. Or did I have to consider this moment itself as the first instance? As a black person, an educated black person, one sometimes has to either be too sensitive to racism or to make a lot of concessions, by being slow to cry foul, by "understanding" the context of any treatment. Although, even at that, there was always a line that never needed to be crossed. Even for the slow "concluders". What that line is, depends on each and every one.

CHAPTER 8

Zero Hour

24 July 2015

I spent the afternoon at the Book Fair. After the presentation of a novel by Victoria Guerrero, she invited me to join her and some friends of hers, mostly creative writers, to a popular bar for literary writers in downtown Lima. Unable to get a cab in front of the entrance to the Book Fair, we walked over a reasonable distance along the Salaverry Avenue, stopping empty cabs along the way till we finally got one to drive us to town. The bar is called Quirelo, a popular place for literary authors in Lima known as *Hora Zero*, literally meaning "Zero Hour", a point of (new) beginning. When we entered, the atmosphere was rather intense with smoke spiralling in the air, preventing a full view of the faces of those who were sitting there. I took a seat near two ladies who were part of the group, but I had not developed familiarity with them like the others. They were rather very quiet, not very engaged in what was the discussion on the table. Noticing my apparent loneliness, Ema and Victoria beckoned me to come over to their side. Both ladies were very friendly and engaged me in discussions on every topic. In a small talk manner, Victoria presented to me the members on our table and the one next to ours. Each one of them was a writer, I came to learn. I continued to engage her on life in Peru. In the course of our discussion, I came to know that she had spent some time in Berlin. She even has a poetry collection titled "Berlin". Talking with her, you do not doubt of her curious and provoking way of looking at what seems bland or benign at first sight. She also has a great sense of humour.

"How many German girlfriends have you had?"

"Only ten of them," I answered, returning the sense of humour characteristic of my friend whom I had known just for a day.

"But I guess you know the difference between a *Meine Freundin* girlfriend" and *Eine Freundin von mir* 'a (female) friend of mine' in German."

"Oh yes, I learnt one should never mix the two up."

"Absolutely, hahaha."

"What about Peru, how many of them?"

"Am still quite new here and am still exploring."

Victoria and I laughed and we went ahead with the drinking. She popped the champagne which a "boyfriend of hers" had given her as a present for her book presentation. A well-packaged bottle, with Victoria's name inscribed on it in beautiful calligraphy.

In the course of the discussion, I asked Victoria:

"How is Mario Vargas Llosa?[1] Is he back home in Peru now?"

"No, he is now with his princess, Isabel Preysler, his newfound love. That is Vargas Llosa for you." I recalled a lecture I followed on YouTube on Victor Hugo where Vargas Llosa gave an account of Hugo's romantic (or sexual) escapades with women even in his early eighties. The ironical, euphemistic and innuendo-ridden tone in which he narrated this aspect of his admired precursor sent his audience giggling all along. But what was even more vivid to me was Vargas Llosa's Nobel acceptance speech of and how he, in an instant outburst of tears, talked about his (then) wife Patricia "the love of my life, someone who has brought order to my chaotic and neurotic life". That was in 2010. Truly, a day is a long time in life, to echo Harold Wilson's saying that a week is a long time in politics. I went on to tell her how my interest in Peru was almost entirely due to the genius I found in Llosa's work that connected rubber exploitation in the Congo with the same gruesome reality in the Amazonian region of Peru. *The Dream of the Celt* a novelistic reproduction of the story of Sir Roger Casement forced me to think about connections between these two distant but close continents: Europe, Africa and Latin America.

Just as we were discussing, one guy came in, accompanied by an old gracious and reverent man, with crystal white and well-kempt hair. Victoria whispered into my ear, "Gil, this is Oswaldo Reynoso, one of the greatest contemporary novelists from Peru." The bristling hair and deep smile of this man were enchanting and seemed to distend a complex observatory sway.

After a round of greetings, the old man and his young friend sat close to me. Victoria's friends had gone out to smoke.

"It is my pleasure to know you, sir. I come from Germany but I am

---

1   Renowned and arguably, the best-known Peruvian author. He was awarded the Nobel Prize for Literature in 2010.

Cameroonian."

"Oh, really wonderful!" Both of them responded as if in a chorus.

The name "Cameroon" seemed to have unleashed the historical memory of his younger friend. He delved into a series of rhetorical questions of which I was the main interlocutor. The old man kept silent, but with a keen sense of interest, followed his friend's deployment of historical knowledge and my responses.

"Roger Milla remains the best player of Cameroon, true or false?"

"Of course, he is. Even at the African level." I responded.

"The squad of the 1990 World Cup was one of the best in this period. They made us proud by beating Argentina hands down. Argentina was warped in a nightmare before they discovered the damage that had been done. If not because of the damn opportunistic Lineker, Cameroon could have won that World Cup! Roger Milla, Cyrille Makanaky, Oman Biyik, Louis Mfede, Thomas Nkono, Stephen Tataw, Joseph-Antoine Bell…" He recalled the names of the entire squad of the Cameroon national team of 1990. I was astounded. I as a Cameroonian could not name as many as he did.

"Cameroon did the unimaginable. The national team is called The Indomitable Lions, true or false?"

"Very true, it is amazing how you retain every detail about our team."

"Do you remember Cameroon versus Peru on 15 June 1982? Certainly, you were not yet born or you were too young, true or false?"

"True, that was before I was born."

"Yes, that was the magic year that stamped Cameroon in the memory of Peruvians. Roger Milla, the magician. It was a draw game but Peruvians could not believe a small African team could stand up so bravely against them. Mila even scored a goal but it was denied. Peruvians will never forget two names: Roger Milla and Thomas Nkono. He frustrated every attempt by the Peruvian attack. There was also one unforgettable incident in that game: a dog entered the football pitch and the referee had to stop the game for some seconds to expel the dog with a red card!!"

All of us were shedding tears of laughter.

"Yes, I now recall that game, I was in China by then. Said the old wise man briefly and withdrew back into his listening position.

"Do you remember Milla's way of celebrating his goals? After scoring, he would run to the corner kick spot and exercise a beautiful dance, spinning his waste around in a very sexy manner!!"

"That is Milla's trademark! You know what? Many people have told me much about this fateful game. I did not know about that before my coming here. I only came to know about it here in Peru."

"I remember in that year, any moment a black man entered a bar while people were discussing, one of the drinkers would hiss, "Husshh, this is a Cameroonian spy." The bard again intervened, speaking slowly but clearly. We all laughed. The other poets sitting near us joined in without really understanding the subject of the matter. Certainly, they were just amused by how the three of us, including the bard, were moved into laughing so synchronically.

"If you ask me now, I will tell you that I was secretly supporting Cameroon. It is then that I bought a book about your country. It was in French. Remind me, next time we are to meet, I will bring the book along."

"Sure, that is interesting. I will certainly like to know about the book." I said with a sense of gratitude.

Some few minutes later, the bard excused himself and took his leave. He had not even been drinking. My friend wanted to see him off but he told him calmly.

"Don't worry, please! Continue conversing with your brother."

Embracing me, he said, "I am 85 years now. My bones are weak. I would have loved to hear you talk more about Cameroon but it is getting late. We will surely meet again". I expressed my desire to meet him again as our schedules permitted. He seemed to have much to say and his taciturn posture that night confirmed that intuition the more. We stayed for about fifteen more minutes. A bit insecure about going home quite late into the night, I also announced to the others that I was leaving. A round of embraces followed and I took my leave.

Carlos, Victoria and Karina, in particular, wanted to know if I needed any help in getting a taxi. I told them Miguel would go out with me. They were assured. Miguel tried successively to stop two taxis but they were going in different directions.

The third car came and the driver accepted to take me. *Lince, Avenida Petit Thouars Cuadra 26, Calle Jirón Soledad 565.*

"I am taking down the plate number of the taxi. If you waylay him I will kill you straight. Take him quietly to his residence." Miguel said to the driver, in an almost threatening voice.

I held tightly to my bag, trying to read the facial expression of the driver to gain assurance from him. I was at his mercy. At that very moment, all the macabre stories I had heard about *delincuentes* in Lima invaded my mind. I felt a need to converse with the driver, to make friends with him, to look at him and to visualize him leaving me safely at my destination. I needed to win him over based on friendship and not for fear of the threats that Miguel had proffered. At one point, I even thought Miguel's threats, though not meant to be provocative, could make matters worse if the driver had evil intentions. The taxi driver was a rather taciturn fellow. His Spanish left much to be desired and veered off any grammatical constraints, avoiding the high hills of full sentences and preferring the planes of brief noun and verb phrases. He drove quite slowly. Sometimes I had the impression he was stopping. When, finally, we came to recognisable places along Avenida Salaverry, I pretended to know every junction we crossed, which contradicted the rather guiding hand from Miguel which proved to every reasonable person that I was a stranger in these parts.

Finally, I reached home. Relief!

I called Miguel to inform her of my safe arrival and that the driver was not a *ratero*, (thief). Rather he was just a calm *Serrano* (mountain-dweller), from what he told me. Fortunately!

At night, I sketched a rather simple, naïve poem.

Soy Gil,
Niño del otro lado, de todos lados
Quiero tocar mi hermano peruano

Soy chinchano,
Si, venido abrazar mis hermanos
Hermanos del otro lado, de otra orilla

Soy chino, si, mi nombre es chino,
Ahora estoy aquí, estoy aquí, si, estoy aquí
Contra la historia, para encontrar la historia

Soy gitano, gitano negro, me pierdo en tus ritmos
En tus tambores, tambores de memoria, me muero.

(English translation)

Am Gil
A child from another side, from everywhere
I wish to touch my Peruvian brother

Am Chinchano,
Yes, have come to embrace my brothers
My brothers from the other side, the other shore

Am Chinese, yes, my name is Chinese
Now am here, yes am here
Against history, to meet history.

Am gypsy, black gypsy, I am lost in your rhythm
Under your drums, drums of memory, I die.

CHAPTER 9

Café Haití

25 July 2015

I went to interview a Paris-based Peruvian author Alfredo Pita in Mira-flores today. He had lived both in Cajamarca and Ayacucho and knew these regions by heart. Cajamarca is where Pizarro hanged Inca Atahualpa for blasphemy, treason and idolatry on 26 July 1533. The tons of gold and silver, *el reparto*, offered, by the Inca were not enough to satiate the appetite of Valverde's god. Ayacucho was the flashpoint of the 1980s violence in Peru. Ayacucho in Quechua actually means, *el Rincón de la Muerte*, "the corner of death", the title of one of Alfredo's novels. Not only is Alfredo a fine author and journalist, he is also of interest to me for the fact that he lost three close colleagues amongst the five journalists killed near Ayacucho, specifically in Huchuraccay on 26 January 1983: Willy Retto, Jorge Luis Mendívil Trelles, Eduardo de la Piniella, Octavio Infante, Amador García, Pedro Sánchez, Félix Gavilán and Jorge Sedano Falcón. They went to cover the incidents in Ayacucho when reports of violence occurring in that part sounded to Lima audience like episodes in a distant world, like Strange Tales from the Arabian Nights. Till this day, it is still unknown whether they were killed by the government forces or by Sendero rebels. The final report of an independent commission chaired by Nobel laureate Mario Vargas Llosa to shed light on the saga raised more controversy than it resolved.

Back to Café Haití. It is an upper-middle-class bar/restaurant with quite old and seasoned waiters and waitresses. They are quite welcoming and kept me well entertained as I waited for Alfredo to arrive. He came a few minutes after our appointment because he did not easily find parking space. Before we began the interview, he told me we would have to interrupt it at some point because he had asked his nephew to meet him at the Café at a later time. His nephew came when we were thirty minutes into the interview. When Alfredo presented us to one another, we switched to German, turning the former into an admiring spectator. Narbo had spent seven years in Germany, in Bielefeld, studying Geochemistry. He came back more than seven years ago. His German was still quite fluent. After I ended the interview with Alfredo we exchanged more. I told him I was travelling to Ayacucho. That is when he told me he lives there and was in Lima just to visit his uncle who came in from Paris for the Book Fair. He assured me I did not have to look for a hotel. He would host me with pleasure. I was very happy that I had got a friend who would be my anchor in Ayacucho. Before we separated, we exchanged telephone numbers and Facebook addresses. Alfredo very kindly settled all the bills.

After the interview, I was about to cross the road when a smiling security guard passed by and spoke to me very friendly. I stopped and moved close to him. He was intrigued by my Cameroonian grassfield regalia: black jumper with green, red yellow embroidery with the map of Cameroon dexterously knitted on the front.

"I like your dress", he said.

"Thank you."

"Where do you come from?"

"I come from Cameroon but live in Germany." What you have to know by now is that when you travel, different nationalities trigger distinctive and telling facial expressions, pauses, interjections, etc. Sometimes, the interlocutor tries to conceal, but you often get to read the meanings.

"How is Germany?"

"It is fine," I responded laconically.

"Now coming back to Cameroon, let me ask you something. Is it true what we see on TV sometimes? Put another way, do you guys really live with animals on the streets?"

"We also have domestic animals like in Peru of course. Why not?"

"No, no, I mean real animals, lions, tigers, leopards…"

"Oh, as far as I know, those ones are only found in parks. We have some parks in Cameroon, but you have better-endowed parks in countries like Kenya, for example. Actually, I saw my first lion, in Germany, in a park in Hannover."

"Really?" He beamed with surprise.

"Yes, there are some few animals in parks in Cameroon, but unfortunately I have never visited them."

"So, what we see on TV is just exoticism?" I did not feel compelled to respond. As I was talking with him, about three colleagues of his gathered. A police car drove and stopped by us. A black policeman stuck his head out, shoulders all covered with epaulets. He greeted me, asked where I was from.

"Cameroon," I responded.

"Oh, Cameroon!! I like your attire, welcome to Peru. How long will you be here?"

"For one month, but I am thinking of extending."

"You better extend my friend. One month is not enough. Enjoy your stay in Peru".

He asked his driver, another police officer of a lower rank, to drive on. I then bid my friends farewell who stood by and watched me conversing with the black police officer as if awed by his epaulets and the fact that he was discussing with his "brother". I took the bus back to Lince.

I was a bit hungry and I decided to get into a Chinese chifa restaurant. In each *cuadra*[1], you would find at least two *chifa* restaurants. I thought they were manned by the descendants of the late 19th century Chinese immigrants, most of whom came from Taishan in Guangdong Province. No! After visiting about four *chifas* in my first days in Lima, the very strong Chinese accent of the waiters convinced me that these were recent immigrants. As I often engaged the waiters in small talk while consuming my *lomo saltado*, I used the fork not just to bring under control the slender and elusive Spaghetti but also to extract elements of Spanish grammar from their very strong Chinese intonation.

---

1   Block

CHAPTER 10

From Book Fair to Homes

27 July 2015

In the morning, I visited Octavio Santa Cruz, the nephew of the famous Santa Cruz siblings, i.e. of Nicomedes Santa Cruz (1925-1992), Afro-Peruvian poet and public intellectual and Victoria Santa Cruz (1922-2014), intellectual and performer. Octavio is a mid-fifties gracious looking man with well-kempt blades of white hair, the kind we used to admire as kids in Nelson Mandela, Colin Powel and Kofi Annan. He is as laid-back and soft-spoken as the latter. I had first met Octavio at the Book Fair where he presented a book *Mi Tío Nicomedes (My Uncle Nicomedes)*, dedicated to the family life of his venerated uncle, a seasoned hand at *cumanana* chants and *decimas*, ten-verse poems filled with memories of slavery and the experience of Afro-Peruvians in modern-day Peru. As for Octavio, he is a seasoned guitar player, cartographer and Arts teacher of the Faculty of Arts and Letters, San Marcos University. He is the most popular living member of the Santa Cruz family after his brother Rafael (1960-2014), actor and author (of *The Afro-Peruvian Drum*), passed away last year.

He came to pick me up in front of the San Marcos University Campus. He drove a *Volkswagen* Beatle which we call *toroki* in Cameroon pidgin. It was my first time to be driven in a VW Beatle. The last time I saw it was in the Second World War Museum in Bonn, Germany in 2011. But I have never doubted the magical strength of this car. In pidgin we say, *small-no-be-sick*, i.e size is not usually synonymous with power or strength. More so when it comes to a German car. Colin Powel testifies of the prowess of the Beatle in his autobiography *The Child from the Bronx*, 1995. After serving as commanding General of US Fifth Corps in Frankfurt, West Germany (1986-87), he confesses his *Beatle* remains his most valuable gift and intimate friend from the country. He has bought and re-sold some of his cars, but never his Beatle. Anyway, to cut a long story short, Octavio's creaking Beatle took us home with great efficiency and comfort.

His housemaid, *la empleada*, served us tea and biscuits. We had a great and informative interview. Asked what his connection to Africa is, he told me: "Actually, for many black Peruvians, Africa is more of an imagination; it is far removed from our reality. We hardly stay connected with it except occasionally through Western media. It is a material for poems, music and more of a spiritual and artistic connection. My uncle Nicomedes was lucky enough to have visited Africa in the 1960s on the invitation of poet and then President of Senegal Leopold Sédar Senghor to participate in a Pan-African conference in Dakar." At the end of our interview, he offered me a copy of his late uncle's *Decimas: Poemas y Antologia* (Decimas: Poems and Anthology), a collection of short stories, two of his CDs and a handbook of essays on Afro-Peruvians' lives and history. We entered the Beatle and he saw me off at the main road from where I boarded the bus back home to Lince. In the car, he gave me a brief history of the slave trade in Peru though time cut us short given that his house was not far from the main road.

Slavery was abolished here on 4 December 1854 by President Ramon Castilla leading to the freedom of close to 20,000 enslaved Africans. The slave masters were compensated with an overall sum of 6 million pesos while the "freed slaves" had to eke out a living as "free" labourers under pay conditions that could not even keep body and soul together. Slavery had been abolished by San Martin when he declared Peru's independence on 28 July 1821 but was later re-introduced by presidents Felipe Santiago Salaverry and Agustin Gamarra to boost agricultural production. Destiny postponed.

When I arrived home, I only had time to answer a few emails and boarded the bus to Avenida Brasil in order to meet the history lecturer who had presented a history text at the feria the week before. On the bus to Avenida Brasil, I asked one guy sitting next to me how many minutes it would take for us to reach. After responding to my query, he, in turn, inquired where I was from. During our small talk, he cautioned me to be careful when moving around Lima, especially at night. He revealed to me he was a soldier under Fujimori's regime. Then Lima was relatively secure, he said, with a sense of longing. The situation has worsened in the past four years or so because of the very weak president, Ollanta Humala. People talk ill of Fujimori now but there are aspects they are not humble enough to acknowledge. He reinforced security. Lima was secure, far more secure than it is today. Now, no single day passes without news of assassinations.

I arrived at the historian's house and was well received. He spoke about the history of his country with great mastery and passion, especially when it came to the War of the Pacific (1879-1883) between Peru-Bolivia and Chile. I remembered the emphatic *Viva el Peru* (Long Live Peru) with which he had ended his presentation at the Book Fair some days ago. He loved to speak French with me since he had been teaching in a French college before going on retirement. After the interview, his housemaid set the table for us. After eating what seemed like a mixture of crayfish and onions, I washed my hands and was almost moving back to the reading table where we conducted the interview. He reminded me what we ate was just the entrée. More was still to come. This is Peru. The housemaid's face wore a permanent smile and she showed utter respect for her master. She responded to every call with Si, *Señor*. There seemed to be mutual respect between them for the man seemed kind and gentle. He told me about the passing away of his wife two years ago and what an emotional cost it meant for him. I can imagine the housemaid was of immense consolation to him. After exchanging emails and Facebook addresses, I left them.

From there, I went to meet another Peruvian historian in one popular bar close to the stadium. We discussed much of the history of Chinese migration to Peru. He was with his wife, a very lovely and funny woman. She cautioned me against the trappings of Lima girls. Some will go out to drink with you, for a party or something, when you are distracted, they put some powdered stuff in your wine and before you discover, you have fallen asleep or even conscious while they clear everything on you, something even your passport! Such warnings sounded funny but delivered with a certain amount of seriousness, almost keeping her cheeky side aside. The husband settled the bills for all of us. After our meeting, they saw me off to my apartment in their car. He gave me a book by Emilio Choy (1915-1976), a prolific Peruvian historian of Chinese origin and one of the authorities when it comes to Chinese immigration in 19th century Peru.

CHAPTER 11

Lenin and...

28 July 2015

It is the Peruvian National Day. I would have loved to witness the parade but many people advised me it was better to watch it on screen at home. The traffic was completely blocked and it would be tedious to trek from Lince to Avenida Brazil. I had passed by the Grandstand the day before. It was well arranged with Peruvian flags all over. It seemed rather calm, with some few police officials inspecting every centimetre of that space for security purpose. You would not imagine that in a few hours that place was going to burble with a national spirit and chants of "Viva el Peru" and the speech by the President, Ollanta Humala. It reminded me of when I visited Chicago Grant Park in May 2012, four years after the famous Barack Obama victory speech after defeating John McCain on 4 November 2008: "It's been a long time coming, but tonight, because of what we did on this day, in this election, at this defining moment, change has come to America." And it was Grant Park that history elected to host this historical moment. One could not imagine that four years ago, this space was the focus of the world, encapsulating the spirit of history in the making, seeming like a breakthrough in race history with all of us. The world had never been so united with the United States of America. From the student quarters of Yaoundé, sacrificing my sleep so as to follow the speech at 3:30 A.M., I answered "Yes We Can" almost unconsciously, seized by the spirit of the moment. There was no better coincidence between the historical moment, the spectacularising power of modern Television and the hyperreal of cityscape montage. But now, the place was disappointingly bare, almost looking as unkempt as a goat grazing land. The modesty of that space, some would say, reflected the aftermath of the victory. It was a true example of the making and unmaking of spaces

Early in the morning, before coming back to watch the parade on

TV with Elena, I went to the market to take my breakfast. There it was business as usual. The fruits section of the market was replete with fruits of all colours, shapes and sizes, some which I had seen for the first time, others which I only knew thanks to primary school English readers. We wrote exams about fruits most of which we never knew in concrete reality. The mixture of so many fruit varieties, ripe, half-ripe and over-ripe, emitted a deep scent, an olfactive aura perhaps akin to the Garden of Eden in the days of Adam and Eve. I had always thought we had much variety in Cameroon until I came face to face with Variety.

After buying a few fruits to take home, I entered a restaurant operated by three young waitresses. I had a very interesting chat with one of them who seemed the most communicative of the three. We exchanged curiosities on life in Peru and Germany respectively.

"But those people do not like us there." She said

"Really? How do you know?"

"We hear it from those who travel to that part of the world and also in the news."

"Well, I am not quite sure. Like in every society you have those who are welcoming and others who are not. It also applies to me here in Peru."

"But Peruvians are very good people, right?"

"For sure, just less than a week here, I have met some nice people."

"Yes, we like strangers, it is not like in Chile."

"Oh really? How is Chile like? I intend to go there after Peru. Have you been there before?"

"No, but my brother has been there. They are racists. Don't even go there."

It was interesting listening to that little girl as she drew the race map of the world in very simple terms. I had wished to provoke her more but customers flooded in and I also concentrated on my food.

Some days ago, my landlady's daughter — Naomi evoked a similar opinion.

"When I was in Europe I travelled only in the poor parts of the continent. In Spain and Portugal and part of France."

"Really? 'Poor Europe'. That is interesting."

"Yes, they are quite poor there. And they do not like us in the other richer parts like Germany, France, Britain, etc. But I hear they like Latina girls. Is that true?"

"I do not have any specific experience with that mindset. But come on, who does not like Latina girls?"

We all laughed and continued with our breakfast.

When I came back home from the market Elena and I watched the parade on the TV screen. But the screen was not very clear, with images appearing more like silhouettes. We tried to adjust to no avail.

Later that afternoon I went to the Book Fair. Again, it was business as usual, with an excess of Peruvian red and white colours lining the walls. I interviewed the Peruvian author and critic based in Maine, US. — Carlos Villacorta. He made one key statement when I asked him a question about *Peruanidad* (Peruvianity): "We Peruvians do not have a common language in speaking amongst ourselves. When I talk to you, we understand each other even better than sometimes when I talk to fellow Peruvians". The second interview with Miguel Effui was scheduled for 6:00 P.M. but he did not show up. I waited for 20 minutes in vain. I called his number but it did not get through. He did not call me back either.

I took a stroll around the area to have a look at some books as I waited for a sign from Miguel Effui. I remember having come to the stand of the San Marcos University Press where I met one detective novelist. He told me his name is Lenin. After noticing a slight sense of amusement on my face, he said to me:

"You seem astonished. Do you know the name of the guy, sitting behind the table?" "The one signing receipts for customers."

"I began to imagine what could come after Lenin."

"He is called Stalin, Diego Stalin."

"I almost burst out laughing had Stalin not raised his head up at the hearing of his name." I shut up. Lenin explained to Stalin that he was just introducing the names of the sales personnel to a customer. Stalin waved at me, with a smile on his face and then continued with his work. I remember two of my acquaintances in Peru were actually called "Ivan".

I returned home by bus in the cold Lima night.

Just before I went to bed, I checked my Facebook, almost half-asleep. Hark on, I saw this timeline post from "Hil Draze":

> See I feel lost in dis world since u left me alone in place wit ur girls n
> I heard dat u in a better place no hurts no pains jst diamonds n pearls
> yes mama yes papa hey mumy have u seen ur man he looks even more
> hansome u shld see ur man done a rili gud job wit ur kids 4real gave us
> a roof n a 3 square meal mom left first n said I was great said I had a
> gift she gave me a tree wen all I needed was a stick. Dad pls tell mom

I'm missx her face I still remba wen we got back from school wait'n
for my mamas spaghetti. Oh, mama oh papa I really feel de pain cos
ever since u left its not been de same thres no sunshine nt even de rain
n no amt of joy here can take away de pain. RIP my beloved parents.

I was heartbroken. "Hi, Draze" is the Facebook name of "Hilton",
the son of Mr. Richard Mbonwe, one of my guardians in my secondary
school days. He had been ill but actually recovered. Though a primary
school teacher, he had very high dreams. He kept telling me about his
wish to foster his education to the university level, in a foreign country. I
remember his friend, the German architect and woodworker, Christian,
who used to teach woodwork in a College in Nkambe, my hometown in
Cameroon. He became very close to Christian. We used to drink palm
wine at Richard's home. He taught me "Guten Morgen" and some few
German expressions which I later forgot! He used to supply Richard
with a monthly magazine "Deutschland" which I basically confiscated.
It enlightened me immensely on life in Germany. I remember, when I
came to Germany, I had written him a mail asking if he was in contact
with Christian and if he could help me re-connect with my first ever-
German friend. I remember vaguely that Christian had told us he lived
in Bremen. But I was not sure. It was more than 16 years now. Now, all
was lost.

CHAPTER 12

When I touch 'her' waist...

29 July 2015

I went out to buy bread. As usual, I scanned at the titles of the Newspapers on the stand in front of the store. Most of the titles are critical of the presidential speech the day before that gave a balance sheet of Ollanta Humala's achievement. The title of *La Republica* was most scathing: *La Republica ficcional de Ollanta Humala* ("*Ollanta Humala's Fictional Republic*). The front page that I read reproached the president for giving a romantic view of his regime's achievements whereas the country's reality spoke of many points of weakness for his regime, such as insecurity, social exclusion, unemployment, etc.

I had a queer experience later on that day. My newly begotten friend Julio invited me to his house. He was visibly of Asian origin. Quite short and stout, low and well-kempt hair and tucked in shirt with jeans trousers. Almost the same style for the few times I have met him. We first met a few days ago when I stopped him on the way to Avenida Arenales, asking for the road to the Book Fair at Jesus Maria.

"Please sir, how can I get to the Book Fair?"

"At Jesus Maria?"

"Yes, please."

"Oh, it is not far from here. If you do not mind, just come with me. I am also going there."

"Is it very far?"

"Not really, we can take about fifteen minutes if we move without any hurry."

I had to make a call to a friend back in Cameroon. Julio patiently waited for me to finish. As we went on, he advised me to take care, absolute care, during my stay in Lima.

"Lima is very dangerous. There are a lot of gangsters around."

"Yes, many people have warned me. I mostly avoid going out at nights."

"Yes, that is better. Or if you do, you should have a trustworthy friend or driver to take you back."

"Thanks for your advice. That is very kind of you." We continued walking. He told me he was from Piura, in the North.

"People are more open, more willing to help. Lima people are very rude."

"I think it is the case with many big cities all over the world that people usually claim to always be in a haste."

"But Lima is an especially unfriendly place."

As we walked he showed me the hospital where he worked. A nicely painted building, two storeys, a hospital adjoined to a pharmacy. He told me he is a lab technician. That day, when we arrived at the cafetería, we took part in one of the panels in the Blanca Varela auditorium. My friend left for work. But the following day he wrote to me, offering to assist me if I needed his help in anything.

The following day, I went to the Book Fair by car at about midday since the presentations in the morning hours did not particularly appeal to me. As I was having lunch in a restaurant not far from the Book Fair venue, my friend of the day before called me. He joined me there, his house was quite close, he assured me. It did not take more than fifteen minutes before he arrived. He told me he already had lunch at home. So he took only a glass of *chicha morada*.[1] He offered to show me his home before we come back together to follow some of the panels at the Book Fair. That was timely because I still had about an hour left before a panel on Jorge Besadre, one of the most famous Peruvian intellectuals. We walked to the place. He lived on the third floor of a storey building. A well-equipped apartment, I thought.

"You seem to live like a bourgeois." I complimented.

"Oh, not that. Life is not easy in Peru."

"Yes, but it seems you are not doing badly."

"Well, my present job is relatively well-paid. My last job was slavery; it was in a clinic in Piura. Then I moved to Lima when a former classmate of mine who furthered his education in Boston, USA, came back and opened a big clinic here, very modern. He convinced me to work with

---

1 A sweet Peruvian beverage made from purple corn, a variant of Zea mays native to the Mesoamerica, and spices. Non-alcoholic, it is a type of chicha usually made by boiling the corn with pineapple, cinnamon, clove, and sugar.

him. That was a gift from heaven. That is how Peru works. Connections."

"Lucky you. Some classmates are friends for life."

"Otherwise I would really be suffering in Piura."

"How big is the town of Piura?"

"It is about one million."

"So, it is not a small city anyway."

"Well, in comparison with Lima."

"Of course, I know Lima is incomparable."

He removed his shirt, complaining of the weather. I had also removed my jacket and held it in my hand.

"You can leave your jacket on the bed, no problem. It is really hot!" He implored. "Even what you are wearing on you looks too warm. Don't you have a singlet inside? At least to take some fresh air before we go back in some few minutes." I began sensing something amiss in this long treatise on weather and clothing. Deep down in my habitus, something was beginning to sound familiar to me. But the other way round.

"Have you already met someone in Lima?" he asked, grinning uneasily but benevolently.

"What do you mean?"

"I mean to ask if you have found love here?"

"I came just last week my friend. That would be too fast of me." I responded, trying to sound funny, unsure of where the discussion was leading us to.

"Do you also do it with men or just with women."

"Why ask?" I asked, conceding that the "it" was common knowledge. No need pretending.

"It is because blacks are known here to be very strong and interesting in these things."

"Well, it's a global stereotype. Please, can we go? I need to attend a panel discussion in fifteen minutes." I said.

"Do not even mind. We Peruvians do not respect time too much." And then he continued. "In our clinic, we also do massage." He moved closer to me, pressing his hands on my back, smiling, moving his hands gently over my shoulder and then my waist. I felt squeamish, what should I do? I remembered Achebe's *Things Fall Apart*: "If I hold her hand she says, 'Don't touch!' If I hold her foot she says 'Don't touch!' But when I hold her waist beads she pretends not to know." My case was different. I felt the corrosive effects of hands on my poor skin, awkwardly trying to ignite flames that would not heed. I could not be rude, I played calm.

Here was I, reminded of those initial secondary school moments: those moments of positive denials, of affirmative withdrawals, of affective pushing of hands and of angry smiles. I restrained myself, appearing almost meek. It was a moment of great psychological ambiguity that I managed with incredible calmness. I had to be calm and modern.

"Please, let us go. It is almost time. I am even late."

"Ok, if not today some other day." His face was rather imploring. "Let me see you off then."

From the house to the Book Fair, I doubt if we exchanged any word. I was disappointed with his intentions. But I did not hate him for his attempts. It is just that I had hoped for an encounter of a different nature. When we arrived at the Book Fair, he simply bade me farewell and we separated. He did not even enter the gate. I never heard from him anymore. Leaving me with the marks of his bland, rough, stiff, and slightly irritating hands on my skin and my memory. I remembered my naïve poem at the beginning of my stay. I came to touch my Peruvian brother, my Peruvian sister. I came to emb-race. But not this kind of emb-race. I remembered his prior warning to me: "Beware of Lima. It is a tricky place!"

CHAPTER 13

Weapons Square, Lima

31 July 2015

Elena and I went to the central town. We visited Amazon, a second-hand bookstore where books are sold at exceptionally cheap rates. I do not know if it is named in connection with the online shop or with the natural Amazon forest region. I saw nice titles that I would have loved to purchase but I was still intrigued by the question: How was I going to transport the books back to Germany? I had thought Elena equally wanted to buy some specific books. That was not the case. After conversing with one of the booksellers about a specific sociology text she was looking for, she bid us leave. The bookseller did not have that title. Instead, he proposed two other similar books that Elena did not really like although they were quite cheap. Just S/2 per text.

We went past the main market. It was quite different from a typical Cameroonian market, a little better organised, I must be honest. The stalls were divided into small narrow corridors, *callejones*. Just opposite the market, there is a giant entrance portal with marvellous murals, something like expressionist painting.

"It is a school of art, part of the University of Lima," Elena told me.

"It is quite impressive. I like its location above all. Right near the market, a very creative location for popular arts."

We continued down until we came to the rear of the House of Congress.

"Here is where the robbers congregate," Elena said in a rather dry tone, venting her consistent dismay towards the politicians of her country.

"No, Elena that is being too hard. Some of them are working hard for a better Peru. Those working for the common folks."

"Of course, you are right. The truth is that there are some of them who were genuinely good men, but power has gradually corrupted them. You know how much they earn?"

"How much?"

"About S/900 as a monthly salary. Compare that with the average earners of this country. You can understand why there are so many feuds amongst politicians battling to occupy congress seats. There have been assassination attempts on several mayors and deputies or candidates for these posts. It is a terrible fight for power."

"Politicians are roughly the same everywhere. However, the culture of assassination attempt is something still rare in my country, no matter the level of antagonism."

Elena and I went down to the frontage of the Congress House. I took some pictures. Then we came to the Inquisition Museum. We were just a few minutes before the opening of the museum. Others had seemingly been waiting for a much longer time.

Then came the guide, exquisitely dressed lady with a typical public relations smile, but trying to convey the gravity of the topic of inquisition. She led us to the docks and the courtrooms. Gradually, we were led into the dark labyrinths of the torture and hang rooms. In these complex catacombs, the figure of death assailed me at every millimetre. I sensed awe, a chilling atmosphere of nihilism, pain, anguish all convulsing in my being. I was faced with the imprints of the barbaric transmission of culture. At that very moment, I was there in the Inquisition Museum of Lima. But I was elsewhere. It conjured images of elsewhere, of some of the spaces, the walls of Auschwitz, the Birkenau slaughter fields, the Rampe[1], the death March unto the gas chambers, the moving dead, the sun, the air, life. Of other places, heard or read about, cardinal points on my agony road map. The space was dim-lighted, even though I still engaged in the dangerous game of photo making. Here, the intermix of the crepuscular moment and areas of darkness, the finicky passages underground, the crevices and the figures inside, leaning on the wall, man turned into stump, life as mocking reality in a space where death ruled king. In such a passage, my mind was warped, I lost the power of thought and it is when I came out that I began to figure out what I had just gone through. I had heard about the word inquisition in my secondary school days. It almost sounded cosy, appealing to the ears like most religious words. This rather euphonic name made me relate it in my mind to something beautiful, something laudable, something worth

---

1   A train stop in Auschwitz II, Birkenau where deported Jews, Sinti-Romas and other victims of the Holocaust alighted.

imitating. Nothing of its macabre connotation.

In this cave, the mind was less concerned with the word of the guide. The silence of the human objects crowded and echoed. When I finally came out of the underground cells, I could not trace Elena anymore. I looked around disturbed and tried to dial her number. Perhaps she was underground, in the curated cells, where there might be network problems. Suddenly, Elena tapped me on my back. She usually had a charming smile, but this time, her demeanour lost its lustre, perhaps worn down by the disconcerting experience we had just gone through. Elena easily became emotional whenever she talked about forms of human discrimination and denigration. I knew the experience would strike her too, although she had been through it several times. Usually, after every site we visited, Elena would ask me if I liked it. This time, she did not. It was not worth asking, I guess.

After the museum, Elena and I parted ways since she had to catch up with her appointment at the dentist. I was left alone to tour the *Plaza de Armas*. She promised to meet me at the *Casa de la Literatura Peruana (House of the Peruvian Literature)* in about an hour.

I went to the *Plaza de Armas*[2] also known as *Plaza Mayor (Main Square)*. There were certainly riot police, with large armours and apparently poised for rapid intervention. The Plaza de Armas, in Lima, just like its counterparts in most places in Peru, is a site of memory, where many historical events have taken place. In Lima, it is located just next to where San Martin declared the independence of Peru. But it was also a commercial area, where people met to exchange goods, one of the policemen told me. By that time, goods were also human.

"So, the slave trade took place here?"

"Yes, exactly. Enslaved Africans were bought and resold here. Their registration by the council also took place here. Permit me to ask: I guess you are from Brazil, Aren't you?

"I am from Cameroon, but I study in Germany."

His colleagues began to show interest in our discussion. They came close but rather just listened while I continued conversing with their colleague.

"Oh, that is great. When did you arrive?"

"I have been here since a week ago."

"And how long will you be in Peru? Do not leave from here without

---

2   Literally "Weapons Square" but the equivalent in English is "Parade Ground"

going to Machu Picchu."

"Oh yes, I can't afford to miss that. It is on my plan. I still have close to two weeks left. Please, can I take a picture with you guys?"

"Yes of course, with pleasure."

One of them took my phone and took some pictures of me, sandwiched by heavily armoured policemen. I have never been so secure before! They were all smiles and as I leave, they wished me the best in Peru.

As I left them, I was enticed to take a picture of the colony of pigeons flying freely around. There were myriads of them. One of the policemen quickly judged that I needed a photo and came to my service.

"Thank you very much. That is so kind of you guys!"

"Thanks for the compliments." He grinned with gratitude.

* * *

On this same spot, on the morning of 29 June 1823, in the heart of the American wars of independence, a Peruvian of African descent was tortured and then hanged by the Spanish Royal Forces for acting as a conduit between the government of Callao and the Patriots in Lima. At the point of death, he uttered: "If a thousand lives I had, gladly would I give them for my nation." His name was José Silverio Olaya Balandra. A street, el Pasaje Olaya, some two blocks away, is named after him, but many Peruvians are not aware of this figure. Forty-seven years earlier, on 22 Sept 1776, in the heart of the American War of Independence, a young spy from Connecticut was arrested and hanged by the British Royal Forces for treason. "I only regret that I have but one life to lose for my country." were his last words. His name was Nathan Hale, considered an American hero and, officially designated in 1985 the state hero of Connecticut.

* * *

Facing the *Plaza de Armas* is the *Palacio de Gobierno*, the office of the President of the Republic. Days later I would comment to Elena about this.

"Your government is very close to the people. Congress is basically in the marketplace whereas the president lives next to a popular park."

"Elena smiled. I know what you mean."

"I mean it seriously Elena. In Cameroon, the presidential palace is a no-go area. It is a sacred space."

"In spite of that, we are all the same," Elena said. She later told me that the palace was the seat of government right from the conquest. It was Pizarro who constructed it in 1536 and the subsequent viceroys and presidents of Republican Peru lived there.

I moved along the left flank of the Presidential building, still marvelled by its proximity to an assortment of activities, hawking, petty trading and all kinds of survival strategies going on around there. However, within the fenced yard, the protocol of power was rather unmistakable. The still attentiveness of the sentinels conveyed the officialdom within. Two on the presidential steps and four on the yard, human pillars in a well-marshalled state choreography. Some bodies are strong, almost impervious to basic reflexes, I thought. I stood there for close to fifteen minutes watching the body, wondering if no heady fly could disrupt the postures. Or this kind of benign but sharp pinch that sometimes assails our bodies, making our bodies adjust instantly.

Adjacent to the palace, were stores selling indigenous Peruvian handicraft. Colourful shoes, handbags, wool purses, ponchos, etc. As I was wondering whether to get into the stores to kill time while waiting for Elena, a stout guy came and greeted me.

"*Boa Tarde. Brasileiro?*"

"*Falo português mas não sou Brasileiro. Sou dos Camarões mas moro na Alemania.*"[3]

"*Guten Tag, wie geht es dir?*"

"*Sehr gut, oh du sprichst Deutsch !*"[4]

"Yes, I do." He replied, in German.

"From which part of Germany?" He switched to Spanish.

"From Bavaria, Bayern."

"Bayern München. We have a Peruvian player in Bayern. Pizarro."

"Oh yes, I know." This was a bit of an overstatement because I came to learn about Pizarro while in Peru. I had a rather vague idea of a Bayern-Munich player by that name. He went ahead to narrate more football stories.

"Cameroon Vs Peru 1982: your country played a great game against Peru." "Cameroon has a great team, right?"

---

3   "Good day, Brazilian"
     "Good day. I speak Portuguese but am not Brazilian. I come from Cameroon but I reside in Germany"
4   "Good day, how are you doing?"
     "Very good, Oh you speak German"

"Yes, somehow, they used to, but now things are a bit different."

"Roger Milla, Samuel Eto'o. Sure, old and new generation. Although Eto'o is almost on his way out too."

"Very often I have met Peruvians who know either Roger Milla or Samuel Eto'o, depending on their age group, but hardly would they know both. And again, you seem to know so much about Germany."

"It is because my brother lives in Karlsruhe."

"Oh, I see!" I exclaimed, though that did not seem to me as ample justification. The guy seemed a bit impatient, wanting to say something perhaps not in the direction in which I was pushing the discussion.

"There is a bar around here where many tourists drink. At this moment, there are so many of them there. Just around the corner."

My first instinct was to resist the invitation. I asked him if he knew the Catholic Church where there are *catacumbas* (*catacombs*).

"Oh yes, it is just opposite the bar. They let in groups of tourists after every thirty minutes." I still did not want to follow this guy. But then, we were in the middle of the city and only an extremely paranoid mind would insinuate any sinister outcome. More so, there were many security agents around. We were within the perimeter of the presidential palace. Having a bottle of beer to kill time as I waited for Elena seemed logical. It would be good to have a taste of Peruvian beer.

We entered the beer parlour. It was a snack bar with a restaurant. A smartly dressed waitress came up to me.

"Good day, sir. What do you take for beer and food?"

I quickly made it clear that I would take just a beer.

"No food." I felt a sense of disappointment in the eyes of my new-found friend.

"How many bottles of beer? Two or just one?"

I did feel a bit bemused at the entire setting. What did he mean by two bottles of beer? Was I also going to pay for my friend? Of course, this was something I could do but I was not compelled to. I had started confirming my doubts when the waitress failed to ask my companion about his choice of food.

As I opened my mouth to say "one", I felt the eyes of my companion on me. And he said:

"Two, am sure". Trying to be suggestive.

"What kind of beer do you want to drink, sir?"

I dabbled at the available options which the waitress listed and described to me.

"I need something typically Peruvian."

"Ok, I think Cusqueña would be okay for you. It is a good beer. Many people like it."

My friend ordered for a foreign beer, Pilsen, certainly more expensive as I would later see on the bill. As we drank, he engaged me on a fast-track interview to gauge my preferences on some things.

"German girls are very beautiful, aren't they?"

"Well, it's subjective. Some are very attractive, of course."

"Have you ever had a German girlfriend?"

"Sure. I have been living there for five years now."

"I also had a German girlfriend here." With almost a sense of boastfulness. "She was a tourist who came to Lima two years ago."

"Oh, that was very smart of you." He smiled, with a sense of pride. "But I have about two Peruvian girlfriends now."

"Aren't you married?"

"Me, no, not yet. I am still waiting for the right person. I prefer just girlfriends for now. Here girls are very cheap. If you need anything just tell me. There are some high-class places meant for people like you. There you can have a very decent sex. The street prostitutes are criminals. Just watch out during your time here. They lure their customers, make them drunk and seize their belongings."

I began to gauge the intentions of my companion. I tried to be as diplomatic as possible in proving to him I was not interested in his implicit offer. But he did not seem to give up. Suddenly, he jumped out, telling me hurriedly:

"Those girls outside are tourists. Let me talk to them."

Minutes after, he came in, accompanied by three ladies and one guy.

"Meet Gil, he is also from Germany."

I could sense the subtle doubts on the girls' faces. They hesitated for a while before one of them came over to greet me. She was in dreadlocks, slightly thin. I inquired about her hometown or village in Germany. They were University students from the Wuppertal, but they came from neighbouring villages. While she had just come straight to Peru for a two-week holiday, the other two girls and the heavily bearded man had lived in neighbouring Ecuador for six months before touring Peru with her. The other three joined in, inquiring in which city I lived. Later they told me their trajectory. They planned to travel to Ayacucho and later on visit some colleagues in Trujillo, up North. They ran out of funds for Cusco and felt so thrilled when I told them "I would go to Cusco in little less than two weeks."

"Happy you!" One of them said.

They seemed to be in haste. One of them had dashed to the restaurant latrine nearby. She came out and all hurried to the taxi waiting for them outside. We bade farewell and they went off. My friend, who had been quiet, curiously listening to us speaking in German followed them outside. When he came in, he confided to me.

One of those girls, the one with the Rasta hair smokes weed.

"How do you know?"

"She asked me if I had any lead-up. Unfortunately, my friends who do that business are not in town today. Me, I don't do that."

My phone began to ring.

"Hi, Gil. I am at Casa de Literatura."

"I am coming in a jiffy, Elena. I am a minute away from there."

I beckoned and the waitress brought the bill. I paid for the two bottles and bade farewell to my friend. He looked a bit disappointed that I was leaving, partly because of the friendship that had developed between the two of us, but also because I had not responded to his trappings. As I was settling the bills, he wrote his number and name on my notebook which I held all along.

"Please call me at any time and I can arrange something for you. Anything of your choice. As you wish."

"Ok, my friend. Thank you. See you next time."

CHAPTER 14

Tschüsss again

1 August 2015

As I went out to the Chinese-Peruvian restaurant for lunch, I met this man on a different street. The *Tschüss man* who told me more than a week ago that being black in Peru is problematic. He recognized me before I could recall that he was the one. He was about to cross the road. No time for us to meet again and talk. In the haste of crossing, he put his index finger under his eyelids. I found it hard to deduce the meaning. In my language, it would mean "you will see". But within the context of our last discussion, it could mean "you will see what I told you". It could also have been an inquiry, have you already started seeing what I told you?". As usual, there was no emotion on his face. It made it difficult for me to know how to accord meaning to that interpretation. If I see him next, I am sure I will recognize him before he recognizes me.

Hay negra y negra-retinta

De Guinea, Senegal,
Congo, Angola y Camerún
Desciende el negro común
En el Perú colonial.
Llamado "negro bozal"
Por su expresión tan sucinta,
El mestizaje despinta
Su oscura pigmentación;
Por esta misma razón
Hay negra y negra retinta.
Nicomedes Santa Cruz (Decimas: Poemas y Antología)

(English translation)

Black woman, darker black woman

From Guinea, Senegal,
Congo, Angola, Cameroon
Came the common blacks
To colonial Peru.
Known as "bozal"
For their very succinct expression
Miscegenation removes
Their dark pigmentation;
For this reason
There is black woman but also very dark black woman

Nicomedes Santa Cruz (*Decimas: Poems and Anthology*)

CHAPTER 15

To Be is to Move

3 August 2015

I left the house that evening a bit earlier. I knew from my two-week experience that, though the distance to the travel agency was not very far, Lima's murky traffic called for a sense of caution. My intention was to be at the *Cruz del Sur* station at least one hour thirty minutes before departure which was set for 9:15 P.M. Some few steps to the bus stop, I met an Afro-Peruvian I had greeted a few days before right in front of my flat. He recognized me instantly though it was getting dark. I told him I was travelling to the southern towns of the country. He advised me to buy some pills so as to guard against high altitude in Ayacucho. Yes, Juan, Elena and other friends had given me the same advice. We exchanged numbers so that we could meet and have a drink after my return to Lima.

I proceeded to cross the road. There was an endless line of vehicles trooping down the road with no chance for pedestrians to cross. The traffic lights were then of no use. Even when it was green for the pedestrians, the cars kept their course. I was a bit confused.

"What is happening, *señorita*? Is there no consideration for pedestrians?" I asked the lady who stood near me. She pointed to a traffic police agent in the middle of the road, about twenty-five metres from us, waving a staff as a sign of controlling traffic. He kept ushering the cars to continue down irrespective of what the traffic lights indicated.

At this time of the day, traffic lights do not mean anything and you must always watch out. The lady told me. Some impatient young boys saw a slight thaw in the number of cars coming down and quickly crossed though the policeman was still ushering cars to keep on. I found it pretty dangerous. A truck almost knocked down one of them.

After what seemed like an endless process of waiting, our turn to cross finally came. A few minutes later, a heavily crowded voice came and amongst the various destinations that the motor-boy composed in his song, there was *Javier Prado*. The bus was suffocating. When I arrived at the travel agency, I made a sign of the cross.

I arrived forty-five minutes to the departure time. We were asked to wait as the passengers from Chiclayo made their arrivals and claimed their luggage. The buses looked very impressive. The whole set-up, the agents, their attire, their body language, and the entire atmosphere smelled of the airport. The Marco Polo-marked inter-city buses made a very good impression. I reflected over names: *Marco Polo, Cruz del Sur*. Every single name breathes history. Coincidentally, a passenger passed by me with a trolley bag. On it, in nice calligraphy: *Simon Bolivar*. In the street of Lima, I had felt surrounded by this historic mist of founders, revolutionaries, etc. etc. The names are so eloquent that a curious mind would not find rest until meaning is made out of them. I also admired the fact that certain avenues, as if in a Pan-American spirit, carry names and towns of other Latin American countries. *Avenida Brasil. Avenida Venezuela. Avenida Bolivia*. Also names of other Peruvian towns like *Avenida Arequipa, Avenida Ayacucho*. Just like in Germany.

We boarded the bus at 10:40 P.M. and departed ten minutes later. I sat on the front seat of the second floor, close to the window. This was ideal for someone who wanted to have a night view of Peruvian countryside. Next to me was a tall guy, seemingly in his mid-30s. The two front seats on the other column were occupied by two young lovers who kissed all through the trip, an exercise they had begun at the agency as we waited for boarding time. I guessed the trip must have been too short for them. I thought sustained public kissing was so peculiar amongst German youths. I had not seen a lot of such during my trips in the US, France and other parts of Europe. Seemingly, Peruvians were similar to the Germans in that aspect.

Some hamburgers were served on board as soon as we kicked off. I quickly consumed because I had not had enough time to dine that evening. After having a bite, I took out one of the books I carried along. It was a pamphlet on Afro-Peruvians, their histories and contributions to the Peruvian national culture, an interesting review put together by the CEDET[1], an Afro-Peruvian research centre based in Lima. I read the first few pages but was just too exhausted to focus. Sleep gained the better part of me. I woke up about three hours later to discover that the

---

1   *Centro de Desarollo Etnico* (Centre for Ethnic Development)

bus was stuck in traffic. We were going to spend nearly three hours in one spot. When we finally pulled out of the traffic, it did not take long before the driver announced that our bus had a slight technical problem. That again took him not less than two hours to put the bus on the move. At daybreak, we were still far away from Ayacucho, where we were supposed to arrive at 5:30 A.M. according to what the lady at the ticket counter had told me the day before. The truth is that we finally arrived at Ayacucho at five minutes to midday.

I remember one thing about that trip. As the bus flashed its headlamps on turning one curve, between wakefulness and sleep, I caught sight of the statue of the Virgin Mary by the road. Though it was protected by a rectangular cage with a roof, I had an ample view of the statue as the bus slowed down around the corner. For over a long time, I had not seen the face of Mary at such close quarters. What I saw was slightly bigger than the Virgin Mary of my childhood days. It used to be held by Catholic Christians during the Feast of Christ the King across the whole village with solemn sounds and measured steps, with young children marching in front in white gowns. These were some of the things that as a child made me envy my catholic neighbours whom I saw as having a better experience and contact with God than those of us from the Baptist church. I was jealous of my Catholic friends who were mass servants and had the divine favour to be close to or even carry such divine figures. Sometimes when we stood by the roadside and watched our friends in this holy company, there seemed to be a wide gap between us. I could not even wink, or whistle at my friends as we used to do in those days amongst peers. Their place in heaven was somewhat guaranteed even if we engaged in the same childhood crimes and desires during break time at school. Sometimes in school on the following day, one could not dare talk about the holy procession of the previous day. Back to the Virgin Mary on the road to Ayacucho, upon arrival in Ayacucho, one of the passengers told me that these roadside statues meant that an accident had occurred on that spot, that someone or many people had perished around that vicinity.

CHAPTER 16

Ayacucho, the Corner of Death

Ayacucho seems more closely tied to death than life… it has always been a place of battle and death. Revolutions begin in Arequipa – an old saying goes – but when they reach Ayacucho they are serious matters.[1]

Ayacucho has quite a different topography from Lima. While the main parts of Lima are situated on a plane, Ayacucho, on the other hand, is found in an undulating and relatively low landscape. The greater part of the city is located in a basin and the traveller from Lima appears on a hilltop and then spirals down to the city. There seemed to be a striking topographical similarity between Ayacucho and the headquarters of my region in Cameroon, Bamenda. Just like the up-station hill in Bamenda, the hillside surrounding Ayacucho offers you a bird's eye view of the entire town. More so, Bamenda somewhat synthesizes Arequipa and Ayacucho. When she coughs, Yaoundé has to listen, for a Bamenda man does not live under a culture of fear and intimidation. No doubt did the fall of the Berlin Wall reverberate in Bamenda more than elsewhere in Cameroon, leading to the Operation Ghost Town.[2]

As we almost entered the main town of Ayacucho, I was greeted by a signpost with the inscription *Avenida Javier Perez de Cuellar*. It took me down memory lane, to the days when we used to cram names of past United Nations Secretary Generals for our General Knowledge classes.

---

1   Carleton Beals, *Fire on the Andes*, 1934.
2   On 25 June 1991, the Cameroonian opposition announced "Operation Ghost Town" in a bid to force the Biya regime to call for a national conference as a crucial step in the country's democratization process. Religiously observed in Bamenda, the stronghold of the main opposition party, the Social Democratic Front (SDF) headed by Ni John Fru Ndi, it involved the voluntary closing of businesses, shops and taxi services, and the refusal to pay government taxes. The regime in place often responded with violence and that led to several deaths. Ghost Towns have equally been used as a political strategy by the separatist movement in the two English regions of Cameroon between 2016 and 2019, and it has been most effective in Bamenda.

I remember Javier Perez de Cuellar was from Peru. By that time, that name "Peru" seemed so far-fetched to me, a land I never imagined in my wildest dreams to visit. By then it appeared to me like an Asian country!! I remember I used to interchange the country of UN Secretary-General U Thant, Burma with the Peru of Javier Perez de Cuellar. By then, from the name, I was never sure whether Peru was in Asia or Latin America. In my puerile consciousness, I had always associated the country with these nice-sounding names –Venezuela, Brazil, Argentina, etc. Like most Hispanic names, I considered the name to be too long. Little did I know that even that was a short form of a noun phrase that reads *Javier Filipe Ricardo Perez de Cuellar y de la Guerra*. Later I was to learn that Simón Bolívar was a short form for Simón José Antonio de la Santísima Trinidad Bolívar y Palacios; Gonzalez Prada for *José Manuel de los Reyes González de Prada y Álvarez de Ulloa* and Flora Tristan for *Flora Célestine Thérèse Henriette Tristán y Moscoso Lesnais*.

The streets of Ayacucho are quite narrow. Most of the houses are in brown bricks. Very few structures were cemented or painted from outside. Most of the streets were being dug by a group of construction workers. I later learned the town council was renovating its water and drainage systems.

Upon arrival, I called Narbo who was still at work. He promised to meet me at the Plaza de Armas under an hour. I thus decided to go to the tourist agency that my friend Miguel had recommended to me. Miguel had informed me that upon my arrival, he would be in the countryside of Ayacucho and would only be able to meet me on my second day in town. I paid for three days of guided tour of the city and its environs. Narbo came and met me at the agency and we went together for lunch. We both took *puca picante* an Ayacuchan delicacy that many of my friends from Lima recommended to me. Narbo took me to his house, a big three-room apartment. He showed me my room and bid me to feel at home. I took a bath and changed my clothes.

I put on something warm as Ayacucho was colder than Lima. We took a taxi-cholo, a three-seat cart powered by a motorcycle engine, back to town. Narbo left me at the *Urpillay* tourism office and went to the office. He wrote down the address of his house to me so I would easily find my way when I come back.

We visited the *Museo Hippolito*, located near the university. We were told it is a gift from the Venezuelan government. There were various artisanal relics from the Wari, Chanka, Nazca and Inca cultures. It was quite a rich museum with high-quality preservation kits and lighting system. During the uprising in the eighties, we were told, the museum was sealed since it is just adjacent to the Universidad San Cristobal de Huamanga, the original flashpoint of the violence.

We later went to the artisanal centre in the inner-town of Ayacucho. There, we were able to visit some artisanal, embroidery, weaving and carving workshops. I found it genial. I was quite amazed by this old man, a nationally recognized artist whom we visited. He carved all sorts of religious and national paraphernalia with incredible dexterity. It was like visiting the factory where the nation and the church were produced. He used a particular clay material that is found in a remote part of Huamanga, Ayacucho. He demonstrated to us the entire procedure, with a complex array of fine tools. I looked at the statues and statuettes of Virgin Mary, Jesus Christ, John the Baptist, Pope Benedict and Francis standing there in his factory shop. I figured them on the church altar and was amazed about their auratic potentials. Myriads of these objects were exposed on the table in the fore room. His wife and children were there. Like many Peruvian businesses, it looked like a family business. The restaurants in Lima almost had a family dimension to them. I wanted to buy one of the objects but changed my mind. Rather, when we visited the handicraft shops close by, I bought a small flute band, made of a dozen individual flutes yoked together in two columns of six by a fine and colourful thread. I had seen it in the musical performance in Lima where I was entranced by its musical power. I just loved the sound of it and the dexterity of the flute players. When blown by experts, it produced an eclectic and contrapuntal sound that synchronised all the twelve flutes in a tensed and beautiful unity. It reminded me of the *Rkongni* group, my village dance that came to be part of my identity. I imagined how members of that group would react if I presented this type of composite flute to them as a gift from Peru upon my return to Cameroon. From the artisanal centre, we visited a church and a seminary. In one of them, there were nuns. We were not allowed to see them but you could stand in front of the window and converse with them. It seemed quite strange to me, it reminded me of the mystery we used to attach to Catholic priests and sisters in our childhood days.

I came back in the evening at about 7:30 P.M. and found Narbo on the phone with his wife. It seems he was trying to explain something to his wife who unfortunately did not seem to share his perspective. When he was through, we chatted and laughed over family politics, especially amongst young couples. Soon, he tilted his laptop screen to me and said:

"This is the kind of job I do. I told you, right?"

With raised eyebrows, I carefully looked at the image on the screen. It was the picture of a shallow shaft into the earth. Standing around it was a group of people, mostly men, with human skulls in their hands.

I was taken aback for a few seconds. I tried to conceal my astonishment.

"Oh yes, I remember you had told me at Lima that you are a geologist." But at that time, I had not figured out the exact nature of the profession.

"Yes, I am a forensic archaeologist. We are presently exhuming the corpses of the victims of the 1980s violence from the mass graves. We do thorough DNA tests and all other forms of verification and family members come forth to identify their relatives."

"It must be a very difficult task."

"Yes, of course, it is. We need to talk with the villagers who help us in identifying the sites. The team verifies their claims and decides whether to start the digging. It is done in the presence of many officials: state counsel, church leaders, village heads and representatives of victim families. And then the bodies found are taken to our laboratory. That it is when the real work starts."

Narbo explained these in a very relatively low tone. But he tried to be as equanimous as possible. By saying it must be a difficult part, what I meant deep in me was the emotional challenge of even the professionals involved in the task. Not just the procedures and stages. From this time, my view of my friend changed, I would say. His face then began to have a much deeper meaning to me. Narbo has seen it all. Humans reduced to things. He was, a huaquero[3], not for gold or silver prospection. Rather, a huaquero of human skulls, human bodies in an attempt to restore their human dignity.

"After tomorrow, there will be a hand-over ceremony of the mortal remains to the victims' family members. Perhaps that could be of interest to you. I still need to confirm the time. But it will take place at the St. Francis Cathedral, just beside the Plaza de Armas."

"Please do and tell me. I am ready to sacrifice one of the trips to attend the ceremony.

---

3   Adjective derived from *huaquerismo*, the tendency of some Spanish colonial authorities in Peru to order the unearthing of the graves of indigenous dignitaries in order to recover the gold and silver with which they were buried. This practice was the order of the day during the viceroyalty of Francisco de Toledo (1569-1581).

"Ok! It could be helpful to you."

CHAPTER 17

In the Footsteps of the Inca

Day 2 in Ayacucho

We had a guided tour to the ruins of the Inca Empire in a locality called Vilcashuaman. I needed to wake up at 4:20 A.M. because I was meant to be at the *Urpillay* tourism agency at 5:00 A.M. The day before, for security reasons, I had asked the tour guide to give me the numbers of some trustworthy taximen whom I could call to pick me up. She gave me two numbers and assured me they were customers of her agency. I woke up on time, thanks to my alarm clock. I then dialled one of the numbers and was told it was out of network. I dialled the second one. It rang continuously but no one picked it up. Something was wrong. However, there was no time to waste. I went to the bathroom, rinsed my mouth quickly and took a fast and warm shower. Hopefully, I would get some taxi along the road in the next *cuadra*, some two minutes' walk from Amancais, where Narbo's apartment was located. What If I fall into the hands of a *ratero* masking as taxi man? For security reasons, I decided to take just the necessary things I needed for that day. I kept my maestro/visa bank cards at home. Took a banknote of S/50 and went out, making sure I closed the door as stealthily as possible so as not to wake Narbo up. When I went out of the gate, I saw two guys and a girl just alighted from a taxi. Seemingly, these guys are from a party, I said to myself, judging from their outfits and their drowsy utterances. The taxi was already zooming off when I closed the gate.

Please, taxi!! I shouted.

Noticing my attempt, one of the guys shouted at top pitch for the taxi driver to stop. It did stop and reversed to where we were. I ran up and said to the driver:

"Good morning sir. Please, can you take me to the *Plaza de Armas?*"

"No problem, my good friend. He sounded quite cosy."

I entered the taxi. Playing the same game as in Lima whenever I took a taxi during dark hours, I tried to sound like a town boy with full mastery of urban life and the townscape of Ayacucho.

"Streets are quite small here in Ayacucho. It is not like in Lima."

"You are right. Lima is much bigger, you live there?"

"Yes, I have been living there for years, although I also visit Ayacucho quite often." My uncle lives here." I claimed, making sure that I rehearsed my phrases thoroughly in order not to commit grammatical mistakes.

"But Ayacucho does not have many *rateros* like in Lima", I purported.

"Yes, here it is much more *tranquilo*."[1] He responded, seemingly happy with my good words for his home city. Since Lima, by its stature, basically bullies every other town in Peru, claiming mastery of this Leviathan enhances prestige. Lima has no match, Gulliver amid Lilliputs. But I needed to balance things, to bite and blow. My positive remarks about life in Ayacucho only came when I was confident that we were finally approaching the Plaza de Armas. When we arrived, I paid him S/5 and he drove off. I was relieved.

Opposite the tourism agency, there were silhouettes of human figures on a bench, leaning against the iron bars that fenced the Plaza de Armas. They were about five of them, wrapped up in thick jackets. I was not sure whether they were fellow tourists waiting for the agents. I went and leaned on the wall of the agency building. One of them moved towards me with very cautious steps. A thousand ideas crossed my mind but I was compelled to stay put.

"*Good morning.*"

"*Good morning.*"

"Are you one of the tour guides? Or you are also a tourist like us?"

"I am also a tourist. I am sure the agents will come very soon."

"Oh, that is great. I came with my family, they are sitting over there. They said at 5 A.M. I hope they will respect time."

He told me his wife and two sons were coming along. We went together to where they were sitting. We shook hands. Even in that darkness, a sense of a common destination gave me assurance and security. Some few minutes later, a mini-bus parked in front of the tourism agency. We all moved closer. It was the manager and the driver. We waited for a few minutes as other participants arrived.

At exactly 5:05 A.M. we were on our way. Altogether we were 12 persons, of all age groups. I sat in front as suggested by the boss of the

---

1 Calm

agency. Since I came from far, he wanted me to have the fullest view possible of the landscape. It was really cold and my doubled sweater and overcoat were helpless as the driver began to speed across the mountain chains just after we came out of the narrow streets of Ayacucho. As the wind flapped against the windows of the vehicle, we were almost freezing. It was drizzling and a thick fog covered the mountain chains as we spiralled along. The driver treated us to one huayno after another. Huayno, even when it is about love has this whining tone. I was told it used to be a music of celebration in these communities, but the war changed everything and huayno became *wanka*, funeral dirge in Quechua. The driver put one of the moving songs to which I had listened in Lima a week before, when Elena invited her friend, the *chino*, to her house. The song *"Flor de Retama"* (Flower of Broom) captures the horrors of the Peruvian civil war in the specific community of Huanta, one of the flashpoints of the armed conflicts.

Vengan todos a ver

¡Ay, vamos a ver!
Vengan hermanos a ver
Ay, vamos a ver!
En la Plazuela de Huanta,
amarillito flor de retama,
amarillito, amarillando
flor de retama.

Por Cinco Esquinas están,
los Sinchis entrando están.
En la plazuela de huanta
los Sinchis rodeando están.
Van a matar estudiantes
huantinos de corazón,
amarillito, amarillando
flor de retama;
van a matar campesinos
huantinos de corazón,
amarillito, amarillando
flor de retama.

En donde la vida
Se hace mas fría que la muerte misma
taita inti arde indignado
las grandes nieves se descongelan
y los grandes lagos comienzan a colmarse
el gran aluvión, esta por llegar
para sepultar, mundos que oprimen
y sobre la tierra nueva; florecerá la retama
y así las palmas que suenen arriba
ta ta ta

Donde la sangre del pueblo,
ahí, se derrama;
allí mismito florece
amarillito flor de retama,
amarillito, amarillando
flor de retama.

La sangre del pueblo
tiene rico perfume;
la sangre del pueblo
tiene rico perfume;
huele a jazmines, violetas,
geranios y margaritas;
a pólvora y dinamita.

¡Carajo!
¡A pólvora y dinamita!

(English translation)

Flower of Broom
Come on and see you all, yeah, let's go and see!
Come on and see you all, yeah, let's go and see!
In the little square of Huanta, little yellow Flower of Broom!
Little yellow yellowing Flower of Broom!
In the little square of Huanta, little yellow Flower of Broom!
Little yellow yellowing Flower of Broom!

In every corner they are, the Sinchis are entering
They're going to kill students, hearted people of Huanta,
Little yellow yellowing Flower of Broom!

Where life becomes colder than death itself
Tata inti is fuming with indignation
The big snow is defrosting
The lakes get full to the brim
And the alluvium closes in to bury
The world of the oppressor and in its place,
Shall flourish the flower of broom
With its palms sounding above

Where the people blood Yeah, is shed!
Just there it flowers little yellow Flower of Broom!
Little yellow yellowing Flower of Broom!

The people's eyes dream beautiful dreams
They dream wheat in the barnyard, wind in the meadows
And above every child a star.

The people's blood smells a rich perfume,
It smells of jasmines, violets, geraniums and daisies!
Of powder and dynamite!
Damn it! Of powder and dynamite!...

This area was amongst the worst hit by the guerrilla in the eighties. Many were decapitated here. Many supposed terrorists were arrested by the anti-terrorist police, never to be seen again. As I looked at the rugged mountain slopes, cliffs, the screes, the pinnacles, the brinks, I began to imagine how this difficult topography might have played in favour of the deadly battles thirty or so years back. Along these slopes, many heads rolled. Many hopes dashed. Much blood, much. Bodies were left to decay under the fog of the misty valleys some metres away from me.

The road was so rugged that at some point, the minibus was basically walking along. Given the twist and turns of the road, it was difficult to foresee a car or bus coming in the opposite direction. I remember our minibus almost collided with a bigger bus around a very sharp curve.

Seemingly, neither of the drivers was aware that there was a bus around the corner. Both realized just seconds away and the two buses missed each other by a hair's breadth. I could see the shock on the face of our driver. He made a rapid sign of the cross. Later, he confessed to me he was not a Catholic, not to even say a Christian. But at that moment, he thanked God for his life and ours.

We passed several road construction workers on the way, with all kinds of machines digging and transporting soil, sand and pebbles from the quarries onto various points on the road. By the roadside were so many tarpaulin tents, with temporary markets popping up at the junctures where the road constructors worked. We crossed many bridges, I am sure one of them was the famous River Bamba. I did not want to bother the much-focused driver with questions. The smaller streams, only superficially deep, did not have bridges. Our minibus simply rolled across them with its tyres, splashing water onto the adjoining shrubs, leaving me with a childlike sense of pleasure.

We continued for close to three hours and arrived at Vilcashuaman at about 8:30 A.M. We alighted in front of the restaurant where we took breakfast. The wife of the man that had first met me in the morning beckoned me to move from my seat and get closer to them so we could share some food she had brought along. She had come with a whole package of various food items. She passed some bread and glasses of *chicha* as they were preparing our breakfast. I felt very grateful. We exchanged for some few minutes about the common food items in Peru and Cameroon. They were amazed at the similarities between the uses of maize grains that can be consumed as fried, boiled maize, liquor, flour, etc. All these transformations had their cognates in both cultures. Our food was served. I had chosen to eat Trucha, a mixture of fresh fish, salad and Irish potatoes. This was upon recommendation from the generous woman. All of us on that table ordered the same dish.

We finished eating and went down a few metres to the Usnu, a very important administrative site of the Inca Empire. The most important Inca architecture in Vilcashuaman is the Usnu. Constructed in the shape of a trapezium to shield it against volcanic explosions, the Usnu is 25 metres wide and 27 metres long. It has 5 doors and one of them is only used by the Inca. It is claimed that its edges and walls used to be covered with golden laminas. It has five floors with outlaying terraces at the flat top of which is a stone-carved royal throne where the Inca would sit and address his people. The assembly ground at the foot of the pyramid could contain more than 40,000 subjects at the time. The guide had a commanding mastery of the narratives. To initiate any important political event, every Inca would assemble the mummies of his ancestors by his side. It granted ancestral legitimacy or blessing to his decisions. Vilcashuaman comes from two words – *Vilca* (sacred) and *waman* (hawk). The llama, puma, snake, condor and hawk are some of the most symbolic animals in the Inca cosmology. Vilcashuaman was made an important administrative centre by Inca Pachacutec, one of the most expansionist Incas.

It is believed that the city has the shape of the hawk of which the Usnu stands as the head. The location of any cultural structure in the Inca Empire had a very deep rationale. Cusco, for example, has the shape of a Puma with Sacsaywaman as its head. Coming back to the Usnu, it is built with large and black volcanic stones, square-shaped and carefully chiselled. Vilcashuaman was one of the most important administrative centres of the Tawantisuyu. It is equidistant to the southern and northern poles of the Inca Kingdom: 40,000 kilometres to Ecuador and 40,000 kilometres to Mendoza, Argentina. It is therefore very symbolic in the trajectory of the Inca, *el Camino Inca*. The tour guide explained to us the meaning of the structure and its importance in the Inca Empire.

After visiting the Usnu, we went up to the town square of Vilcashuaman. There were many inhabitants lined up in front of what seemed like a group of registration officials. Perhaps it was some public sensitisation or identification campaign. One of the men on the line saw me and tapped his neighbour on the shoulder. Not before long, a whole string of curious eyes was gazing at me, accompanied by smiles of apparent amusement. I could feel the eyes on my back as we climbed up to the sun temple of the Inca at the top of which was the Catholic Church, *San Juan Bautista*, i.e. John the Baptist Catholic Church. The Spanish conquest had the policy of erecting a Catholic church at the helm of any important Inca site. The same exists in Coricancha in Cusco. This was a sign of the change of times, the triumph of the new order over the old, to say the least.

What remained was a touristic simulation of the original sun temple. As we approached the Cathedral at few minutes to midday, there was a well-dressed man who walked rapidly past us, elbowing us to the side of the road as he moved towards the bell. And then came the bang. It roared with barbaric intensity and almost sent me dumb, almost tearing my eardrums. The weight of time, its strident intensity.

When we came down from the church and sun temple, we sat down at the Plaza de Armas for a few minutes of rest. I was intrigued by the term, *huaca*, the sacred sites in the Andes. The sun temple was a *huaca*. In Quechua, it is spelt *wak'a*. I remembered my Ethiopian colleagues who did their research on holy shrines in Ethiopia. They referred Waka as a name for "god", if I remembered well. It made me see the interconnectedness of cultures. In my two Quechua sessions, I had the intuition that the flair of the language was somewhat similar to Limbum, my language. I had not been able yet to pin it down to particular words but I was sure that these languages had something in common. It took me four years in Germany to discover the basic fact that "wir", the German word for "we", is the same as "wir", the exclusive "we" in Limbum. In the same light, "si", the exclusive "we" in Limbum is merely doubled to obtain the Kiswahili equivalent – "sisi". The same applies to all the personal pronouns in Limbum and Kiswahili.

As I was reflecting over these linguistic affinities, two ladies, fellow tourists travelling in my group, came and sat by me. They inquired where I was from and what I was doing in Peru. They listened with amazement as I told them my research work that connects Africa and Latin America. They went further to inquire if I enjoyed my time in Peru. I answered in the affirmative as usual.

"Tell me, what kind of food have you been eating?"

"Most of the time, I have eaten many nice things, but I sometimes forget to register the name in my mind. But mostly, I have been eating *chaufa con pollo, lomo salteado, frejol, arroz y papitas de Huancayna*. And last but not the least, I have been eating *Chucha*. It is what I ate this morning." I said with a strong emphasis on *chucha*.

"Oh really? So *chucha* is all you have been eating ever since you came here?"

"Not all the time, but many times. I ate it this morning." I repeated.

"Wow!" The lady exclaimed and laughed continuously for about a minute. I was dumbfounded.

"It is *trucha*!" They corrected my pronunciation. They told me what *chucha* means in Peruvian slang. I started giggling. I excused myself for the wrong pronunciation but the damage was already done. It was my rite of passage.

We boarded the minibus back in the direction of Ayacucho. We were to visit more touristic sites on our way back. After about a forty-five minutes' drive, we came to an area known as Vischongo where there is a large archaeological complex. We alighted and went to the *Pumapaqcha*, a Puma-shaped lake. Thanks to the lagoon, it is a very fertile area and is purported to be the *chacra*, farm of Túpac Amaru for the growth of several crops like maize, coca leaves, *hoja de coca*, etc. About a hundred metres from the banks of the lagoon, there is a fountain where the Incas used to bathe with the belief that it had rejuvenating powers. To climb up to the fountain was not an easy task for the gradient was pretty steep. We passed around a stone that functioned as the solar clock, *Oloj solar Inca*, Intiwatana, a three-angled stone that was used to measure the rise of the sun. The lagoon area, called the *acllahuasi (house for the chosen women)* was where a select group of women carried out weaving and brewing activities for the Inca.

The spring flows on two channels, finely carved in stone, looking more like two modern pipes. Those of us who made it up to the fountain imitated the Inca gesture by washing our head under the refreshing shower of the Inca fountain. Since the weather had become extremely hot, it was a pleasure letting the cold drops from the mini waterfall soak parts of our shirts and inner wears. It was cold and refreshing. Purportedly, we were rejuvenated. After all, is coming to America not a ritual act of newness in itself? Don't we all come to America to renew ourselves in its waters, its nature? We made a lot of fun about that exercise. It was like a baptism, in-between aspersion and immersion. We all kept laughing as we shared jokes while descending from the fountain.

One of the ladies said, as a matter of fact, everyone comes to the Americas to remain young, eternal youthfulness. Nueva España, Nueva Grenada, New England, Nouvelle France, Nouvelle-Orléans, New Amsterdam, New York, New Hampshire, Nueva Germania ... Civilisation, evangelization, partnership, aid, human rights etc. etc. For Old Europe to remain young, it can be a heavy cost for its body parts and for the body parts of those, those ones whose bodies need to be used for her plastic surgery. The Mandinkas, the Inkas, the true and mistaken Indians, the "chinos", and other brown majorities without any projects need to be brought into the fold by benevolent others. For Europe to remain young, its old bones need to rest in union with the mammary glands of the sweet sixteens, so that when they reached maturity, their body was as vast and barren as T. S. Eliot's "Wasteland", as old and young as Ayi Kwei Armah's "Abroliga the Frog", "the Old Man Child".

When we descended back to the lagoon many of the fellow sojourners walked round it up to where the bus was parked. However, some young men were at the mouth of the lake offering us the service to sail with us on the boat through the swampy lake unto the site where our bus was parked. One of the women who teased me on my favourite Peruvian food was with me in the same boat. She assailed me once more.

"You seem to be travelling all alone. Where is your family?"

"I have been asked this question several times."

"Are you married or single?"

"I am married since about 3 months ago."

"Then what are you doing here?" This question made me feel guilty.

"So, no time to *pachamanquiar*!" One of them said, smiling.

"What is *kachamanquiar*?"

"In Peru, that is how we describe what people do during the honeymoon."

"Oh, I see. This is the second vocabulary I am learning for today. I will take it down!"

"Yes, take good note of that." They were so funny, these ladies.

We arrived at the other bank and paid the boatmen their S/2 per passenger. We waited for those who trekked around the lake to join us and then continued the trip back, stopping at one village called *Madre de Dios* for lunch. Interspaced with some Quechua names, most names of villages here somewhat bear the marks of God's miracles and revelations in this part of the world: Jesús Cristo, Asunción, Concepción, Juan el Bautista, San Pedro, Santa Rosa, San Francisco. It is not for nothing that Ayacucho, even though "the corner of death" is surrounded by thirty-three churches that mark the years Jesus Christ spent on earth.

After lunch, we went around one hill, parked our bus and climbed a steep escarpment to one waterfall, *las caratas de Pumapaqcha*, Cusibani and Alpachaca. After having taken pictures under the close to 40 metres high waterfall with its refreshing showers, we walked back to where our bus was parked, passing through the farm of an Indian woman. She was tilling the soil and burning a heap of dry grass. Some ten metres from her, was a young kid in a grey *sombrero*, squatting near a brown-coloured lamb. Meters away were a small violin, partly covered by dry grass. The child bore the colour of the earth; covered with the dust of the soil his mom was tilling some meters away. The true child of *Pachamama*. This atmosphere reminded me of those childhood days when my mother was everything to me, she still is. Then, the earth had a particular scent, especially when it welcomed the first rains of the season. That scent, I have long lost. Think of the taste of the vegetables cooked on the farm, with the dry stem of the maize plant as an *extempore* spoon, adding a particular flavour to the *njama njama*, (huckleberry). Then, the world itself had colour, texture and taste. Then, I expected with certainty the feast of life when the people of the earth will gather around a bonfire and celebrate life. Then, Life had meaning. Life was like a Christmas gift by then and I believed that the Lamb literally died to save young, innocent and sinful children like us.

With his left hand, the child was stroking the mane of the lamb slowly and tenderly. The lamb stood there immobile, seemingly enjoying the hands of the young boy. It was surely his best friend. When I passed by the young boy stared at me steadily into my eyes. I am sure he asked himself a lot of questions. I came close to him, and we had a brief conversation.

"What is your name?"

"Juan Sabastian del Salvador."

"Juan Sabastian del Salvador, how old are you?"

"I am 9 years old."

"And in what class are you?"

"Second year."

"Oh, that's good."

"Where are you from?"

"From Africa, from Cameroon. Have you heard of Africa?" He shook his head.

"Have you heard of Germany?" He shook his head again.

His eyes were still fixed on me. It was difficult to explain to him. I felt like spending more time with him, but my friends were already a distance from me. I bade him farewell. I left him with an assignment. He also gave me an assignment and I have not stopped thinking about this child, my friend. We both wanted to know more about one another. The encounter with him reminded me of an incident in my church in Bayreuth, Germany. At the beginning of the service, it is ritual for our pastor to bid Christians greet their neighbours with a handshake and welcome them in God's house. My neighbour to the left shook my hand, with prior hesitation but gradually held my palm tightly against his, letting it go only after many seconds. After the handshake, he whispered in my ear: It is just like any other hand. Let me tell you honestly that I am now seventy years old but I have never come so close to a black person or touched their hand. Smiles. But you will bear with me that the smile of an old man with wrinkles is a labyrinth, we only call it smile for lack of a better word. I "smiled" back. I turned right to greet the other lady by me. The old man was still itching to talk to me but we were in the church. Unfortunately, I was in a haste and left after church service. Perhaps, had I stayed back, I would have heard more of his "experience".

When we left the waterfalls, we spent merely about 30 minutes on the way to reach Ayacucho. The bus became quite lively, with passengers conversing with one another. It is like the visits to the Inca springs and the waterfalls had taken its due effects. The driver and I were in front, silent, only following the album of Edwin Montoya to which the driver treated us since we left Vilcashuaman. One of the songs was outstanding with its sense of longing: Hola mi amor (Hello my love)

Hola mi amor que tal
Hermoso volver a verte
Hora mi dulce amor

Hola mi amor que tal,
Me muero por estrecharte
Hola mi dulce amor,
Que deseos de tenerte
Necesitaba tus besos,
Me hacia falta tu amor
Necesitaba tu aliento
Para volver a vivir...
Que hermoso es volver a verte

Hola mi dulce amor,
Que lindo es volver ha verte
He contado los minutos,
que ausente estuve de ti
He contado los segundos,
Pero al fin estoy aqui
Por tu amor no se que hacer
Sin tu amor es de morir

(English translation)

Hello my love, how are you
How sweet is it to see you again

Hello my sweet love,
I long to come close to you
Hello my sweet love,
I long to have you with me
I needed your kisses
I missed your love
I needed your breath
To come back to life
How lovely is it to see you again

Hello my sweet love,
How nice it is to see you again
I have counted the minutes
The time I was away from you,
I have counted the seconds,
But alas I am here
For your love, I do not know what to do
Without your love, it is better to die.

CHAPTER 18

Ayacucho, Thirty Years After

6 August 2015

In the morning, I got ready before Narbo. His wife had come the previous night and he had a longer morning than expected. She had informed him she was going to arrive in Ayacucho at around midday on Thursday. However, she wanted to surprise him. She had called him and he picked her up on his bike. He told me she complained that he did not show any or enough excitement on meeting her. Narbo is a naturally composed person, not very jocund at flaring up in amazement.

While his wife was still sleeping, Narbo and I dressed up and rode on his motorcycle to the Cathedral for the ceremony. We arrived at the church at 9:00 A.M. when the service was scheduled to begin. He was actually supposed to be there an hour before. The previous evening, he and his colleagues had brought in the mortal remains to church. But as an archaeological team member, he was supposed to be in church with his colleagues one hour before the commencement of the handing over ceremony. Certainly, there was to be a pre-briefing on the tasks they still had to perform during the ceremony.

When we arrived at the church, Narbo joined his team while I lingered outside for some time. I tried to get in touch with Miguel, my friend who had coordinated my trip to Ayacucho through email. The day before, through text messages, we had agreed to meet during the ceremony. I was very grateful for his recommendations with regard to the tourist agency and the sites worth visiting in Ayacucho.

While waiting for Miguel, I contemplated the figures of police officers in neat uniforms, looking very serene, conveying the very gravity of the ceremony at hand. There was also a martial band. It has been long I had not come so close to these since my primary school days. And then my eyes fell on the Church bell hanging at the left flank of the Cathedral frontage. The bell. This has always been a queer object to me. Sometimes, it does not only mark time, perhaps the call for devotion time, but also the Time, the final moment. In my community, most bells are made up of a car wheel drum. But when that wheel drum is turned into a church symbol, it carries a different meaning. Perhaps things have changed, I have not been home for a long time now. Our house is very close to the Baptist Church, so the bell always had an immediate effect on my sensibilities. Whenever you heard the bell ring at an odd time of the day, then tragedy has befallen the village; a soul has answered the final call. As I stood there, lost in memory, John Donne's poem, "When the Bell Tolls", came to my mind. Huamanga thirty years back. How many times did that bell ring in those dark days? What message did it carry? For whom did it toll? Were they even able to gather and murmur a prayer to the son, daughter, mother or father, killed under heinous conditions? Could a soul answer the bell's call without the risk of convening a second meeting? What did the golden gods on the church counter say, when tens of thousands bled to death under their noses? What was the fate and how was the faith of Ayacucho's thirty-three cathedrals in this time of smoke?

With these questions in mind, I entered the Cathedral. It was full to the brim, with people dressed in different attires and uniforms. On the edge of every pew, there were youths dressed in white T-shirts and black trousers or skirts. They supposedly belonged to a support team, present to offer any form of assistance to the audience, mostly made up of members of the victims' families. There were numerous sachets and bottles of water lying at the four corners of the church, with an armature of First Aid kits brought in by members of the Red Cross team. Not mastering the seat arrangements in the cathedral, I came and sat near an old lady, who recognized my presence with a nod of the head. I responded with the same body language. Few minutes thereafter, one of the ladies in uniform came to me and inquired.

"Are you also one of the victims' family members?"

"No, I am visiting." The word "visitor" echoed like a bell in my mind. It accorded me the privilege of the researcher, unconcerned with the fate of the victim, an objective observer drawing scientific material from raw data. I felt immersed in the moment. If that space was only reserved for the victims, then I was one.

* * *

(Auschwitz, 2 July 2012. There is a commemoration ceremony in the International Youth Meeting Centre, in Auschwitz in memory of about 500,000 Sinti-Romas, i.e. "Gypsies" who were massacred by the Nazi in the Auschwitz concentration camps alone. I am the only black person in the hall, most of whom are German and Polish Sinti-Romas. A short stout man meets me on the corridor, shakes my hand and with a smiling face asks me:

"Nice to meet you, my friend. Are you also Roma?"

No time to think, only the face, there in my front, there for me.

"Yes, I am Roma."

That evening, there was a reception in a guesthouse/cultural centre at the heart of the Auschwitz forest. It was dusk, there was Roma/Polish cuisine and music. I danced to the tune, they laughed from the beginning, then appreciated my learning skills, then cheered... I was happy.)

* * *

The lady welcomed me and moved away to attend to the women seated behind me. Certainly, she had wanted to talk to me, to counsel me as I saw those similarly dressed talking to some members of the audience. Deep in me, I was moved by the fact that someone thought I could be one of the victims' family members. This question touched me to the core. Yes, I was part of the family members. They are human beings. Their loved ones lying at the altar were human beings too.

Again, John Donne's poem assailed my memory, this time even more strongly:

No man is an island
Entire of itself;
Every man is a piece of the continent,
A part of the main;
If a clod be washed away by the sea,
Europe is the less,
As well as if a promontory were,
As well as any manner of thine own
O thine friends were;
Any man's death diminishes me,
For I am involved in mankind.
And therefore send not to know
For whom the bell tolls;
It tolls for thee.

Behind the altar lay several rows of carefully arranged coffins. Sixty, as my friend had informed me the previous night. As I was lost in thought, contemplating the ghoulish sight of the coffins, my phone rang. Miguel. I bowed down and in a low tone, I was able to inform him I was inside the Cathedral. He too was in, he said and stopped the call. I looked around and saw one man, in spectacles, craning his neck as in search of someone in the crowd. I was not sure if he was the one. Quite different from the Facebook pictures of him. Less hairy, I would say. He noticed me, came and got me by the hand and we moved quietly to the corner of the cathedral, at a safe distance behind the column of pews.

"Finally, we have made it."

"Welcome Gil, so happy that you are here."

The atmosphere, the circumstances of our meeting, did not give room for an outburst of joy. We kept it low key.

"Thank you for informing me about this event. I was not aware since I was not in town. Please, let's move over to the other row so you can greet my friend."

I took my bag and crossed over. Many eyes were on me. Perhaps because of the heavy backpack I was carrying. I had taken my things along in case I was late for the bus station in the evening. I did not need to go back to Narbo's house.

"Gil, here is Gabriela, my very good friend."

"Very delighted to meet you, Gil."

"Same here, Gabriela." She shifted for Miguel and I to sit by her.

Gabriela was born and bred in Ayacucho and can tell you so much about this town.

After this brief chat, we sat and followed the mass that had just begun. Some few minutes afterwards, Miguel moved closer to the altar where the coffins lay. A forest of cameras was there, trying to capture in the closest detail possible the images of the coffins and the names inscribed on them.

"I need to stand a bit closer for some shots. My camera is not very strong." I told Gabriella.

"That is ok Gil. I will take care of the bag."

I knew that Miguel would send me the pics later on. I merely wanted to have as many close-up shots from as many angles and perspectives as possible.

The ceremony began. The Peruvian anthem was sung with everyone on their feet followed by a very vivid and rapturous "Viva el Peru". Then, many speeches were made by the authorities gathered: the mayor, the State Counsel, the chairman of the Protestant and Evangelical Association, the provincial governor, the chairperson of the council of victims and families. The Archbishop of Huamanga was the last to speak. All speeches were summarized in Quechua since most of the victims' family members were from rural communities with limited knowledge of Spanish. Messages were full of compassion for the victims, the need for justice, the responsibility of both the terrorist rebels and the Peruvian army in the killings, the need for communal healing, the need to have faith in the Peruvian judiciary system, the commitment to a new Peruvian national spirit where such crimes will never, never again happen, etc.

"We know that the soldiers, supposedly acting in the name of the Peruvian State, committed excesses that are unacceptable in a state of law. I ask for forgiveness from the family members' victims and that never in the history of the Peruvian military and police force shall we repeat such atrocities. The army is committed to the protection of civilian lives and nothing else. I plead for forgiveness in the name of the Peruvian state."

The voice of the governor was emotive and empathetic. There, he was the State in its human and emotional form. I later gauged from my discussion with Gabriela and Miguel that many Peruvians have lost faith in the country's judiciary system and its willingness to deal with the responsibilities of the army in particular regarding the crimes committed during the guerrillawar. Corruption and lack of political will were enormous cogs in the Peruvian judicial system and other key sectors of the society.

After the speeches, the names of the deceased on the coffins were read out and the corresponding family members came for them. Amidst a solemn atmosphere, the coffins were heaved out of the cathedral in Indian file. Looking at those white wooden cages and imagining they each contained what was once a human being with dreams, hopes, friends, suffering, pain, happiness, anxiety, made me reflect on the meaning of life. In my childhood, the sight of a single coffin coloured my nights in grey, making me confront the despair of existence, asking myself why I was created in the first place, doubting whether I would go to heaven if I were the one in that coffin. Surely, I have grown up and the question of hell and heaven is less of a preoccupation. But the question of life has stuck on me like chameleon faeces in times of bliss and grief. Anyway, under the Ayacucho sky, family members loaded their coffin on the carriages of vehicles and took different directions, to start a new phase of mourning after thirty years of waiting.

We passed at the tourist agency to inquire if they had gotten enough subscriptions for a midday tour to the Wari Archaeological Complex and other touristic sites. They told us it was possible. The previous evening, I had informed the agency I need to attend the ceremony in the cathedral and was not going to be able to undertake the tour in the morning hours as earlier planned. They told me if enough people subscribe for a midday tour that would still be possible. Otherwise, they were going to refund me for the trip. Fortunately, about ten persons had subscribed for an afternoon tour. Since we still had about an hour and a half to go, we decided to visit the memorial museum dedicated to the victims of the 1980s' violence.

This museum was the effort of a group of women united under the banner of ANFASEP, National Association of the Relatives of the Kidnapped, Detained and Disappeared. The association is composed mainly of mothers who lived through the nightmare of losing their children or other loved ones in the war. Prominent amongst them was Mama Angelica whose son, Archimedes, "was disappeared" during the war. They fought for the representation of this painful memory. The initiative did not get instant government support but these women were not deterred. They maintained their efforts to represent the trauma of the time and the responsibility of both government forces and the elements of the *Sendero Luminoso*. The tour guide, a lady in her mid-30s was quite emotional in her explanations. Most often, one is faced with certain plasticity in the mood of tourist guides dedicated to memories of death, violence, massacre, and genocide. Having to tell the same story over and over, coupled with the fact that one is merely doing a job for which they are paid, can sometimes remove the emotional charge of the narrator's account. But it was not the case with this lady. She conveyed the grim nature of the dark times through a trembling voice and a grief-stricken face. One of the curated sceneries was the torture chamber operated by government forces, where persons suspected to belong to *Sendero Luminoso* were detained. The half-lit nature of the spaces, the half-view that its dent offered, rendered the imagination of these moments loaded with primeval horror. Blood could be seen trickling down the face and the entire body of the victim as the military officer mercilessly clamped down with the barbed whip. I thought of the images of the Inquisition. My nerves raved instantly. The deafening silence of that crepuscular space conveyed in my soul the helpless yelling of the victim. That cry went unheeded, both to the torturer and the entire world, no one listened to that strident scream, and that soul perished, in the world, the apocalypse of the moment, the end of the world. I went around continuously taking photos of the faces and the biographies appended to them, of people leaving the house for work and never returning, of children going to play at the marketplace never to be seen again, of mothers going to the farms and being buried with their crops under the fertile earth, of college students going to college to learn the hard lessons of death.

We went through the besmirched pair of clothes displayed on the wall, figurally dripping with fresh blood, those clothes conveyed bodies that were there and then no more. The image of the clothes left behind brought back those macabre images of the shoes of the victims of the World War II victims which I saw in Dresden museum way back in 2010. There is something in the remains of mass massacres that numbs your sense of being, especially when what is left behind used to fit into a body, a body like yours, like mine, now absent. I thought of the piles of infants' clothes, shoes, dolls and feeding bottles in Auschwitz museum.

I came across one T-shirt with a mishmash of inscriptions on it. The guide narrated the story behind this exceptional T-shirt. "This shirt belonged to Manuel Calvaro don Carlos, a young teenager, a talented artist, student of one of the best arts colleges in Ayacucho. It was the custom of the school that during the graduation ceremony a cloth-book is offered to the graduate. It is a shirt on which textual passages could be inscribed with the wishes of friends and loved ones for the graduate. On Carlos' shirt there were many wishes and laudations for his talents, well wishes for a long career and happy life." But that career was to end two weeks after graduation. That young, promising soul was to leave at dawn, squashed by a pistol, never to see the day. The cloth was there, hanging in the museum, thick with the wishes of friends, family, and teachers on the young Carlos. Now, it is a book for all to read, a cloth for all to wear, to share the dream of this young boy, to share the dream of his well-wishers, to share the dream of humanity. This shirt fits all sizes, beyond gender, beyond race, beyond immigrant and indigene, so long as you have a body. The cloth fits you.

When we came back to the tourist office, we had just about twenty minutes before the trip to Wari. Caught up in my hunt for the memorial events and spaces, I had not eaten anything since morning. Miguel pleaded with the tourist agency to give me a few more minutes to take a fast lunch. We went to a restaurant facing the Plaza de Armas. I took a plate of roasted chicken with plantains. It was delicious but I almost choked as I was battling with time. I hurriedly tore the chicken into pieces and drank the soup. I didn't want to be the one to delay the entire group. Gabriela bade me take it easy. I was through, ready to go. Miguel opted to see me off at the tourism agency. He had asked the waiter to cover his plate of food.

"We see each other later in the evening Gabrielita."

"Yes, Gil. Have a nice tour."

In two minutes, Miguel and I were there. I was the last to get on the bus, though I was just about two minutes late. Sometimes, Peruvian time is very punctual! When I entered the bus, Miguel then went back to his friend. I promised to call when I come back from the tour.

The Archaeological Complex was about forty kilometres from the central city of Ayacucho. It was extremely hot and I had to tie my jacket around my waist. The amazing philosophy of the Wari, the stone clock, the complex graveyard, etc. converged to make it one of the great cultural phases of Peruvian history. After about forty-five minutes of guided tour around the Archaeological Complex, we continued forth to the Pampas of Quinua where the famous battle that pitted Simon Bolivar's liberation army against the loyalist forces for the viceroyalty took place. I took some time to climb up the monuments and take photos. The battery of my phone was by now completely flat and I pleaded with a Peruvian man to take photos of me with his camera. I gave him my Facebook address so he could send the pictures to me. This he did instantly since he had an Internet connection. As I moved back to where our bus was parked, a group of young boys trailed after me, offering to narrate the history of the battle of Ayacucho. They were about seven, aged between seven and thirteen, I guessed. I randomly chose one of them to "do" the historical account for me. I was highly thrilled by the musicality of his historical narration.

La batalla de Ayacucho comenzó a las 9 de la mañana del 9 de diciembre de 1824. Aquí se enfrentaron las fuerzas del virrey José de La Serna contra los patriotas al mando de Antonio José de Sucre. Los españoles iniciaron el ataque desde el cerro Condorcunca. La división peruana que comandaba José de La Mar luchó por contenerlos y con la ayuda de los montoneros de Marcelino Carreño los obligaron a replegarse....

(English translation)

> The battle of Ayacucho started at 9 A.M. of 9 December 1824. The
> royal forces of Viceroy Jose de la Serna confronted those of the patriots
> under the command of Antonio José de Sucre. The Spaniards launched
> the attack from the Condorcunca mountain. The Peruvian division
> led by José de la Mar fought to repel them and with the help of the
> guerrilla forces under Marcelino Carreño, the royal forces were obliged
> to retreat…

The boy presented several pages of history in a musical narrative. In
the end, I gave him S/2. He seemed quite satisfied with the tip as his face
beamed with joy, followed by a merry gracias *señorito*. My gesture, perhaps
generous enough, opened a Pandora's box. The other boys swarmed in on
me, each offering to sing history to me in a different and distinctive tone.
Others said the history that their friend-competitor had just narrated
to me was false and that they were ready to give me a fuller account of
the battle of Ayacucho. I said it was enough for me and quickly hurried
off, complaining my bus was about to leave.

The man who had helped me take the photos was leaning against a
pick-up. He was from Lima. We had a nice chat about Peruvian food,
life in Lima compared to the countryside, etc. All along my trip, the
astonishment of accompanying Lima dwellers when faced with realities
in the hinterlands of Peru would sometimes make me feel they belong to
a different country. In the course of our discussion, my young historian
came around, in humility and an almost imploring tone, and said to me:

"Now I want to just narrate the history to you, without singing this
time around."

"It is ok my friend. Not now, what you did was enough. I enjoyed
it. Perhaps later…"

The young boy reluctantly left, seemingly frustrated. Some few minutes later, he came back to me, still interrupting our discussion, telling me.

"Is it ok now *señorito*? Now, you said later, can I do it now?"

I did not realize that by saying "later", I was merely postponing the
services of my young historian.

"Please, leave us alone. It is enough for today, sing or tell the history
to other people since you already told him." My Peruvian friend said,

forcefully.

It is then that the boy calmly went off, for good. We kept discussing Peruvian food and musical cultures until the other fellow sojourners started coming back. It was time for us to get into the bus and start driving back to Ayacucho city. My friend was still hanging in front of his pick-up, waiting for his wife and two sons who were enjoying a horse ride on the pampas. Luis Ronidel became one of my most consistent Facebook friends. He kept sending me messages about my whereabouts and my research, inviting me to come back to Peru whenever I had the chance. I hope to see him again someday.

We arrived at about 6 P.M, nearly an hour and thirty minutes before my trip to Cusco. I called Miguel to tell him we had arrived and I was waiting for him at the agency office. He had carried my backpack for me since it was too heavy to take along to Wari and Quinua. He came rather punctually. He was not far from the city centre. We discussed briefly about the tour. Time was getting close. I had bought my ticket to Cusco the previous day and the trip was in about one hour thirty minutes. I bade Miguel farewell and took a taxi to the Chankas agency located at a distance of about fifteen minutes away from the *Plaza de Armas*.

CHAPTER 19

All Roads Lead to Cusco

What does it matter that a drop of my blood falls off in Cusco's central square, where the forefather of our independence Túpac Amaru, was killed! … I want the people to know that I am not only willing to shed some drops of blood from an unimportant wound, but also to give my life to underscore the lies of the Apristas and the Communists in Cusco![1]

When I bought my ticket the previous day, the young lady at the counter asked me to be at the agency at 8:20 P.M. before departure. However, I came at 8:00 P.M. to avoid any infelicities. I felt a bit hungry and decided to get into a nearby restaurant to have dinner. The travel agent promised to inform me when the bus arrives. I finished eating at about 8:30 P.M. and the bus had not yet come. I decided to get into a nearby store in order to buy some pills against high altitude and *some* juice to sip along the way. When I came back to the agency, I did not find the girl at the counter. A young man sitting outside in front of his cargo told me the bus had just passed!! He suggested I go to the curve some 150 metres away to check if it was still there to finish uploading cargo. How could this happen? I ran helter-skelter, with my bag on my back. When I reached the curve, someone told me a bus had just packed some 200 metres away, at the next curve. He asked me to turn to my left and see if I could find any large bus painted black with the inscription CHANKA VIAJES. I almost ran out of breath. Around the curve, there was a large bus parked by the roadside and passengers were trying to get in. Two men were loading cargo on the bus carriage. I got to the door of the bus and presented my ticket. I explained to him how I almost missed the bus even through I asked his colleague at the agency to give me a shout when the bus arrives. Fortunately or unfortunately, the girl in question was on the other side of the road discussing with someone.

---

1 Speech by Terry Belaúnde (president of Peru 1963-1968, 1980-1985), during a political campaign as the presidential flagbearer for the Popular Action party in Cusco on 21 May 1962 where he was attacked by purported members of the rival APRA party. He won the elections but was overthrown by the military in 1968. (See *The Shining Path.* by Gustavo Gorriti, 1999. p 222.

I just calmed down and got into the bus.

It was damn hot inside the bus. The seats were not too uncomfort-able, but far below anything I had met in Peruvian inter-urban transport before. The space between the rows was very small and my legs were not comfortably positioned. The thought that we were going to spend 16 hours on the bus made me sick. I just hoped to get some sleep since I could not even pretend to peruse any of the books I had put close to the surface of my backpack. Neither was I able to open my laptop due to the tiny space. I just felt weary under the excruciating heat and the thought of the long journey ahead, with all the uncertainty due to the nature of the roads. I prayed silently as we began the trip.

The guy seated next to me was already sleeping before I got in, with his head resting on his knees. I did not even have the possibility of seeing his face. Travelling with a complete unknown. With the per-sistent warning from my friends about the risks of theft, this made me again insecure. On travelling, one is nearly at the mercy of the other, in every dimension. But sometimes, the sense of fear conceals from us the gentleness of the heart of the other. After long hours of driving, we came to a place called Andahuaylas. Some passengers alighted and we spent about 1 hour at the Chankas agency in this area. It looked like a very big town, a sleeping giant, but from the intermittent flashes of incom-ing buses at some ensconced couple returning from a night party. Some few new passengers climbed on board but there were many empty seats left. My unknown companion had also alighted. I had enough space to stretch out and even find a more or less sleeping position. At some point, I was awoken by the noise of passengers who seemed to be alighting. I inquired from a lady in front of me about what was happening. The vehicle has a breakdown and the driver says it may take some time. So, people just want to catch some fresh air. I remembered lamenting the fact that I chose that agency in the first place. He told me it was notori-ous for breakdowns. But Miguel had a different impression. It was one of the few agencies that went straight from Ayacucho to Cusco. Some minibuses take you from Ayacucho to Andahuaylas and then you take another minibus to Cusco. I saw that as a strenuous option.

The bus was almost empty, but for one old man who was snoring on the seat behind me. I put on my jacket and alighted. People were standing in groups, talking in low pitch. Someone had lit a fire on the roadside and a group of people, covered with ponchos, were catching some warmth. It was a beautiful sight. I went over to join them. Not all were passengers. The fire had been lit by a young couple dressed in party wear, on their way from an all-night party. It was on a Saturday. During travelling, I had almost lost the sense of time and days of the week all dissolved in the landscapes I came across during my trip.

The fireside in the middle was a curious sight. At first, the flames raged, and then the glows gradually began to wane. Since it was quite dark, as the flaccid embers began to flicker out, the human figures were somewhat converted into strange silhouettes. One lady asked us to move closer together, to literally form a circle around the fireside. As we did, the flames suddenly regained vigour, saved from the effect of the midnight zephyr. The fire sparks, in harmony with the hissing of fireflies and the half-audible voices, created a sinisterly idyllic affect. We looked more like survivors of a shipwreck, a plane crash, or members of Noah's Ark or perhaps, a circle of pioneers on a decisive mission, labourers of the future or fellow sojourners on a distant journey. In the moment of waiting, we shared stories, some heart-rending, some funny, some shocking, some doleful, others hilarious. I learned new idioms. As the waiting continued, I gained faith and trust in my new community.

> Groupés pour la nuit sur cette grande place de notre village, ce coupon de sable où nos caisses versaient une lueur tremblante, nous avons attendu. Nous attendions l'aube qui nous sauverait, ou les Maures. Et je ne sais ce qui donnait à cette nuit son goût de Noël. Nous nous racontions de souvenirs, nous nous plaisantions et nous chantions. Nous goûtions cette même ferveur legère qu'au coeur d'une fête bien preparée. Et cependant nous etions infiniment pauvres. Du vent, du sable, des etoiles…Mais sur cette nappe mal eclairée, six ou sept hommes qui ne possédaient plus rien au monde, sinon leurs souvenirs, se partageaient d'invisibles richesses. Nous nous etions enfin rencontrés.

(English translation)

> *Sitting in the flickering light of the candles on this kerchief of sand, on this village square, we waited in the night. We were waiting for the rescuing dawn - or for the Moors. Something, I know not what, lent this night a savour of Christmas. We told stories, we joked, we sang songs. We tested the light fervour akin to a well-prepared feast. Meanwhile, we were infinitely poor. Wind, sand and stars… But on this badly lighted cloth, a handful of men who possessed nothing in the world but their memories shared invisible*

riches. We had finally met each other. (Antoine de Saint-Exupéry. Wind,
Sand and Stars.)

When the driver finally asked us to get back to the bus, I almost felt
resistant. I saw the same expression on the faces of my new friends as
we dragged our feet to the bus. Just as I got into the bus, it occurred to
me that Andahuaylas was the birthplace of one of Peru's most popular
writers: José Maria Arguedas. The moonlight and the aura of the environment made me instantly connect with the sense of locale so vividly
captured in some of his works like *Los Rios Profundos* (The Deep Rivers),
El Zorro de Arriba y el Zorro de Abajo (The Fox from Above and the Fox
from Below), *Todas las Sangres* (All Bloods) etc. His works stress the
indigenous roots of Peru and the need for the integration and respect
of the indigenous people and other minorities in the country's national
cultural project. Tragically, Arguedas committed suicide on 12 December
1969, after a sustained depression. His life was lived in a painful limbo.
Born to a mestizo family, he was raised in the heartland of Andean cultures. In his life, he was a victim of the existential malaise of the Peruvian
nation, at times rejected by both the mestizo and indigenous peoples for
not being fully in any of the camps. Hybridity was particularly painful
and tragic for him. One of the statements he made during an interview
with Hofmann of the journal *Trilce* popped up instantly in my mind:

> He asimilado la cultura llamada occidental hasta un grado relativamente
> alto; admiro a Bach y a Prokofiev, a Shakespeare, Sófocles y Rimbaud,
> a Camus y Eliot, pero más plenamente gozo con las canciones tradi-
> cionales de mi pueblo; puedo cantar, con la pureza auténtica de un indio
> chanka, un harawi de cosecha. ¿Qué soy? Un hombre civilizado que
> no ha dejado de ser, en la médula un indígena del Perú; indígena, no
> indio. Y así, he caminado por las calles de París y de Roma, de Berlín y
> de Buenos Aires. Y quienes me oyeron cantar, han escuchado melodías
> absolutamente desconocidas, de gran belleza y con un mensaje original.
> La barbarie es una palabra que inventaron los europeos cuando estaban
> muy seguros de que ellos eran superiores a los hombres de otras razas y
> de otros continentes «recién descubiertos».

(English translation)

> *I have assimilated the so-called Western culture to a relatively high extent;*
> *I love Bath and Prokofiev, Shakespeare, Sophocles and Rimbaud, Camus*

and Eliot, but I enjoy much more fully the songs of my people; I can sing, with the authentic purity of a Chanka Indian, the harvest song known as harawi. Who am I? A civilized man who, deep down his marrow, has not abandoned his indigenous and Indian self. As such, I have walked down the streets of Peru and Rome, Berlin and Buenos Aires. Anyone who has ever listened to me sing has heard totally unknown melodies, of great beauty and with an original moral lesson. Barbarity is a word invented by the Europeans when they were very convinced that they were superior to people of other races and from "recently discovered" continents.

I stayed awake along and as we drove past villages and hamlets, I wondered what life could be like in these places. I had the feeling of travelling from Yaoundé to Bamenda in Cameroon. Traveling between Yaoundé and Bamenda, most buses stop at Makenene for passengers to stretch out their bodies crammed for hours between tiny seats and also to chew or sip something. Drivers who headily refuse to respect the unwritten constitution are faced with a volley of curses and insults in the many languages that flourish in my country. But those cases are rare. Before the bus finds a comfortable spot to park, you are greeted by some entrancing olden days tunes by the impeccable Makenene disco. Tunes and tubes by the Rumtas, Sally John, Sam Fan Thomas, Kassav, Charlotte Mbango, Bebe Manga,[2] etc. resuscitate long memories of the bygone heydays. "We have twenty-minutes and if anyone does not respect the time, we will leave them behind," announces the driver or his "motor boy"[3]. Half-awake, you scape and elbow your way through the crowded and gullied alleys of the market looking for your choice amongst roasted fish, egusi pudding, roasted plums and plantains, bush meat, in fact, everything, depending on the season. Some people prefer to gulp a fast bottle of beer, one for the road. It happens that you meet an old-time friend you have not seen for years at that moment of passage. Or you greet an old friend with elation, just to discover that s/he is not the one. Some hop into the wrong bus after the boozing and the

2   Prominent Cameroonian musicians of the 1980s, and 1990s with the exception of Kassav, a Caribbean musical group from Guadeloupe. It was formed in 1979, consisting of Jacob Desvarieux, Joyceline Béroard, Jean-Philippe Mathely, Patrick St. Eloi, Jean-Claude Naimro, Claude Vamur and George Decimus.

3   The driver's assistant in charge of maintaining order, settling conflicts, checking tickets in the bus, and sometimes he is the one to negotiate with the railway police on behalf of the driver.

quarrel over seats begins. When the latter finally finds his/her bus that has been blaring for the missing passenger, s/he, both tipsy and drowsy, is faced with invectives from the impatient passengers. Some answer back, while others remain provocatively silent, (un)consciously. The music, the night, always turns Makenene into a somewhat surreal space and I wonder what life is like beyond the utosphere of that market spot and the night. The transient disjuncture caused by that time-space procures a certain inexpressible jouissance. The last time I was in Makenene, I could not avoid singing Olivia-Newton John's "Country Roads, Take me Home", a song on the state of West Virginia:

All my memories gathered 'round her
Miner's lady, stranger to blue water
Dark and dusty, painted on the sky
Misty taste of moonshine
Teardrops in my eye

Country roads, take me home
To the place I belong
West Virginia, mountain momma
Take me home, country roads.[4]

Our next stop was at Abancay. We arrived there at about 7:00 A.M. and the streets were already beginning to bustle with inhabitants making their way to the marketplace and offices. After a brief stop of about ten minutes, we got new passengers on board. But as we started to ascend the cliff, getting out of Abancay, our bus came to a standstill; a long queue was ahead of us. After waiting for about fifteen minutes without movement, our driver came down. Some passengers followed. For close to thirty minutes, I also felt it was time to catch some fresh air. I came down the bus and tried to enquire from one guy wearing the CHANKA T-shirt what the matter was. The guy told me there was heavy traffic due to road construction a few kilometres ahead. We were going to wait for close to two hours. I looked in front of our bus, there was a long line of cars queued up. Some passengers had come out and occupied the road-side, others gathered in small groups, discussing, eating fresh foodstuffs bought from the women who moved around with basins on their heads

---

4   The original song is by John Denver.

hawking around the occasional public space.

I went back into the bus, took out a book, *The History of Peruvian Literature* and sat, leaning against the wheel of an abandoned huge truck by the roadside. About fifteen minutes later, there was the hurried movement of passengers back into their cars and buses. Seemingly, the traffic had been cleared.

We were back on the road. By now many of the passengers were wide-awake. Now I had a full view of my fellow passengers, recognising some who shared the fireside with me hours ago. I continued reading the book; though at some points the jolt of the car frustrated my efforts. I put it aside and just threw myself into the flow of the journey. Sometimes, the best form of reading when travelling is merely to look at the evanescent elements on the way, nature, the people, the plants, the animals whistling past as the bus continues its spiralling along the Andean mountain chains. Sometimes, it is also the best moment just to have a free mind, to think, even about nothing.

CHAPTER 20

The Open Wounds of the Túpacs

We arrived in Cusco at about 4 P.M. In terms of the building structures, the outskirt of the town was a little bit of a disappointment
to the Cusco of my imagination. It seemed as if all the buildings were
under construction and the sewage disposal was apparently a problem. As
we moved inwards, the site was much better, though. When we arrived
at the bus station, I easily found a taxi to take me to the hostel. It took
us just about 12 minutes to reach there.

Hostal Acosta is a relatively small hostel with a capacity of 34 rooms.
I was asked to tarry a bit longer at the reception while they cleaned my
room. I waited for about 15 minutes during which I engaged the manager with some questions about the trip to Machu Picchu. As promised,
she bade me not to bother for there is someone to inform me of all the
modalities involved. She called the person on the phone and he promised
to come immediately. Some few minutes later, the travel agent came
in and demanded to know the exact number of days I had to stay in
Cusco and how we could maximise my time in the city and the visit to
Machu Picchu. We settled on the following schedule: A bus would pick
me up from my hotel the following morning at 7:30 A.M. for the near
6-hour trip to *Hydro-electrico*. From there, we would take the train to
Aguas Calientes where we would spend the night. He said it was also
a walkable distance. All depended on me. The following day would be
the trip up to Machu Picchu and return to Cusco that same evening.
Initially, I intended to go down to Arequipa from Cusco but the agent
wisely advised me to consider passing through Puno, an equally beautiful
town, before getting down to Arequipa. I found his orientation worthy
since Puno had much to offer in terms of the variety of Peruvian culture, especially its cultural affinity with parts of Bolivia. It was another
distinctive facet of Peru, I was told. After this orientation, the manager
sent a little girl with the key to my room. It was now ready for me to
pack in. It was a small room with a medium-sized bed. The room was

almost threadbare, but fortunately with thick bed sheets and a blanket. This was essential because it was dead cold in Cusco, much colder than in Ayacucho. I checked the bathroom. There was a slightly discomforting odour. Coincidentally, the manager knocked and suggested I could get into the next room that was slightly more comfortable.

It was not much better but the bathroom was cleaner. I packed in my things. After all, it was just for that night. After taking my bath, I met up with the tourist agent at the reception so we could go to his office at the *Plaza de Armas* where I was going to complete the payment and get the due receipts. The streets seemed very tiny, in fact tinier than those in Ayacucho. Packed with hawkers selling handicrafts, foodstuffs, not to mention the restaurant waiters almost assaulting one with their menus. The Plaza de Armas was quite modest, but I could not avoid thinking about the memorial thickness of this seemingly benign space. Manco Inca. Amaru I. Amaru II. His black wife Micaela Bastidas Puyucahua. Hipólito, their son. The spectacle of conquest, the passing of the old order and the advent of newness. Plaza de Armas in Peru is a curious place. Apart from being a meeting place for people, it is a meeting place for memories. Not every encounter is peaceful, some meetings leave wounds, bruises, stains, impressions, long-lasting changes, at the personal and communal levels. Wilfred Owen in his poem "Meeting" has left a great challenge to humanity wherein he and his "enemy" recognize their humanness in a First World War trench and decide to work together for peace.

We entered the office on the second floor of a modest storey building facing the Plaza de Armas. It was a very tight office, full of maps of Peruvian towns on the walls, reminding me of our boys' rooms in those days which were packed with images of stars, popular film captions, football stars, pretty girls, and picturesque landscapes. This culture was rather disappearing. These walls have been replaced by screens and virtual walls. The images on the walls included touristic hubs and superlative expressions describing them, making Peru an indispensable touristic destination.

After completing the deal, Alfredo directed me to the road to the Cusco Museum and how I could get back to my hostel from there. The museum was just one scuadra away from the central cathedral. When I passed at the Plaza de Armas, I was confronted by memories of the fallen Incas and the various commercial agents enticing me with all kinds of offers.

"Good morning sir, massage?" She addressed me in English. The stark touristic English with rough edges that point to you its immediate borders and limits and that collapses at the least stretch. It was a rhetorical question because, before waiting for my response, she was already squeezing a handbill into my palms.

"Thanks, *señorita* but I do not have time now."

"Ok. You can come back later. My shop is behind the tourism office you find there to your right." As she took her pains to explain to me, I made haste to the museum. It was supposed to close at 6 P.M. and it was already 4:50 P.M. I needed about an hour for the guided tour around the whole place.

I passed in front of a discotheque called *Mama Africa* and was deeply intrigued. What inspired the owner to name a discotheque in the heartland of the Inca kingdom after a far-off continent? Under the signboard with the well-carved name of the club, there was another sheet in English spelling out in bold:

MAMA AFRICA
Salsa training with Cuban maestro
9:00 P.M. -11:00 P.M.
After that, Disco Non-stop

I arrived at the museum at five minutes to 5:00 P.M. The lady at the office told me the tour was S/10, without a guide. I could get one if I was willing to offer a tip at the end of the guided tour. I conceded and her colleague accompanied me around. She seemed quite versed in the history of the prehispanic civilisations. It was quite a big museum, one-storey but quite a large building, one of the biggest I have visited in Peru, with about 26 rooms. We could only visit half of that, the main ones. I was loaded with information on a wide variety of Inca, Wari, Nazca cultures, etc. It had the same collection of artefacts as the museum I had visited in Wari archaeological site but more advanced in the degree of technological preservation of the artefacts. I left the museum a few minutes after 6 P.M. I gave the guide S/10 as tip and she seemed very satisfied.

Upon coming out, I passed in front of the cathedral. Some kids were performing cultural dances on the space between the steps of the cathedral and the fence around the Plaza de Armas. It was a well-choreographed performance. The kids were dressed in beautiful Andean colours, performing drills under the tutelage of three adults, two women and a man. I took some pictures of them. It was a beautiful sight. I asked one lady standing close to me on the cathedral stairs to take me some camera shots before I leave for my hotel room. I realised I needed at least a picture of myself standing at the Plaza de Armas of Cusco. I intended to capture the Plaza de Armas of any town I visited in Peru. A young guy was standing nearby, looking idly busy. I wanted to kindly request him to take a picture of me. The guy pre-empted my request and came towards me asking:

"You need a photo?"

"Yes, please. Thanks very much."

After he took about three photos of me, I collected the phone and thanked him generously.

"Please, do you need anything?"

"Sorry, I did not get that."

"Am asking if you need something, marijuana, perhaps. I have it here, just if you need."

"Oh thank you, I don't even smoke common cigarettes."

"Sorry, no problem. See you, my friend. Enjoy Cusco." He smiled amicably at me as I went off. I was told Lima was dangerous. Perhaps I also had to be careful while in Cusco. Or perhaps this was part of the cultural shock. It looked like normal here. For a Cameroonian like me, it was a shocking possibility.

I badly needed some rest. As I slowly moved to my hostel, my memory was again crowded by the historic weight of the space I had just trodden. This time, I did not only think about the Túpacs. As I moved closer to my hostel, my memory also moved closer to my present, both in space and time. I thought of Duala Manga Bell of Cameroon, I thought of the Kenyan chiefs buried alive by the British colonialists in Kenya, as narrated by the Kenyan novelist Ngugi wa Thiong'o in his novel *A Grain of Wheat*. And many more. My legs were now heavy, weighed down by fatigue from my long trips and the memories of colonial cruelty. But all along I was pestered by this question: How does one write about a place like the Plaza de Armas of Cusco without losing his or her sanity? Perhaps to live in or/and think about the postcolony means to come to terms, no matter how hard it is, with one's historical conditioning, the historicity of one's place in the world. The masters of this world prefer the postcolonial subject to sleep, to forget, to forgive, to accept their condition as given. The etiquette in modern social and human sciences is for the subject to be moderate, to be postmodern, to relativize, and to see every process as dynamic, dialogic, open-ended... But the truth is, even under the opium of forgetfulness and the scientific habitus of moderation, sometimes in the depth of your soul, the grey facts of the excesses of history flash up in your memory, assailing you with an unfathomable forcefulness, making you look at the world with the interrogative eyes of an innocent child. Perhaps it is with such eyes that one can better appraise man's inhumanity towards man because of race, ethnicity, class, etc. All underlined by the curse of humanity: greed. Perhaps it is in America that the history of oppression based on race/class has taken its most obscene forms. Here, the history of blatant exploitation has led to the permanent seduction of the "heroic act" (el gesto heroico), the historical decision (la decisión historica) "setting the prairie on fire" (incendiar la pradera) and the "war to death" (guerra a la muerte). While responding to the strident call of history has launched some nations on the course of considerable freedom and equality, others have had mitigated and even catastrophic outcomes. The Túpacs, Ches, Sankaras, Cabrals, and Lumumbas of this world sought to face the colossal challenges of their time and met death. The Fujimoris, Mugabes, Kenyattas, Salva Kiir and so on ended up entrenching conditions of inequality against which they initially fought. In these two continents, life remains a burden, an unfulfilled promise to a large percentage of the population while the few lavish in wealth. In many ways, the question posed by an Indian subject in Inca Garcilaso de la Vega's[1] *Comentarios Reales* (Royal Commentaries of Peru) remains valid in these parts of the world, four hundred years after: "Shall we not know what the fruits of our master's lands taste of?"

"Plaza de Armas", the bellicose name itself sounded with renewed queerness to my ears. What does Plaza de Armas really mean in popular Peruvian meaning-making? I needed to ask some of my Peruvian friends later on.

---

1   Inca Garcilaso de la Vega (1539-1616) was a mestizo chronicler and writer born in the early years of the Spanish colony in Peru. In *Royal Commentaries*, a bitter treatise on colonial atrocities and the destruction of Inca cultures in Latin America, he refers to the anecdote of two subjects sent by their master with melons as a gift to his friend. The master also sends a letter along and warns his non-literate subjects: "If you touch of these fruits, this letter will report to my friend and he will tell me." The irony is that the melons were cultivated by the subjects on land from which they were dispossessed by the colonial regime. On the way, under the spell of hunger and curiosity, one asks the other: "Shall we not know what the fruits of our master's lands taste of?" They hide the letter temporarily and devour some of the fruits. Then they continue their journey and hand the melons and the letter to their master's friend. You can guess the rest of the story.

I elbowed my way through the packed tiny street that leads to Hostal Acosta, ignoring the reckoning and beckonings of the hawkers lined up along the handicraft shops in the *Choquechaka* alley. I arrived at the hotel feeling a bit weak and weary. I fell in my bed and not before long, I was deep asleep. I had just had a nightmare. While on a trip to north Cameroon our bus is intercepted by a terrorist group. They speak in a language that none of us passengers could understand. But from the husky voices of our malefactors, it was clear that our minutes were counted. No amount of supplication could save us from the grim fate. We are all wailing in different languages. Like a stroke of magic, another bus full of passengers appears on the scene splashing lights onto our faces. Our captors disappear into the nearby bush. It is then that I woke up, discovering my feet on the ground, with my shoes on. Oh, what a nightmare. I almost jumped up in celebration. Dreams, some make you wake up and say a prayer of thanksgiving to God to celebrate the fact that it is just a dream after all. But others transform you into a state of perfect bliss, you wake up and curse the real world, wondering why good things, truly good things, only exist as desires or dreams.

Perhaps my dream was borne out of the reality coming from my country in the past days. News of the Boko Haram suicide attacks in Maroua, Cameroon the week before had shaken me right down to the marrow. I remember myself telling my Peruvian interlocutors about the calm and peace that reigned in Cameroon in spite of the economic difficulties. After the series of attacks in Maroua, my discourse had to change. Cameroon was in fright. Why should people be killed in such horrific circumstances for no just reason than the psychopathic mindset of criminals? I lived in Maroua before going to Germany. I taught in a village very close to the border with Nigeria. Thus, the attacks struck a particular chord in my being.

I could not sleep anymore. I went to the bath, cleaned my eyes and brushed my teeth. The streets were still very buoyant with people moving up and down. I felt tempted to go out, especially because of the information about salsa in the Mama Africa nightclub. It won't hurt having some experience of Cusco nightlife.

I put a few *soles* in my purse, made sure I left all valuable belongings in my hostel room. I did not take the risk of going out with my visa card. However, I took my German residence permit along. I slowly went downstairs. The attendant had left. At the reception desk, I met a young boy with a smiling face.

"Tell me, my friend, how is it attending a disco here at night? Is it very dangerous?"

"No, not all. All the *discos* are quite close. And this street is busy till dawn."

"That is reassuring. Do you know Mama Africa?"

"Sure, it is one of the most popular discos here. There you can meet tourists from various countries killing the night. Most of them are either on their way to or are from Machu Picchu."

"Great. I will go there though I do not intend to be long. But I hope you won't lock me out. Do you stay up all night?"

"For sure. I get to sleep but the bell outside is connected to my room. When you come, just ring the bell and I will open, without delay. There are also some of the guests out partying now. So, I go to sleep at night but I have to always be on the *qui-vive*."

"Oh, I see. That must be damn stressful, man."

"Don't mind. It is my job. I try to cope."

I wished him courage and left. I went past the busy tourist shops at Choquechaka. It was getting to 10 P.M. and the shopkeepers were closing down. The restaurants were rather still packed with customers and the streets were still filled with hawkers.

"Please, have a look. Don't miss this." A young man in straw heart assailed me with a bunch of very attractive *tableaux*, the famous retablos of Cusco and Ayacucho. Without waiting for my consent, he began unrolling them.

"Here is Machu Picchu. It is a handmade tableau. It took me three weeks to finish it but I am giving it to you at just S/50."

I did not allow him to go through the complete bundle. I told him his tableaux were great masterpieces but I was on my way to a club and it would be needless buying anything since I would not have where to keep it. He dexterously rolled the tableau and it shrunk into a tiny sheet.

"Look, it is simple! You can just slide this into your pocket and it won't even affect your dancing feats."

I smiled at his sense of humour and went off, bidding him a friendly *Adios hermano* (goodbye brother). The *Plaza de Armas* was getting empty, with the few people around dispersed in little groups on the public benches. Some couples could also be found kissing and ensconced in one another's arms. Few hawkers were moving from customer to customer with their load of touristic products.

I came to the gate of Mama Africa. The guard greeted me and asked me to go up to the second floor. Entry was free of charge. The salsa class was going on at the moment. As from 11:00 P.M. entry was going to be S/10, he told me, imploring me to make hay while the sun shines.

I entered and slowly climbed up the stairs. As I got close to the door, the walls were lined up with a thin plastic with hyperreal tigers. I began to feel squeamish. I have a phobia for feline creatures. Blake's "Tyger" in the Songs of Experience came to my mind:

> Tyger, Tyger, burning bright,
> In the forests of the night;
> What immortal hand or eye
> Could frame thy fearful symmetry?...

But the bustling at the door meant it was interesting getting inside. My curiosity edged over my anxiety. As I made my way into the club, I was greeted with nice tunes of salsa. A multitude of young men and ladies were lined up, responding imitatively to the swinging body of two lead dancers, a boy in a T-shirt with the map of Brazil at the back and a girl-in-black whose slender body seemed to be made of spring. The two were ingenious in their steps and movements, born to do it. The apprentices appeared to be having much fun learning. Though there was a wide gap between the masterly steps of the two frontliners and the rest of the group, one could see the salsa fervour in the eyes and bodies of these youths. But there were also casualties: those ones who could not tune their bodies to the complex and rhythmic acrobatics. They simply fell off and humbled themselves on the benches as envious spectators. There seemed to be some affinity between most of them. Perhaps they were from the same country. I heard some of them speak Spanish with a rather foreign accent. Some also spoke English with an American accent.

Though not a good drinker, I felt I should not just be standing there and watching whereas almost everyone had a drink on their lips. I went to the counter and inquired about the price of beer. It ranged between S/10 and S/16. I went in for half a litre of *Cusqueña*. I had drunk it before and liked its taste. Well, I am not a beer connoisseur to recommend anything to anyone. As I sipped the beer, I decided to take a break from the salsa performance, to gain a better view of the nightclub. On the wall close to my right was a frightening sculpture of a lion with its full horror features. I was startled by this image. It was staged behind a grove-like background that accorded it its full terrific aura. It was very close to the second beer counter. As you ordered for beer, Big Brother Lion was looking at you, roaring at you, drinking the beer before you. There were two empty seats close, just adjacent to the DJ box. I went and occupied one of them, near some two chaps. I thought it could be a good angle from where to watch the salsa display. It is when I sat down that I discovered the images on the wall facing me, where there was a raised escarpment, like a small podium. They were images of black women in a luxuriant setting, in full gyrating posture, voluptuous buttocks radiating with sensual intensity, albeit with a slightly burlesque tilt.

Once again, I arrested my consciousness back to the salsa scene before me. The music went on for close to an hour and the two lead dancers moved from one style to the other. The steps got more and more complicated and some natural selection had taken place, but the very zealous apprentices followed, with varying degrees of awkwardness. Any change of style almost meant the elimination of some apprentices. The male lead dancer made the ambience even more climatic with his intermittent and extemporaneous re-mixing and orientation:

"Two steps right, front, hold your partner tight. Right again, three steps back and swiiiiinnnnnggggg." His voice switched from one pitch to the other, depending on the nature of steps. When it was all through, I approached the chap to exchange a few words with him.

"Wow, congrats my friend. You are a real maestro. Are you from Cuba, or maybe Brazil?"

"Oh no, a Peruvian. It is just a T-shirt. And you?"

"I am from Cameroon."

"That is wonderful. Samuel Eto'o Fils. You know salsa already, right?"

"No, not really. I just admire your mastery of the game. In my University, we have salsa classes on Wednesday evenings but I have never had time to attend".

"It is a beautiful dance. How long will you be here? We practice four times a week."

"I just came in today. I will be going to Machu Picchu tomorrow. When I come back I will continue straight to Puno."

"That is fine. Most of these folks here are from the US. They organise and travel to Machu Picchu in groups. But most of them just like to have a nice time here at night."

As he was talking to me, the DJ beckoned him to come. Seemingly he needed his assistance for the disco selection. The disco had begun but the floor was still empty as the salsa dancers were taking a sip after what seemed like a challenging exercise. I quickly gulped down my bottle. I won't be here for long because I still needed enough rest for my trip. I elbowed my way to the counter amid Sean Paul's "Hold my Hand". It is one of my favourites and I was tempted to take a second bottle to tarry much longer but I summoned the courage to say no to myself. I came down the steps under the poised fangs of my tigers. I bade farewell to the three guys at the gate. But before leaving, I tried to be inquisitive.

"Please, is there any particular reason why this place is called Mama Africa?"

"Well, I can't really say. Perhaps my boss will answer your question much better." He pointed to one man who was busy arranging some cartons on the corridor leading to the dance floor. He moved them outside and was giving orders to the boys on where to carry them. I patiently waited for him to finish. He finally came out and leaned his back on the pillar. I approached him, as cordially as I could.

"Please, sir. I really enjoyed the salsa dance here."

"Nice to hear that."

"I am told you are the boss here. You look like one."

"Thank you, my brother. Where are you from?"

"From Cameroon. I am travelling to Machu Picchu." I pre-empted his question so as not to veer off from my point of interest.

"That is fine."

"Please tell me, how did you come about the name Mama Africa?"

"In reality, it is just a name. This place has been operational for over 10 years under this name. It is just a name."

"I see." I did not want to sound too pushy or to sound like the Policeman of Africa. I thanked him and went off. The *Plaza de Armas* itself was virtually empty as people were concentrated at the entrance to the major nightclubs and main restaurants surrounding it. There were two other main discos in that vicinity.

I moved along the street to my hostel, intermittently battling for space with some incoming taxis on the Choquechaka alley. I arrived at the hostel and rang the doorbell. There seemed to be no response. I placed my ear on the door for any sign of movement inside. None. I rang twice, thrice… A couple passed by kissing profusely. I felt almost guilty, like a thief trying to force a door open. I felt like a night thief trying to break into a building. After about three minutes of waiting, I heard the inner door creak. I heard steps moving close to the main door.

"Please make sure you keep the cat in check," I said while the door was still closed.

"The cat does not sleep here. It went home with my sister." He opened the door to my greatest relief. He stretched his joints to creaking points as he closed the door. Though relieved I was still not sure the cat was not in the hostel. I thanked him and went up to my room. I quickly went through my email and Facebook. Thankfully, nothing much, even on Facebook. Sleep.

CHAPTER 21

Lost in the Andes

At 6 A.M. the alarm woke me up with a wailing sound. I was not aware I had put the volume so high. Usually, I hushed it down to allow me some time to relish the sweet spasm of morning slumber. But this time, the circumstance was different and like a prompt soldier of Machu Picchu, I had to respond to the call with steadfastness. I stood up and quickly went to the bathroom. I turned on the faucet gently, testing the warmness of the water with my right palm. It turned into a dangerous game between the water system and me. When I felt it was the right temperature, I swayed my entire body under the shower. I prayed for the joy to last. But after enjoying the grace of warmth, a rather deadening cold shower rained on me. I almost shouted in my bath. I closed it up and stepped outside of the shower a bit. I took the testing process all over. It got a bit warm and again I stepped under the shower and felt the warm water plastering the wounds of the previous damage. Now, with peace of mind and body, my thoughts again travelled to the unhappy events in the northern part of Cameroon that happened a few days ago. I was still to chat with my Cameroonian friends on Facebook or to read properly about the happenings and the effects on the popular sentiments in my far-away country. But I could imagine the trauma of a whole nation, a nation not used to blood of that sort. After bathing I dressed up, putting on two T-shirts before my colourful grassland Jumper, with the Cameroon map on it. Machu Picchu was certainly going to be a marvellous experience. I packed a few necessities in my backpack - extra pairs of underwear, singlets, socks and a notebook. I was hesitant to take my MacBook along but finally gave in. I thought I could be able to surf more comfortably on it than using my telephone if my hotel room had an Internet connection. At exactly 7:00 A.M. I was out with my backpack in front of the hostel waiting for the mini-bus. It finally came ten minutes late. That was not late anyway. I jumped into the back seat after a warm *buenos dias* to the other passengers. There were three ladies in the middle row. Directly by my side, there was an averagely old man, certainly in his 50s with two adolescents, whom I was to learn were his sons. One of the boys was talking to his dad in English, with a strong American accent. Judging the man quite friendly, I asked politely:

"Sir, where are you guys from?"

"From Peru", he answered.

"I thought as well until I heard you guys speaking English so fluently."

"That is how I train my boys. We mix English and Spanish, sometimes even in the same sentence. Haha!"

He confessed. Nevertheless, they all spoke very fluently. The two boys seemed to share much with their dad, judging from the body language between them. Where could their mom be? I wondered.

"Where do you come from?"

"I am Cameroonian."

"I see. Welcome to Peru. I hope you like it so far."

"Yes, it is a great country and I hope to see still much more."

The bus stopped at the Plaza de Armas and two ladies hopped in, speaking Portuguese. The chap who was acting as the motor boy dropped off, bidding us a safe trip.

CHAPTER 22

Machu Picchu

On the way to Machu Picchu, in the thick of the Andes, I had a better view of Cusco this time around. It was the first time I went beyond the Plaza de Armas. Though it was still early, the whole city was already busy with people going about their business. Five hundred years ago, all roads led to this place. They still do, perhaps more so for those who want to witness its ruins than its greatness.

We drove for about an hour and came to a spot where the driver halted and told us we had 30 minutes break. It was an opportunity to get to the restrooms in a nearby mini shop. Many other buses had stopped there and the place looked like a temporary public space, with tourists smoking, chatting in small groups, sipping a bottle of beer, cracking jokes, etc. I entered the shop and got a piece of cake and a sachet of orange juice. I bought a set of gloves and a protective hood, in view of the unknown temperature alterations in the course of our trip. I thought of going to the restrooms, but the urge was not very strong. More so, there was a long queue and I did not think I could make it before the thirty minutes that the driver accorded us. When I came out, a short smallish girl was leaning on our bus. She was on the same bus but I did not catch a full glimpse of her since I sat far behind.

"Good morning, where are you from?"

"From Cameroon."

"Oh, so you speak French?"

"Sure, also English."

"Oh yes, I know in Cameroon there is also an English-speaking population, though I sometimes forget."

"Since when are you in Peru?"

"Since about three weeks now." As we were talking, one of the Portuguese ladies came out of the store and on passing by me, I greeted her in Portuguese. She was quite surprised.

"Oh, you speak Portuguese. Brazilian, Angolan?"

107

"Am from Cameroon and I live in Germany."

She introduced me to her friend as we quickly entered the bus to get set. We drove off at higher speed. We were still very much within settled areas, which means we still had a long way to go. The driver put some Peruvian huayno. The disc seemed to have a problem for it was playing in stops and starts. He replaced it with an MP3 of some of the most classic soul and R&B tunes. Though some of the passengers started dozing off, the younger ones seemed to answer the call of the rhythms. From time to time, a particular sound would arouse a chorus from the bus. I also sang along. I did not know who was singing, but most likely the French girl and one of the Brazilian ladies seemed to be our lead singers. My knees played anchor to the head of one of the boys. His brother also leaned helplessly on the shoulder of his dad.

Gradually, we came out of the settlement and began spiralling up and down the mountain chains of the Andes. More than anything I had seen before, the topography was spectacular. Roads were built basically along the slopes of the mountain chains. Though they were in a very good state in most of the cases, the topography made short distances seem endlessly long. It took a whole hour to spiral around a mountain chain to find a favourable bridging zone to cross to the next mountain chain ahead of us. Given that this was the first trip I was undertaking in Peru during the daytime, I bore the full brunt of the Andean topography. I was close to the abyss. Almost throughout this trip, just about a metre off the road was a descent into the unknown. I stopped looking outside for it brought undesirable thoughts to my mind. I could not recede from thinking how many people might have perished on that road chasing the shadow of Machu Picchu!!! In my turbulent mind, I reviewed the reason for the trip. My family, if they think I live! My friends in Cameroon, in Germany, in Lima! Life became so precarious. It sufficed only for a second of inattention from the driver to send us down memory. I resorted to praying but my scrambled mind could not formulate a single coherent sentence to the Almighty. Anyway, in the most dangerous times, God does not expect us to form full sentences of supplication. He is forced to receive our prayers in rhapsodic forms. From the raw material of our wish, since he reads our heart, soul, and mind, he can fashion out his remedy. We had reached a point of no return. I envied my fellow sojourners who could find peace in their sleep. I imagined the horror of the two front seaters, so close to the driver and being able to see more clearly the precipice on which we trod.

On such a road, the driver has to be a superman. Mistakes are paid cash and on the spot. I found the face of the man near me, filled with awe though he struggled to maintain a false calmness. Descending was more awful than when we were ascending, coupled with the fear of having to meet an unannounced bus coming from the opposite direction. The road was just too narrow to host two buses bypassing and one had to retreat to a point slightly wide enough for both cars to pass. After every curve, it was a new world with different signs. Worse, at some point, the snow covered the road and the driver had to slow down his pace considerably. There was rarely any communication in the bus, music was the only source of solace for us. I also tried to read one of the books I had bought from the Book Fair in Lima, *El Virrey Toledo, gran Tirano del Peru*[1] by the anthropologist Luis Valcarcel. However, the macabre thoughts that crossed my mind made it difficult for me to draw any logical conclusions from the passages I was scanning through.

> Tu avais disparu depuis cinquante heures, en hiver, au cours d'une traversée des Andes, rentrant du fond de la Patagonie, je rejoignis le pilote à Mendoza. L'un et l'autre, cinque jours durant, nous fouillames, en avion, cet amorcellement de montagnes, mais sans rien decouvrir... « Les Andes, en hiver, ne rendaient point les hommes. » Et lorsque, de nouveau, je me glissais entre les murs et les piliers geants des Andes, il me semblait, non plus te rechercher, mais veiller ton corps, en silence, dans une cathedrale de neige. (Terre des Hommes, Antoine de Saint Exupéry)

(English translation)

> *You had gone missing for fifty hours, in winter, during a flight across the Andes and on my way back from Patagonia I met up with the pilot in Mendoza. For five days on the plane, together we searched for you amongst this chain of mountains, all in vain ... "In winter, the Andes did not render account of people." And when again I slid myself in between the walls and*

---

1   *Viceroy Toledo: The Great Tyran of Peru.* Don Francisco de Toledo was one of the most memorable viceroys of Peru in the 16th century. His rule dated from 1569 to 1581. Though considered by many as a great administrator, his regime implemented unpopular policies like the reduction, that reorganised indigenous communities in a way as to supply efficient labour for Spanish mines. The tax system and forced labour were considerably intensified due to his policies.

the gigantic pillars of the Andes, it seemed to me that I was no longer look-
ing for you. Rather, I was keeping watch over your dead body, in silence in
a cathedral of snow. (Antoine de Saint Exupéry. Wind, Sand and Stars.)

As we coursed through, one could see inscriptions of political slogans on the poles and the stones at the roadside. *Vota Keiko, el alcade*
Dr. Victor Mendoza, ¡adelante nuestro deputado![2] and so forth. One of the
party emblems was in the form of a white football with blue net lines
across. I had seen those on the walls of so many houses across the road,
some bare mud walls. Some of the inscriptions were done on the tip of
rocks facing the abyss. Democracy on the precipice, hope on the brink.
I wondered how a party supporter cum graphic artist had managed to
inscribe these political signs and slogans on such a risky terrain that did
not offer any safe foothold. One could hardly imagine that there was
a human community, not to think of a radically political community
behind these mountains. The inscriptions were quite polarising and they
spoke volumes of the intense political battles that went on within these
communities. Whether the elections for which these political messages
stood had already taken place or were still forthcoming, I could not
tell. The inscriptions were relatively fresh, though. On these roads, we
hardly found any single soul, once in a while we bypassed white hikers
on their bikes, looking damn tired and exuding thick streams of sweat.
They were certainly *gringos*. Also, the roads were covered with thickets of
oranges, red ripe, abandoned fields of plenty. A Peruvian friend told me
some weeks later that it was the orange season and that the prices had
completely slumped. Harvesting these oranges for commercial purposes
was not a lucrative business. You would spend money on transportation
only for them to rot in one little shop in Lima or one of the other cities
around. Gradually, like in a dream, we came around a settlement. A big
one for that matter. It was a very beautiful town: *Santa Teresa.*

"Here we are going to have a thirty-minute lunch break in a restaurant
we have reserved for you guys. It is a good place and I am sure you will
like it. After that, we will be left with just two hours or so."

I received this announcement with mixed feelings. I was happy that
we were going to take some breath and break from the frightening

---

2   Vote Keiko! Ahead of Our Mayor Dr. Victor Mendoza, Ahead our deputy! (Keiko Fujimori
      is the daughter of former Peruvian president (1990-2000). She has represented her party,
      Fuerza Popular (Popular Force) for two presidential elections (2011, 2016), each time losing
      in the second round despite impressive lead in the first rounds

experiences on the road. But again, the thought of having two more hours to go was not fun. They *also* could become an unquenchable and ravenous consumer of minutes and even hours. For me, it was better we finish the trip once and for all. I was not hungry, but I knew others were. I had never straight jacketed my life to the untameable dictatorship of breakfast, lunch and dinner. Stepping out and then having to climb on board with all the images was like re-enacting my fears all over.

We settled down to eat. It was spaghetti with a very spicy soup. That was upon reservation from our tourist agency. No other option. The French girl came and sat near me and we got to know each other better. Both of us went in for a bottle of Inca Cola each. She was a development studies student, doing her masters but at the same time working with an international NGO. Botswana was her area of interest, she told me. As we were chatting, one of the Brazilian girls took her plate and a bottle of coke and sat near us.

"How do you guys feel? Tired?"

"A bit tired, but I'm used to it, I have been travelling the whole of Argentina and Bolivia", Claire said.

"Am also a bit tired, but hopefully two hours aren't that much," I said, trying to be optimistic.

"I felt awed when the driver tried to double the speed and then almost brought us down the cliff", said the Brazilian lady, Rosa. She was on the front seat of the bus, near the window. This meant she had an ample view of the dangerous motorway we were treading on.

"Yes, he seemed to be driving too fast but after that incident, he slowed down, fortunately", Claire remarked.

"I ravished him with my eyes after that incident. I did not have to say anything but he just understood my state of fear and anger," said Rosa.

I wanted to ask Rosa how she felt sitting so close to the driver and seeing the deep ravines and valleys inches away from the roadside. The question stuck in my mouth. We still have two hours to go and this might just be an underestimation by the driver, psychological plasma to soothe our fears. Also, I discovered Rosa wanted some sense of psychological security by sharing with us her fears. As we were still finishing our food while conversing about the trip, the driver came out and asked us to hurry up, it was time to continue. He was apparently strict on time. Perhaps, then we could believe his estimation of time left. Some few guys were still smoking. We hurriedly emptied our plates and proceeded to the counter to settle the bills.

We all entered the car and began the second lap of the trip. Everyone seemed refreshed but lacked the brightness of demeanour that one would expect. The two boys sat near me and we waited for their dad to come back from the toilet. He was the last to enter the bus. We took off in slow motion. It is only as we got out of the settlement area that the driver increased the speed. Same landscape. With sweet music in my ears, the book in my hand, tired in my body, I took a propitious and natural refuge from my fear, slowly dozing off. When I opened my eyes, we were at the gates of *Hydro-electrico*. Sometimes, we do not need to worry about the future if we are able or lucky enough to have proper sleep. Sleep can have redemptive powers.

Hydro-electrico is where tourists alight and either take the train or trek to the village of Machu Picchu, Aguas Calientes, as it is called. At Hydro-electrico, there are two different rates for foreigners and Peruvians respectively. Peruvians pay a mere one-quarter of what foreigners are meant to pay. Claire and the Uruguayan guy who was with us on the bus convinced me that we could just walk. It was a good idea but I needed to talk with my agent in Cusco. It was not very clear to me if the guide would take me from Hydro-electrico or if I was to meet him at Agua Calientes. I called my tourist agent and he asked me to wait for the guide at *Hydro-electrico*. Claire and the Uruguayan guy thus went ahead, on foot. I took Claire's number and promised to join them in Aguas Calientes itself for a drink or something.

Ten minutes passed. I called the agent again. It rang but no one was on board. I stood in front of the ticket office, impatiently looking around to see if anyone would come asking for me. I was quite disturbed. I spoke to the lady at the ticket counter about my situation. She said the best way could be to trek if I had the energy. She made it look like a doable distance.

It could be a bit tedious if you are not used to trekking but it is altogether fun. Many tourists prefer to trek. It is about one hour thirty minutes. She told me.

At first, I was a bit indecisive. But then I told her:

"I'm going to try. But I hope there are many people on the road. I hope I won't get lost."

"Oh no, you can't, many tourists are trekking to and from Aguas Calientes. You will meet many companions. No qualms." She assured me.

I set on the road. After a few minutes' walk, I met two French guys trudging in the same direction, looking exhausted. After a brief self-introduction, we moved on together. I had found companions. We continued, answering breath for breath. I had to slow down my pace if I wanted to trek in their company. I wondered why they were so tired. Is it that they were humbled by the journey ahead or we did not set out on the same playing field, I wondered. They confirmed the second hypothesis: they had been travelling right from another town between Santa Teresa and Hydro-electrico. It was about one hour walk to the latter. They had about thirty minutes rest before setting forth for Aguas Calientes. After some kilometres away, we joined the company of two Argentines, a boy and a girl, seemingly a couple. We inquired if they had a clearer idea of the road ahead and how many minutes we still had to arrive in Aguas Calientes.

About thirty more minutes. That is what two guys we met on the way told us.

That was somewhat a consolation. We continued and this time around, we engaged in some civic knowledge about our countries. Football, Messi, Eto'o, Evita, Peronismo, Kirchnerismo, etc. I found it a bit difficult understanding the accent of my Argentine friends. They seemed to replace the "jod" sound with the 'sh' making "Yo" sound like "sho", and the "llamar" come off more like "shamar". It made some of their words sound like Brazilian. I thought it might be due to the affinity between Brazil and Argentina, just perhaps as one of the reasons. Chatting with my newfound Argentine friends, I understood why Ernesto Guevara de la Serna was nicknamed by his Cuban comrades as El Che for his frequent use of "che" which in Argentine slang means "pal".[3]

It was getting dark and the insects began their nocturnal chorus. It enlivened my spirit, reminding me of crickets which we used to hunt as children. We would hear the sound and then try to find the insect or its lair in the thicket. Sometimes when you got close to it, it stopped and you had to stay put, keep silent and sooner or later, it would recommence its creaking, thinking its predator had left. The music of the cricket provided a nice soundtrack or anthem to our new nation, the nation on the move. After having left the railroad, we came to a spot where the road split into two, without leaving us a clear indication as to which one led

---

3   Another explication of the origin of the name "Che" is related to "chancho" pig, in Spanish. Other sources purport Che cared less about hygienic matters and nicknamed him "el chancho" the pig, reason why he did not like the name from the very beginning. Che is also the short form of "José" which however did not figure amongst his original name which was Ernesto Rafael Guevara de la Serna.

to Aguas Calientes. We noticed a streak of light shining from a nearby compound, some twenty metres from the roadside, behind a thicket. We also heard human voices coming out from there. The Argentine girl opted to hurry down and ask the voices which of the roads led to our destination. She was just too steadfast and went off before we even thought of any risk involved.

She came back minutes later indicating the way to the right.

"We are not gentlemen, shame on all of us. Especially on you, my friend. How could you allow your girl to go down there alone? If some animal or something attacked her, what will you tell your friends back home? I joked and we all laughed.

We went on for about 15 more minutes and we were at Aguas Calientes! Lights shone from hotel verandas onto the main road. Restaurants were lined up the entrance to the city and groups of tourists moving up and down the main road, speaking in a variety of languages. I met a couple that travelled by the same bus to Hydro-electrico with me. They told me we had to meet our tour guide at the *Plaza de Armas* at 7 P.M. I separated with my Argentine and French friends and hung around with the couple. We decided to take a stroll around the shops just to squander the few minutes left. It was made clear to us that the prices of the artisanal products were much higher than in Cusco. When we passed in front of one shop, two saleswomen looked at me and started smiling. One greeted me:

"*Mi cuñado*[4], *how are you?*"

"I am fine," I responded.

"Where do you come from? You do not look Peruvian." I pre-empted her question by asking her to present her nationality.

"I am a daughter of the soil. You are the one who does not look Peruvian. Oh, do you come from Chincha?"

"Yes," I lied.

"My husband is *moreno*[5], just like you. Do you also eat cats? In Chincha they eat cats, right?"

"I don't know. I have never seen that. Does your husband eat cats?"

"He is not from Chincha. He is from Nazca, those from there do not eat cats."

The discussion on cats could have continued, but time was against

---

4   My in-law
5   Dark-skinned.

us. We had five minutes to be at the Plaza de Armas. After nearly ten minutes of waiting, one young guy came with a T-shirt and petticoat with the inscription Machu Picchu Tours and asked if I was *Gil Noli Shang*. I accepted but asked him to correct the middle name.

"I am Juan Carlos and I will be your tour guide for tomorrow's trip." He explained to the others waiting that I was the only one in his group. He bid them wait patiently for their tour guides, who were his colleagues. They would not fail to turn up, he assured them. It is then we understood that though we took the same bus from Cusco to Hydro-electrico, we belonged to different tourist groups.

Juan Carlos took me to a hotel room with two beds where I would spend the night. It was of good standard, quite neat and the water system functioned efficiently. I was going to share the room with another tourist, he notified me.

"You can have some rest and meet us later in the restaurant at the entrance to the hotel, let us say in thirty minutes. There will be a general orientation on the trip tomorrow." I took a warm shower, cross-checked if my personal effects were all in order and put on a warm sweater. I then went down to meet the rest of the group in the restaurant. We were served a modest dinner. I took a plate of rice with chopped meat, *chaufa con arroz* and *papa de huancaina*. I bought a small bottle of pineapple juice to drive it down.

Juan Carlos, our guide welcomed everyone and started the orientation. We were going to meet at the entrance to Machu Picchu at 6.30 A.M. There were two options, either to take the bus up to Machu Picchu or to trek. For those willing to trek, they would have to meet in front of the restaurant at 4:30 A.M. for tea. Otherwise, one could also get there by bus. The bus station was quite close to the hotel. Those who preferred to take the bus needed to be at the bus station at 5:30 A.M. In that case, they could come to the restaurant for breakfast thirty minutes before. He had bus and train tickets for sale, S/8 for foreigners, S/3 for Peruvians. As for the train tickets, S/28 for foreigners and S/8 for Peruvians.

"I will be there at the top quite early so as to wait for you guys. Our group is called *Grupo Juan Carlos* and our symbol is the Peruvian flag. Our tour will last for about two hours and you can have time to go around alone or in your own groups and take pictures. But remember, for those of you who have to go back to *Hydro-electrico* by train, it leaves at 1:30 P.M. Thus, make sure you are back here at least thirty minutes before this time. If anyone needs bus or train tickets for any of these rounds, feel free to meet me soon after this."

I bought the return train ticket to Hydro-electrico but was not very sure if I should descend from Machu Picchu with the bus. I finally decided to, after thinking that it would be quite exhausting for me to trek down the hill after the close to two hours trip from *Hydro-electrico* that evening and the fact that I was going to trek up to the mountain the following morning. Both tickets cost me S/36 altogether.

I went back to my hotel room where I met my roommates - a man in his fifties and his daughter of about 10. We introduced ourselves to each other. When I told him I was to visit Puno, he revealed to me that Puno was his home city.

"A beautiful place and do not fail to go to the lakes."

"For sure, I have it on my schedule."

We chatted briefly and I went to the bath as his daughter lay on the bed manipulating the open laptop. I also turned on my laptop to check my emails and to sleep early enough to wake up at 4:00 A.M. The internet connection was hitch-free. I set my alarm clock accordingly. It did not take me long to sleep off. I woke up at the sound of the alarm clock. I made sure I put it on the vibration option and I reduced the volume of my phone so as not to disturb the man and his daughter. My technique worked and when I woke up to the tickle and tune of the alarm, it was 4:02 A.M. The two bodies on the bed were deep asleep. Understandably, they would take the bus, the little girl could not be suffered to trek up the hill. I took a quick warm shower and made sure I arranged my necessities in my backpack. I tiptoed so as not to wake my roommates up. When I reached the restaurant, there were about 10 persons already taking their breakfast. The table was set well in advance. I took a glass of tea with a piece of soft bread and made out for the hike. I met four Brazilians. We walked up together for about twenty minutes before I went ahead of them.

The gradient up to the hill is one of the steepest I have ever climbed. The stone-built footpath is almost vertical. Most of the steps have worn out, probably due to the high number of pedestrians who have trodden on them. It was dawn and most of our fellow sojourners had headlights affixed to their fez caps and *sombreros*[6]. Little or no talking is heard, panting answers panting, cough answers cough. The exhausted ones stand, hands on the waist, gain some breath and others overtake them.

6   Hats

I trudged on, though my body was gradually losing its stability. I had already emptied the bottle of water I took along before we attained half of the trajectory. On such a trip, you discover the individuality of human effort. Up there, you cannot borrow one's breath; you cannot lean on someone else, for even the strongest body becomes a pillar of straw. The bus road spirals up the mountain and from time to time, intercepting the footpath at several points. When you happen to meet the passing bus with passengers comfortably seated, it makes you wonder why you chose trekking in the first place. At that time, it seems like pure foolhardiness. Really, at some point, I regretted not taking the bus.

I continued the upward climb, struggling with a dry cough as my lungs were being stretched to limits. I heard some noise just a few metres away. There was one lady in front of me, basically crawling, knock-kneed, coughing like a hag, as Wilfred Owen would say. The uproar grew more and more real and I knew we were few minutes to arrival. When I stepped on the level platform where a multitude of tourists were gathered, I felt like the ancient Greek marathon legend Pheidippides. A lady, seeing how exhausted I was, quickly handed me a bottle of fresh water. It was a very timely gesture. I thanked her profusely and recommended an additional service - a snapshot. She took the camera and immortalized my moment of exhaustion, but also of triumph. Where there is no trouble in the struggle, there is no triumph in the victory. I discovered that tourism had a strenuous dimension, and that is what gave it its sense of triumph. When it came to Machu Picchu, the sense of triumph carried a peculiar dimension.

There was a multitude, lined up according to the group to which they belonged. I easily found the queue of the members of Juan Carlos's group. We passed at the control point after presenting our passports and entry fee receipts. Juan Carlos proceeded to make a roll call of the group members. After calling each name, he would raise his head and look around searchingly, waiting for the member to answer present. When he called my name, he did not waste time and quickly continued.

"Easy to recognise," I commented. Many people laughed at my comment, but that was true.

Juan Carlos gave us a brief "lecture" on Machu Picchu before we could proceed. The construction of Machu Picchu began in 1450 during the time of the 9th Inca Emperor Pachacutec (meaning, "the hand that changes the world") and was abandoned in 1550 by the time of Manco Inca, the junior brother of the disputing monarchs Atahualpa

and Huascar. By the time of the conquest, Machu Picchu, the Great
(Machu) Peak (Picchu) was still in a process of construction. It was a
place reserved for the elite of the Inca Empire, mostly occupied by men,
leaders, soldiers and teachers. According to the archaeological evidence,
few bodies of women and children were found in the excavated graves.

The ruins of Machu Picchu were "discovered" in 1911 by the Harvard
archaeologist and historian Hiram Bingham III. It came somewhat as
a surprise because the object of his research was Vilcabamba, the last
stronghold of Inca resistance. It was also known as the el Eldorado, the
lost city of the Inca. When Bingham came to a small locality, the inhabitants told him there existed an abandoned city upon the mountains.
Bingham then asked a young teenager, Melchor Arteaga, to accompany
him up to the mountains against some modest payment. They set out
at dawn and when they arrived, they found three families living there
and enjoying the luxury of the ancient structures. Bingham published
his report in a renowned scientific journal and got funding for archaeological work in Machu Picchu with a team of historians, most of them
Peruvians. Hiram Bingham took away some of the golden relics, the
legal battle for the return of the relics, same colonial arguments, it was
finally returned to the government of Alejandro Toledo.

After the brief introduction, Juan Carlos understood from the body
language that we wanted to start the tour of Machu Picchu. He quickly
concluded and we moved on. Most of us, especially those who had trekked
up the mountain, were still exhausted. Legs wobbling, we scraped across
the slope of a hillock and gradually the dreamlike rims of endless terraces
and stone walls embraced us with shocking marvel and beauty. From
afar it seemed like a hill of those equidistant and rhyming patterns of
furrows and ridges carefully carved by village women on a mountainous
maize farm. Then it looked like the green version of neatly plaited hair
which our female peers used to call bakala that could exhume beauty out
of the most plain girl. The lush lawns of the terraces shone green with
enchantment. The intricate architecture of the walls seemed to marry the
landscape so exquisitely, with their labyrinths spread across the varying
temperaments of this otherwise difficult landscape. The walls and terraces descended impudently down the steep slopes and the questions you
would ask are: How was that possible? Where did the Incas stand to plait
these precipices with such adroit stoneworks? By what technology did
they roll these large stones uphill or downhill? How many people could
have died in this endeavour? With their rudimentary instruments, how

did they manage to chisel the stones to make them so plane? On one of
the green terraces stood a llama, fondling the back of its baby with its
mouth. We were told the young messenger of peace was just two days
old. What a beautiful way of welcoming us, visitors from East, West,
North and South to the Machu Picchu sanctuary!

You would imagine what Hiram Bingham, "the discoverer" saw when
he arrived here on 24 July 1914, led by the hand of the young Melchor
Arteaga. Certainly, the whole area was covered with undergrowth and
wild sprawling grass, a mega version of the abandoned compound of
my late granduncle, a veteran of the Second World War who fought
alongside the Britons in Burma. As a child, I often asked myself why
he had to fight in a foreign land, for a foreign land, just to return home
and live a wretched life, like the old man in Oyono's *The Old Man and
the Medal*. Anyway, that is a different story altogether.

Now talking about Bingham, I have seen a photo of him: a face replete
with so much undergrowth that you would have had to re-discover him
out of the thick grass of Machu Picchu that he was struggling to clear, to
make his discovery visible. With his sharp sunken eyes and wrinkled face,
he bore this melancholic outlook characteristic of the great philosopher-
president, Abraham Lincoln. It would have been interesting to see such
a face flare up in euphoria upon making this millennial discovery.

When we arrived at Machu Picchu, the surrounding mountains
were partially visible, dipped in the mist of gently moving thick fog and
we were suspended in the middle of nowhere, almost wondering how
we got there in the first place, with Aguas Calientes lost from sight for
good. I saw dotted figures of some tourists climbing up to Wayna (small,
young) Picchu (mountain, peak), a mountain that takes you further above,
permitting you to look down upon an already daunting height of Machu
Picchu. Wayna Picchu is 2,720m above sea level and 360m higher than
Machu Picchu. I caught chills watching those tourists clamber up the
mountain. Going up there would be stretching my foolhardiness too far,
I thought. The slopes were almost vertical, lined with stone walls. Any
slight slide from those heights might land you in an unknown territory,
perhaps into the Urubamba River. To climb up there, one has to book
a ticket several months in advance and the number of available places
is very limited.

We passed through the complex structures that included the sleeping rooms of the Inca, soldiers, assistants, the section of the educators,
sun temple, and astronomical centres. One curious stone was that which

acted as the hitching pole of the sun (intiwatana), the Torian which measured moments of equinoxes, solstices, etc. It also acted as a compass. Most of the buildings you find here incorporate every aspect of the Inca political, spiritual and cultural beliefs. Life contained three realms: *Hanan Pacha* (life beneath the earth), *Kai pacha* (physical world) and *Uku pacha* (the world of the dead). This corresponded to the three systems of labour that characterised work in the kingdom: aymi (mutual self-help amongst the aylus, villages), *minka* (communal work for public duties like roads, bridges) and *mita* (service to the state, tax payment). Politically, the Kingdom was referred to as the *Tahwaintisuyu*, etymologically meaning "four solar regions". The Inca kingdom was divided into four suyus, regions: Chinchasuyu, Kuntisuyu, Collasuyu, and Antisuyu. Cusco was the royal palace, political and military capital. Up till this day, the great stature and complexity of Machu Picchu have left many questions unanswered. Why did they build the citadel in such a risky and difficult-to-access landscape? What was the precise role of Machu Picchu given that Cusco, the navel of the world remained the capital of the *Tawantisuyu*? Why was it abandoned?

After having taken enough pictures, I went back to the entrance to board the bus back to Aguas Calientes. When I arrived at my hotel, I still had more than an hour and a half left. I decided to go to the thermal swimming pool. It was a nice experience and I enjoyed not only the warm water but also the beauty of the environment. Like most public places in Peru, it was well guarded by two police officers acting more or less like receptionists, with very generous smiles on their faces. After the piscine, I went back to my hotel to collect my stuff and get ready for the train trip. I still had about forty-five minutes left. I went to a restaurant for lunch and was served a dish of plantains with eggs and rice. I took as dessert cabbage salad with pear and a bottle of *chicha morada*[7]. After eating, I passed by the Plaza de Armas. I briefly watched a series of presentations organised by a company demonstrating its corporate social responsibility by donating computer sets to public and private colleges. Julie, the Mexican girl in my group met me there. We moved gradually to the train station. Claire, the French lady also joined us at the station. In the train, we met another Mexican girl, a medical student, who joined in our discussions. We talked about aspects of university life in universities in Mexico, Germany, France and Cameroon.

---

7   Peruvian beverage made up of purple corn.

In a mock and dominantly female committee of four (two Mexicans, one French, one German-based Cameroonian), we came out with the following declaration and counsel for future visitors to Machu Picchu: "When you are in Lima, you are in the capital of the country of Machu Picchu; when in Cusco, you are in the city of the marvels of Machu Picchu; when you can still be able to make it to Aguas Calientes, you are in the village-city of Machu Picchu. But just one thing: when you finally reach Machu Picchu proper, you may not have a single *sol* left to purchase even a bottle of *chicha morada* or a plate of *arroz salteado*. This is America."

Sharing experiences with my newfound friends reminded me again of the joys of being an international student. Unlike ambassadors who "lie" abroad for their respective countries, international students are liable to be more genuine in exchanging knowledge on different cultures and societies. They have no official mandate to represent anyone. I remember my first few months in Germany when I took part in a Summer University language programme. Our German language class of 18 was made up of students from many parts of the world: Bosnia, Egypt, Palestine, Russia, Burkina Faso, Belarus, Ukraine, Israel, Ivory Coast, United States, Lebanon. We had a very kind and energetic teacher who did her best to manage this melting pot. From the beginning, it was not easy, though. I remembered the bitter exchanges between the Lebanese and the US student on the morality of lesbianism; the hijab covered Egyptian girl; the proxy wars between the Israeli and the Palestinian guys, both journalists. One day, our teacher asked us to perform the most symbolic gestures in our various countries. When his turn came, the Palestinian guy, a bit loquacious, made the victory sign, forming the "V" with his index and middle fingers and went ahead to give us a long treatise on the Palestinian intifada. The Israeli guy was not amused but the teacher intervened promptly. In the beginning, we always felt a bit uneasy when political questions in our class arose for they almost unpredictably found their way to the Middle East. However, at the end of the course, the atmosphere became more and more cordial as we came to understand each other's background and culture. The Egyptian girl became surprisingly more communicative and jovial. The interaction with our Russian mates who were in the majority became very cordial. When I look back to this period of my time in Germany, the face of the Muslim Bosnian girl, in particular, comes vividly to my mind. On a few occasions, she tried to talk to me about the conflict her country went through in the nineties.

After describing how life was like in those days, she would shake her head, "it was so awful, to say the least." At this juncture, I would do my best to switch the topic of discussion. The day we obtained our language certificates, she was in tears. I captured this scene in a short article I wrote about my experience during the language programme upon the request of the director of the Language and Cultural Centre. It was my first text in Germany out of the classroom context. I cite here the final sentences of the text:

> Ende August hat mir ein Ereignis einen tiefen Eindruck hinterlassen: Es ist während unseres letzten Unterrichts, eine Kommilitonin umarmt und mummelt uns, Tränen im Augen, „Das werde ich nie vergessen…". Ja, ich könnte sie verstehen. Zwischen uns würden die Grenzen der Rasse, Hautfarbe, Religion, Kontinent, Morgen- und Abendländer, gebrochen. Wir waren nur "MENSCHEN" und die Sommeruni war ein Fest unserer Menschlichkeit durch die Sprache.

(English translation)

> *At the end of August, one episode left a deep impression in me: During our last class, one of our mates embraces us and murmurs, with tears in her eyes, "I will never forget this… "Yes, I could understand her. Between us the barriers of race, colour, religion, continent, West and East were broken. We were just HUMAN BEINGS and the summer university programme was a feast of our humanity through language.*

Writing this text in German reminded me of Henri Troyat's *Aliocha*, an autobiographical text describing the life of a Russian immigrant family in France after the 1917 Communist Revolution. After scoring 15/20 in a French test, the second-highest mark in her class, the Russian schoolboy Alexis Krapivine rushes home to proclaim the news to his parents, astonished by and angry at the streetwalkers' indifference towards the bliss in his heart. Truly, "the essence of language is hospitality and friendship" (Emmanuel Levinas).

Machu Picchu

Machu Picchu, here we come trudging on your ruins,
Not stamping our feet in impunity like conquistadors
But in humility, learning from your bosom,
In tribute to the architects of your citadel.

They say we have no history, no philosophy, no culture
Your ruins bear witness to the tragedy of continents,
For gold-hungry missionary-merchant mercenaries,
Wrecked what centuries of civilizations erected.

Even in this postmortem hearth I find greatness of spirit
Memories etched in stone, laid fallow by terror
Bleak memories of people dipped in slavery
In misery, in the land of their forefathers

I cry, I cry, shedding tears on the stumps
Of severed memories.

Gil Ndi-Shang

Pampas de Ayacucho Historic Sanctuary, constructed in 1980 to commemorate the 9 December 1824 Battle of Ayacucho that saw the fall of the last bastion of Spanish Empire in Latin America. Photo credit, Luis Rondinel.

Machu Picchu, Cusco-Peru. (*Machu Picchu*, 102). Photo credit, Linda Murillo.

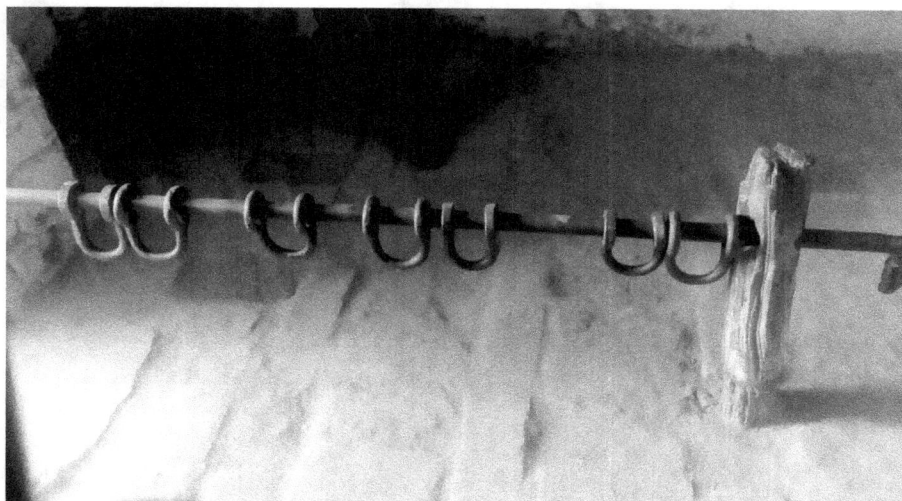

Museum representation of slave torture facility, Hacienda San José, El Carmen, Chincha-Peru. Photo credit, author

Statue of Simon Bolivar, the Liberator. Pueblo Libre District, Lima-Peru. Photo credit, author.

CHAPTER 23

Back to Inca-pital

The trip by train to the Hydro-electrico took roughly 30 minutes. Upon arrival, many mini-buses were ready to take the tourists back to Cusco. The drivers who had just arrived from Cusco had barely 20 to 30 minutes to take the new sets of passengers back. That meant roughly 12 hours of driving, with less than half-hour of rest! I looked at the new arrivals and the anxiety and uncertainty on their faces. Yesterday, I alighted here and looked at those who were returning from Machu Picchu with envious eyes. They had an experience yet unknown to me. Now I was also in their position.

There was one guy on the spot to assist passengers in sorting out their corresponding drivers. Each bus driver had a list of fifteen passengers he was commissioned to transport back to Cusco. The intermediary bade those whose drivers had not yet come to be patient, promising to put things right. Claire and the two Mexican girls had already entered into their buses. I remarked the look on Claire's face when the driver that had brought us from Cusco the previous day called her name on his list. She was seemingly not happy. I recalled her comments about the driver during our lunch break at Santa Teresa the day before.

"Hey, my friend. How are you?"

"Am fine and you?"

"All is fine. Sorry that I am not the one driving you today." He said.

"I missed you today brother. I wish you a safe trip. I am still waiting for my driver."

I responded kindly, with a mixture of regret and discrete jubilation. What I missed was his music selection. It is not that I questioned his driving skill but his attempt to overtake a bigger bus the previous day made us develop goose pimples although, after that, he drove smoothly all the way. However, I wanted someone else. Risks were not supposed to be forgiven on that road. I yearned for my ideal driver. I needed to look into his eyes and find SAFETY written on his face. I needed to safely arrive at Cusco before beginning the trip. I needed full assurance.

One German girl was standing with me. She too was still waiting for her driver. I found her restless and consoled her just to be patient. Her driver came before mine and we bade each other a modest farewell. Finally, the coordinator came and told me he would call one of the drivers still on his way to confirm if I was amongst his passengers for the Cusco return trip.

"Hello. There is a *morenito*[1] here waiting for a driver. His name is *Noli Gil Nchang.*"

I did not know how to react to this description. Coming from Germany where one had to be quite cautious with nomenclatures about races so as not to hurt feelings or appear racist, I found my denomination as *morenito* quite intriguing. Usually, the adjectival diminutive suffix *ito* is used to mark affection for the thing or person thus named. But in some cases, it can also appear pejorative and belittling. I did not know to which category that denomination belonged but I gave its user the benefit of the doubt.

The driver on the phone declared that the *morenito* was his passenger. Minutes after, the driver arrived. Meantime, I went to the toilet so as not to be in any inconvenient position during this trip. When I came back, the bus was nearly full. I was left with the front seat. It was an ambiguous position. I usually prefer front seats, but this was not the time. My legs had more freedom of mobility there than at the back seats. But that also meant that I would be in direct contact with the abyss! The driver was a bit more mature. He had a steady look, slightly sunken eyes with a deep and discrete sight, giving the impression of someone with rich experiences, even including human strain. I felt quite confident. He somehow suited my criteria for the magic driver I imagined and longed for. One lady came and sat in the middle front seat, between the driver and me. She seemed to be the one in control, if not the proprietor of the bus. It was her who gave the order for departure.

"Take good care of that lady!" Said the guy the lady had been chatting with before hopping onto the bus.

"Sure, you can trust me," I responded jokingly. The lady smiled on hearing this. They also have these 'park boys' jokes like in Cameroon, I said to myself. When we started the trip, her phone never seemed to rest. She was calling and answering calls, asking her partners to contact

---

1   diminutive of "moreno", meaning dark-(skinned)

some customers, arrange their logistics and lodging. She owned a tourism agency in Cusco, she later confirmed to me.

I was again awed by the very idea of sitting in the front seat. I tried to bury my fear by engaging the lady in a chat about Peruvian social realities. She was quite responsive and gave me a long treatise on race relationships in Peru. At some point, I decided not to ask more questions so as not to distract the driver in any way. I discovered that now that I was close to the driver, I was able to see the sides of the road, the one-metre distance that separated us from the abyss. Ironically, I felt even more confident and secured. This was not the case when I sat in the backseat the day before. Then, it was as if the car would get out of hand in the next second. About 30 minutes on the road, I found myself dozing off. Gradually, sleep took the better part of me. I was later to wake up at the tollgate when the car stopped in front of two police officers. They asked for the driver's documents. The lady by my side dug her fingers into a sachet hanging on the roof just above the driver's head, brought down the documents and handed them to the police.

As one of the police officers was going slowly and meticulously through the documents, the lady pleaded in a mournful tone: "Please, there is a passenger who has to travel to Puno this night and time is not really on his side."

The police officer did not respond. But he showed his clemency by stepping up his pace and soon handed the documents back to the driver. At that juncture and also in other circumstances during my trips to Peru, I found them quite understanding and polite. Sometimes in my home country, the lady's statement could have worsened matters. The police try to find faults when they know that you are in haste. At such a time, you can easily give in to their pecuniary extortion.

We continued our way. From time to time, the lady would alert the driver, as a matter of caution, that a car was coming from the opposite direction. Given the spiralling nature of the road and the position of the driver, the lady and I had a better view of the road ahead. It was dusk and the weather became a bit foggy, impeding sight on an already difficult landscape. Gradually we left the mountain chains and as we neared Cusco, the situation improved. There were more cars on the way and the traffic signs were more precise. The lady brought out an MP3 from the sachet near the driver's seat and switched on the CD player. It was Peruvian huayno music. The tunes accompanied us right to Cusco. The plaintive tonality of one of the songs has never left my memory:

Sin compasión aquí me tienes sufriendo,
sin compasión aquí me tienes llorando,
sin compasión te has marchado con otra,
no hay sentimientos en tu corazón ingrato.

sin condición mi amor te entregue mi vida,
sin compasión te has marchado con otra,
no hay sentimiento en tu corazón ingrato.

Amor, amor, amor que fue de nuestro,
Acaso no eras feliz con nuestro amor.

¡No! No todo lo malo que nos pasa, es porque lo merecemos,
 a veces necesitamos cosas malas y tropiezos en la vida,
para así madurar y crecer como seres humanos...

(English Translation)

Without compassion, you left me here suffering,
Without compassion, you left me here, weeping
Without compassion, you went away with someone else
You do not have any feelings in your ungrateful heart.

Without preconditions, I offered my heart to you, my love,
Without preconditions, I offered my life to you, my love,
And without compassion, you went away with someone else
You don't have any compassion in your ungrateful heart.
Love, my love, what happened to our love,
Maybe you are not happy with our love.

No! Not every mishap that has happened to us is because we deserve it
Sometimes we need such moments and false moves in life
In that way, we mature and grow as human beings...

Someone had earlier explained to me in Lima that the traditional Peruvian huayno was more about celebration and merriment. But recently, it has become the vent through which artists expressed their frustration with war and violence, not forgetting unhappy love stories.

CHAPTER 24

Puno, Titicaca

We arrived in Cusco around 9:30 P.M. I found a taxi to take me to Acosta Hostal. The bus to Puno was leaving at 10:15 P.M. So I had no time to waste at my hostel. I could not even bathe or eat anything. Thankfully, the traffic in Cusco was not as intense as in Lima. I needed to be at the park at least 30 minutes before time. I pleaded with the same taxi driver to take me to the bus station if he could just give me 5 minutes to bring my stuff down. I promised to be punctual and he gave in. I quickly moved my luggage down to the reception and settled my bill with the waiter. S/90 for three nights. In less than fifteen minutes I was at the park. I did not have much difficulty locating my bus agency. The control officer indicated to me the passage to the bus. In front of the entrance, a short and stout man came to me, proposing to sell me the entrance fee for S/1.5. I did not have the least idea about such a procedure. He explained to me and offered to save my time. I told him I would verify from the police officer. Yes, it was the procedure. The police officer directed me to the counter where to buy the ticket. There was a long queue and I would certainly not make it in time for departure. I came back to the boarding gate of *San Luis Travel Agency* and complained to the policeman at the entrance. He called the guy who had proposed to retail the ticket to me. He told him he had no more tickets. The policemen asked me if I had any cash on me. I hadn't. I showed him the S/20 banknote in my palms. He looked at it lethargically. Finding me already getting anxious about missing my bus, he just let me pass, wishing me a safe trip.

The bus was a huge inter-urban carrier, a double cabin operated by the San Luis agency. I had paid for the semi-bed option to rest properly after such an exhaustive trip. A camera on a tripod was stationed beside the bus door, taking footage of each passenger as they entered. In the Cruz del Sur bus which I boarded from Lima to Ayacucho, we equally had our faces photographed by the security agent. I found these to be a laudable security measure.

My seat was the first seat on the left column of the ground level cabin. Quite comfortable, I felt. I swept my backpack under the foot stretcher and comfortably leaned on the backrest. To my left were two young guys, conversing in very low tune.

"Good evening my friend, where are you from?" Asked the one just nearer to me.

"I am from Cameroon, and you?"

"We are from Spain, from Malaga, precisely."

"Oh, I see."

"So you speak English and French. I know Cameroon was colonised by France and Britain, right?"

"Not really. Cameroon was colonised by Germany between 1884 and 1916. After that, she was administered by Britain and France under the League of Nations and later under the United Nations system. We speak French and English as official languages but we have about 280 mother tongues."

"Oh, you mean dialects?"

"No, I mean fully independent languages."

Gradually, our discussion delved into a long historical treatise on colonialism. He seemed to have world colonial history at his fingertips. He talked about Spanish colonialism, the relationship between Portuguese and Spanish crowns at the time of the Conquista, the legacy of Spanish colonialism in the new world, etc. He was my type of person. But just the body was weak, from my supine responses. He was almost in a monologue. His friend did not even utter a word. I gradually slept off. When I woke up hours later, the other passengers were dead asleep, including my historian friend. I noticed that on the passage floor, there were bodies wrapped in thick ponchos. At some of the stops, the female controller took some passengers on board. They merely lingered on the passages, no spaces left. I am sure those were the extra earnings of the *cobradora* and the driver, perhaps without the knowledge of the company. It reminded me of similar experiences during my trips to Bamenda, my hometown in Cameroon. I was also astonished by the fact that most of those who came in through this method were really old women. I wonder how they could wait along the road so late at night without any fear of robbery. Perhaps, Peru was relatively safe.

I found myself dozing off again in spite of my initial intention to take off my computer and continue reading a text I had left halfway. The thick curtains prevented me from having any view of the surrounding environment. I did not feel the weight of the Andes again on me, thanks to the darkness and the generous sleep.

We arrived in Puno at 4:30 A.M. According to the arrangement with my tourist agent in Cusco, someone had to pick me up at the station. I was quite impressed by the order at the bus station in Puno. The structure was spacious enough and the interior was well decorated. Unlike the smaller station in Cusco, it was well organised and demarcated. I sat on the bench after having looked at the names on the placards held by a group of five tourism agents waiting to pick up their customers. I patiently waited, concluding that my agent in Puno had not yet come. That gave me enough time to clean my face in the nearby washroom.

I came and sat back on the bench. One of the agents who had been there when I arrived turned the back of the placard in his hand. It is then that I saw my name written in bold blue ink. I moved to him and told him I was the one. He welcomed me and requested that I should wait for the rest of his clients to come. Later, more passengers trooped in as more buses arrived from other parts of the country. Three ladies and one guy moved up to him. Certainly, the team was now complete. He beckoned us to follow him. We entered a private car and in some twenty minutes, we were at a guesthouse. We took our shower and cleaned our mouths. Other customers had come before us. However, we had different trajectories thereafter because some had registered for a two-day tour whereas others like myself had only one day in Puno.

At breakfast, two cars took us to the dockyard from where we were ferried to Lake Titicaca.

This is Lake Titicaca

We arrived back at the guesthouse at close to 5 P.M. Vladimir, the gentleman from Russia, and I had some rest at the guesthouse and later decided to go to the *Museo Carlos Dreyer* near the Plaza de Armas. Carl Dreyer was a German painter and collector. Born in Homberg, he spent a greater part of his life in Peru, almost fifty years, travelling around the country and collecting relics of the prehispanic and colonial eras of Peru. He also realized several paintings, especially focusing on the lives of the indigenous populations in Peru and Bolivia. His collections formed the basis of the museum bearing his name, though much has been added to the original collection thanks to the municipality of Puno. Among the paintings of Dreyer is one on Richard Wagner, the most important name associated with Bayreuth, my hometown in Germany. It was a beautiful portrait of one of the most important (but also controversial) cultural/artistic figures in German history. I wanted to take an image of the portrait but the battery of my phone was already too low. The camera of Vladimir's phone had a problem. So, I pleaded with a Peruvian man, a fellow visitor to take a picture of the portrait and other museum objects and send them to me via email.

We were amongst the last guests and the museum had to close at 7:00 P.M. Vladimir complained of hunger. We found a restaurant close to the Plaza de Armas. Unlike Cusco, Aguas Calientes and some parts of Lima, restaurant waiters in Puno were not as abrasive and insistent. We chose our restaurant without any much enticement. Indeed, we did not regret our choice. The food was quite delicious and the salad very rich.

We went back to the guesthouse at about 8 A.M. Upon arrival, the tourist agents had already bought the bus tickets for us. Vladimir had to continue to Cusco, on his way to Machu Picchu. I was heading down to Arequipa. He was however not satisfied with his ticket because he wanted a bed and not a semi-bed cabin. He was quite particular about taste. He decided to go to the station and change it. Therefore, he left immediately; hoping it would still be possible to change. We bade each other farewell, exchanging emails so he could forward to me the pictures we had taken at the lake. I only went to the station thirty minutes before departure time.

There, I happened to meet Vladimir passing by the gate to my bus. He told me he had succeeded in changing his ticket, obtaining a bed option, indispensable to him since he needed adequate rest so as to brave the challenges of Machu Picchu. We embraced each other once more, knowing we would most likely never meet again. We had spent a day together, shared stories, food, space, etc. We were brothers for one day.

CHAPTER 25

Arequipa, the Good and the Bad

The trip from Puno to Arequipa took roughly seven hours. My seat was in the upper cabin and the bus seemed fresh from the mint. The seats exuded the fragrance of newness. The trip was as smooth as that between Cusco and Puno. I had enough sleep and could only read for about an hour before arrival. We arrived in Arequipa bus station, the *Terrapuerto* (land port), at barely 5 A.M. I had tried in vain to reach Mariana with whom I had been in touch for close to a week. Her sister, Camila, whom I knew in Germany, had linked us up when I told her I would be visiting her hometown of Arequipa. I planned to visit touristic sites in town while waiting to catch up with Mariana in the course of the day.

I went to the washroom to clean my face and freshen up. There was a long queue and I had to pay 50 cents of Peruvian soles as the fee. I then entered a bistro to take a glass of tea but also to wait for daybreak. Back to the restaurant, after coffee, I took rice with chicken and levelled it out with a glass of *chicha morada*. I was told that the stores open at about 8:00 A.M. I had to buy my ticket that morning for my return trip later in the night. *Cruz del Sur* was S/110. That was the most expensive. I went in for a cheaper option, S/80. The agency was called *Jalsa*. It was a semi-bed option. Unlike Cusco and Puno, there was just no tourist office at the bus station in Arequipa. The lady at the Jalsa counter told me there is one at the *Terrapuerto* 2[1]. That was also where I would board the bus to Lima in the evening. It was an immense bus station, much bigger than terminal 1 where I alighted. However, I did not seem to see any tourist agency around. Meantime I tried calling Mariana's number and could still not get her. Surely there was something wrong with her connection. I went into a small kiosk and inquired from the salesperson.

"Excuse me, sir, is there any tourism office here in the station?"

"All the tourist agencies are found in the central town. Just get a taxi

---

1   literally land port, meaning bus station.

and it will take you to a good tourist agency."

"Thanks very much. See you!"

Before entering Terminal 2, several taxi drivers were already hawking after me. I decided not to react in any way. That was one of my lessons in Peru. Once you respond, it is seen as an invitation. I remember the incident when I went to the market in Lince and one hawker, a gentleman, followed me right down to the restaurant, coaxing me to buy a piece of the 50 cent biscuits he was selling. I told him I was in haste but he would not listen. When I thought I had freed myself from him, I still saw him in front of the restaurant where I was eating, asking me with his eyes if he could come.

The man who drove me to the central town was quite lovely and soft-spoken. When I told him I would get back to Lima the same day, he asked me:

"Have you already bought your ticket?"

"Oh yes, am travelling with the agency called Jalsa."

"Oh really? That is just the worst you can think of. Why didn't you ask for advice? They have very old buses. Not comfortable at all."

I felt his words like blows. Knowing the topography of Peruvian roads I had travelled so far, I felt like returning with the driver to request a refund from the agency. But again, I thought it is better to seek a second opinion upon arrival at the tourist agency.

"And they took S/80 from you. You could get a good ticket with a better agency for less than that."

"But Cruz del Sur is selling for S/110."

"Forget about them. They are just crazy. They claim too much prestige for nothing. There are better agencies out there." I told him I had no choice than to assume my mistake, hoping the trip would be safe anyway. We got to the agency and the lady had just come in. She was still unpacking her handbag.

"Elisa, how are you today. Julio has not come yet?"

"No, he travelled to Puno for some business. He might be back tomorrow."

"Ok, that is fine. Let me present to you my friend from Cameroon."

"Good morning sir, welcome to Arequipa.

Good morning madam. Thank you very much."

"He wants a city tour. Give him just the best treatment. He is a wonderful gentleman."

"Sure, you guys should just give me a few seconds. I will take ample care of you, ok? Please have a seat. You can place your bag here by the desk."

"Thank you. No problem, take your time." I responded courteously.

"Ok, Gil, you have a nice time my friend. Enjoy the beautiful town of Arequipa." The driver said, poised to leave. I reminded him that I had not yet paid the taxi fare

"Oh sorry. I was so bent on getting you to this office, and most importantly meeting this beautiful lady. So, I forgot to ask for the fare!"

I gave him S/8. He bade farewell and left, promising to come back to the office in the evening.

I was left with the lady in the office. We finalised the tour arrangement and I paid her cash. Four-hour tour of the cityscape of Arequipa, 9:00 A.M. to 1:00 P.M. It was still 8:20 A.M. I asked if I could quickly use her computer to check my message box as she settled down. She conceded. I logged onto my Facebook. Luckily, I did not have so many messages. I had informed most of my friends I would be too mobile to check my Facebook during those days. My sole aim was to write to Mariana on Facebook because she was usually quite prompt in responding to Facebook messages.

I dropped her a quick message, she responded instantly, asking if I was already in Arequipa. I informed her of my day's schedule and we agreed to meet at 5:00 P.M. in front of the tourism agency. She seemed to know the place. Some few friends noticing me online started banging me with chat messages. I resisted the temptation. I did not want to abuse the indulgence of my host. I quickly signed off, apologizing for taking much more time than initially intended. No qualms, she said. She was still trying to fix her look for the day, softening her lips dextrously with very fragrant gel while looking at her face in the minuscule mirror attached to her purse. Knotting her curly hair. Seemingly she had left the house in haste. Quite lovely and gentle, I thought. I saw her in the self-making process. I witnessed, at least in its final phase, the process through which our face, our body transits from its private sphere onto the social and public; the face-lifting process, the fabrication of the social masks that define us in public sight. The process seemed to be endless.

As I sat back on the sofa, my phone started ringing. It was Miguel, asking where I was at the moment and how the trip was moving so far. I explained to him my entire trajectory and we promised to see each other in Lima the following week. Miguel, very kind, generous, patient, gentle, even genteel.

It was about 10 minutes to 9:00 A.M. when one young guy, dressed formally in office suit and a bow tie, stepped into the office.

He will take you to the bus station. It is quite close by. The lady said.

The gentleman turned to me, greeted me with uttermost courtesy and beckoned me to follow him. Less than two minutes' walk. There were few people on the bus. My seat was quite strategic, the front seat of the upper cabin. From there I could have a superb view of the city and take nice pictures of its beautiful landscape.

Fifteen minutes later, the bus was full. Next to me was a lady whose husband and daughter sat immediately behind us. To my left, on the other column, were two South Korean teenagers, looking quite excited about the tour. The guide took the microphone, introduced herself, welcomed us to the beautiful city of Arequipa and promised to use both Spanish and English during the tour.

This is Arequipa

At roughly 1 P.M. we alighted at the bus stop from where we set off. I walked towards the tourism agency office. I was a bit tired and hoped to have some rest on the sofa and even read some few pages as I waited for Mariana. Just before entering the office, I was tempted to pop into a shop selling handicraft objects and some mementos of Peru. I had not bought any single thing in Cusco, nor Aguas Calientes. Perhaps I could pick one or two souvenirs from here. In Cusco, I planned to buy a medium-sized travelling bag decorated with Inca symbols. However, I returned from Machu Picchu too late and had to transit directly to Puno.

I found the exact bag, same size and same colour, but the price was S/40. The bargain was too tough. In Cusco, it was thirty. I decided to try it in the shop next door. It was much bigger. The salesman looked quite friendly, a stout and well-dressed middle-aged man. I found the smaller size of the bag and he promised to bring a bigger one. He sorted it out from an adjoining storeroom. S/35 was the ultimate price and I conceded. I also left the shop with a pair of shoes and a long sleeve shirt, all bearing the stamp of Inca culture.

When I got out of the shop, it occurred to me that I should at least send Elena, my landlady in Lima, a message regarding my trip. The phone was not in the pocket of my overcoat as I thought. I scampered through my two trouser pockets to no avail. Neither was it in the chest pocket of my shirt. I did not want to believe the worst had happened.

It was a cruel joke, I had my Alcatel One Touch on me when alighting from the tourist bus. Could it have been stolen? But how, just how? I could not believe this hypothesis. My wallet was in my trouser pocket, with all its content. I hadn't come into very close contact with anyone in the street. It was not crowdy, in the first place. The probability of theft seemed quite unlikely. But, what other probability?

I got back into the store and with the salesman, we checked around where I had sat to try the shoes and the shirt. Nothing. He was quite meticulous and very empathetic.

"This is not possible. Please, carefully check again in your pockets."

"I have checked and I bet you, it is nowhere to be found," I replied as I put down my bag and scurried through it desperately.

"Give me your number let me try and call." I dictated the number and he dialled.

My heart thumped with expectation.

"The phone is blocked. The number does not go through."

"Was the battery still full?"

"Sure, as far as I can remember, it was about 20% full when I got back to the bus stop after the tour," I suggested to him that I would check in the shop next door where I had first entered briefly. The two saleswomen inside told me they had not seen any phone anywhere. In my wildest imagination, I could not think the phone would be found there since I barely spent three minutes inside there. I didn't sit down, did not pose anywhere. We merely had a brief bargain on the bag and I left. I thanked them for their concern and went back to the next store.

"They say they have not seen it there."

"This is quite strange. It means it might have been stolen."

"Are you sure you haven't forgotten it at the bus?"

"No, I am very sure I came out with it."

He lamented over the issue and told me not to worry. Just be patient let us figure out what might have happened. Some other customers came in and he attended to them while I stood there in anguish. Seeing how busy he got, I kindly told him that I would go to the tourism agency close by and get back to him soon after.

When I entered the office, the lady received me with a generous smile. Her face shone, after having completed the face-making process. But it was not admiration time for me.

"Welcome back, how was your trip?"

"It was quite enjoyable, Arequipa is a beautiful place and with a lot of interesting historical arti/facts."

"Yes, I regret that you do not have enough time to witness the *vuelo de condor*². For that, you need at least two days. But you, what are you hurrying to do in Lima? Why? Lima is not so beautiful, not as beautiful as Arequipa, I mean."

"I have a presentation to do there in two days." All along I tried to maintain a jovial countenance. This lady was not aware of the emotional turmoil I was going through. I would have been interested in small talk of this kind, but…my phone. I was looking for the appropriate moment to break the bad news. At the same time, I did not want to seem miserable. A lady dropped in and engaged her in a chat, before taking her seat close to the wall. They seemed to be good friends, reading from their air of familiarity and their body language.

"You know what? I just lost my phone, with all my pictures from Machu Picchu and all my time in Peru."

"What? Perhaps you forgot it on the bus. Can I call the driver to inquire?"

I narrated my trajectory to her and told her it was unlikely I could have dropped the phone on the bus. But again, all other hypotheses seemed unconvincing.

"Anyway, just call to inquire, one never knows."

She rang and began talking with the driver. I did not expect any miracle from the call, this time around. The driver was already on the second tour with other passengers. He promised to call the bus service and the bus cleaner to inquire. She bade me to be patient and wait for the driver's call before we draw any conclusions. The lady that had just entered inquired about what happened and I explained to her. She was trying to follow our conversation but did not grasp the whole story.

"Do not bother too much. Such is life. I went to Machu Picchu with my husband last year and we have an album full of pictures. If you like I can share them with you. Perhaps burn it on a CD."

"That would be so kind of you."

"I know it is not the same as your *own* photos, but perhaps it can help."

"I know, please it would be a great gesture from you I said, not at all convinced that it would in any way placate my pain. I tried to show my gratitude. It was genuine, but accepting it meant gradually accepting the loss of my phone, with all the images.

---

2   The flight of the condor bird.

The bus driver rang again and the lady responded. I held my breath. The other lady said she had to hurry somewhere. She asked me when I would be leaving and promised to bring the CD to the agency before closing time. As her friend was still on phone, they just waved at each other.

"Well, he says no one found any phone on the bus."

"Thanks for your effort. It means I might have misplaced it somewhere else." My fate was sealed. As she was trying to console me to take it as such, a tall and curly-haired girl appeared at the door. Looking at me, she asked, with an instant air of familiarity.

"Is it Gil?"

"Here I am, Mariana. You are so punctual. I am glad you found this place."

We embraced each other. She was very adorable, with the same soft smile and way of speaking as her sister in Germany. "At least you have got some occasion to put a smile on your face. The tourism agent commented." Perhaps, that was true.

"What is wrong with your phone? It is not getting through."

I narrated to her the entire incident.

"So sorry to hear that. It is an indirect invitation for you to come back to Peru, and visit Machu Picchu once again."

That was funny and provocative in a good way.

Mariana suggested that we take a walk along the streets and think away from the lost phone. It was getting to 5:00 P.M. and the streets of Arequipa began to fill in with people. We went to the Saint Augustine University Museum. Unfortunately, it was closing time. I was both disappointed and relieved. It was my habit to visit museums during my trip as they provided me with considerable knowledge of the culture and history of the people. However, I just wanted to enjoy the fresh air, to enjoy the open sky of Arequipa as the twilight fell on the palm fronds of the Arequipa Plaza de Armas. Mariana was now my guide.

"This is the main Cathedral in Arequipa. There is one narrative that claims that this Cathedral was meant for Mexico City but then it was mistakenly built in Arequipa. When the planners, based in colonialist Spain, realized their mistake, the project was already underway and there was no need to alter it."

"So, this Cathedral is a very pleasant mistake."

We laughed over it as we went inside to take some pictures. There was a mass going on but the worshippers were not disturbed by tourists who came in just for sightseeing and pictures. Looking at the altar and wall statues, one would think that gold was cheaper than wood in those colonial days.

From there we moved to the Library of the Nobel Laureate, the writer Mario Vargas Llosa. It was closed down for renovation, we were told. I was not particularly impressed by the structure. Perhaps the interior was better designed. We left and moved back in the direction of the tourism agency.

"Have you ever tasted pisco?"

"I am not sure. Of course, I know it is liquor, I also know, from my Quechua class that the name is originally Quechua. I learned that in a short Quechua class at the Book Fair in Lima."

"Oh, I see, pisco is one of our typical liquors in Peru. There is a pisco bar not very far from the tourism agency. We can go there and take something. I will write to my dad to tell him where we are so that he can pick us up at about half-past seven. He promised to pass through the city centre after work."

We set forth for the pisco bar. It was well decorated with all kinds of fanciful bottle shapes displayed all over the counters. We took our seats. She inquired about my preferences.

"Here you have many types. Do you like the hard one or the soft one?"

"Well, I guess that which is least strong. I am not very good at alcohol."

"In that case, pisco sour could be the best option."

"Fine, if it is not too strong. She called for the waitress and gave the command."

"Just one or two."

"I am not going to drink."

"Oh no, Mariana. You cannot do that. Let's take two glasses."

"In that case, maybe we take a single glass and share."

That was the compromise. The pisco was really good. I found its taste far better than my experience of vodka and other strong liquors.

We kept chatting until Mariana's father arrived. He looked quite young.

"Papi, this is Gil, Camila's friend from Germany whom I told you about. He is originally from Cameroon."

We embraced each other and he bade me welcome to Arequipa.

He took a seat opposite me.

"Mariana, are you sure this is your dad?" I teased her. "He looks more like your brother. If I had met both of you in the street I would have thought that he is either your brother or your boyfriend. We laughed as her father raised his shoulders and drawing her attention, in a triumphant gesture:

"Have you heard? If it were someone from here, you would have thought that I bribed him to make such statements. He is coming all the way from Cameroon, honest people. And not just that, also from Germany, objective people. So this is an honestly objective opinion!"

His appropriation of my compliments sent all of us laughing out our lungs. It is only after Mariana recovered from it that she found the energy to fire back.

"I agree, behaving like my brother, yes. But looking young, I am not very sure."

Her father closed his ears with the palms of his hands, saying:

"No appeal, the judge has passed his verdict after thorough observation of facts."

He was funny in just every sense of it. There are people in this world, once you meet them for the first time it is as if you had known them throughout your life. I felt similar when I met Camila, Mariana's sister, in Bayreuth during our Spanish speaking/learning sessions. She had this natural air of honesty around her and was so willing to share knowledge about her country. The friendship with her contributed to my choice of Peru as my research interest. I remembered the very first day she told me about Arequipa, her hometown. The only connection I could make was that Arequipa was equally the hometown of the Nobel Prize laureate Mario Vargas Llosa. By then, it settled in my mind that Arequipa was in the northern part of Peru! I do not know why perhaps because my Spanish was quite rudimentary then and I could not grasp everything thoroughly.

I engaged Mariana's dad with a series of questions about Peru, the racial mix of the country, the legacy of Vargas Llosa as writer and politician, the Peruvian civil war and its effects on Arequipa, Peru's relationship with Chile, etc. His response on this last issue was particularly enlightening to me.

"The relationship is now normalizing, although at the level of the government they both have their mutual suspicions. Wait, have you guys already eaten something this evening?"

"Oh no, we were trying to catch up with the visit to the museum. But still arrived there late." Mariana responded.

"I see, then you can order for something to eat. There is a special Arequipanian delicacy here called *salsa en pulpo de anticucho*. I am sure you would like it."

He then called the waitress and passed the order. It was a delicious dish. Mariana and her dad just tasted, graciously.

"It is for you, please go ahead."

I bade them to no avail to eat along with me.

Keen on continuing with our discussion on Peru/Chile relations, I prodded further.

"And how about the people, the relationship between Peruvians and Chileans, generally speaking?"

"They do not have many problems with each other. Of course, in the collective memory, Peruvians have never actually forgotten the humiliation they suffered in the hands of the Chileans."

"Excuse me", Mariana said. "You know what? It is already getting to 7 P.M. and the tourism agent said she closes at 7:30 P.M. Let me go and collect your bag at once. I will be back."

"Oh, great idea Mariana. I did not even notice that the time has moved this fast."

She left and the father continued with the story of the War of the Pacific.

"The war occurred over Bolivian taxes on Chilean companies exploiting nitrate on Bolivian territory. Chile claimed Bolivia violated a treaty signed earlier on with the Bolivian government. When Chile declared war on Bolivia, Peru decided to honour a hitherto secret treaty of mutual defence that she had signed with Bolivia. However, Peru was not prepared for the war whereas Chile had been gearing up for years, with the support of the British forces. It did not take long for Chile to overrun parts of Peru and completely control Lima. It is thanks to the threat of intervention of the French military forces under the command of General Petit Thouars that Chile had to withdraw from Peru."

At the hearing of the name "Petit Thouars", I interrupted Mariana's father. "I live along the Avenida Petit-Thouars in Lima. Since the name did not sound to me as typically Peruvian, I was a bit curious about that. I asked my landlady who he was but for some reason, we did not talk about that."

"Yes, that is the explanation. More so, during that war, Arequipa put up a strong resistance against the invaders. Right from the years of independence, this city was always a bulwark against Bolivar's (Bolivia's) dictatorial tendencies. So, it prides itself on its Republican heritage.

"I see. We had a city tour there today; it is a very beautiful place. I added".

"Oh yes, it is very beautiful, not as polluted as Lima. You know what? There is a popular saying which goes: Everything in Arequipa is very good except its inhabitants."

"Hahaha, quite funny. Unfortunately, I cannot extend my stay here; perhaps, if I stay longer I will experience better things."

"Better or worse things. They already began by stealing your phone. Hopefully, you will come back again. Once in Arequipa, you will always come back." Meanwhile, Mariana came in with my bag and a CD in her hand.

"The lady at the agency says this is from her friend who promised to share her Machu Picchu pictures with you after learning of your loss."

"Oh really? Yes, she promised to. I did not know she would do it so timely. I promised to call the agency later and ask for the phone number or Facebook address of this lady to express my thanks to her."

"That is a good gesture, some Arequipenians aren't that bad." Mariana's dad added, in his usual satirical tone and with a wink.

Vintage Mariana suggested we could start going so I can have some extra time at the bus station. Her dad acquiesced. He called for the waitress and settled the entire bill, including the pisco which we ordered before he came in. I protested to no avail. We all set out for the Plaza de Armas around where he had parked his car. When we passed in front of a memento shop, he asked me.

"Have you got your passport with you?"

"Oh yes, of course. I always travel with my passport to avoid any infelicities, especially when in a foreign country."

"Ok, which nationality?"

"It is a Cameroonian passport. I am only in Germany for studies. No German passport."

He asked us to accompany him to the shop. I saw him hand what seemed like S/2 to the old man at the counter and was given a kind of a passport-shaped booklet wrapped in a transparent paper.

"My friend Gil, here is your passport, to be precise, your Arequipenian passport." He handed it to me with a medal-like object, *characato de oro*[3].

I was bemused. I did not know what meaning to draw from that.

---

3   Literally, Characato of gold, a medallion made "purportedly" made of gold.

He acted without betraying his demeanour. His daughter just smiled and explained to me.

"It is just a memento for visitors to Arequipa. It is meant to sell the image of Arequipa as a peculiar place. It is not valid anywhere, of course. Just for fun."

"Hahahaha. Thank you so much. I was lost, I thought as well it was a joke but I could not imagine a joke about passports." She had acted along with utter compliance and complicity with her dad before revealing the trick to me. Father and daughter understood each other so well! We proceeded to where he parked his car.

"What a nice car you have got. It was a blue BMW Jeep, very sumptuous and of uttermost comfort within."

"Dad, he was saying that we are *pitucos*." [4]

Her father laughed.

I had learned about the word in Lima with Elena, my landlady who constantly referred to Miraflores, the posh district of Lima as a place for *pitucos*, the upper-middle class, the rich, simply put. But later on, a friend told me it could have a slightly derogatory sense. I had no doubts that my host family in Arequipa understood the sense in which I used the word.

"We will certainly pass by the house to enable me to pick up something before we continue to the bus station," said Mariana's dad.

Their house was not far. It took us less than ten minutes to reach there. Arequipa was quite calm at night. Nothing like the cramped atmosphere of Lima's avenues.

When we reached the house, Mariana and I remained in the car while her dad dashed into the house and came back later with something in his hand.

"What did you say was your name again?"

"Gil," I answered, not knowing whether I should say my family name or the given name. At least I met one person in Peru who did not insist on *apellido*, that is, the family name. I had inquired from my landlady why she insisted so much on "Apellido". Each time I introduced myself to a friend as "Gil", "Shang" or "Ndi", she would insist on which of them was my APELLIDO. Later I came to probe the historical explanation of this phenomenon in colonial Peru, the preponderance of family heritage that has remained crucial for many in that country.

Mariana's dad wrote some few words in the book. This is for you.

---

4   Posh. It is used in Peru and Bolivia to refer to middle-class persons.

It was a novel written by himself. – *El Principe Vicunzo.*[5] "To you my good friend Gil, with love from Peru."

"Thank you so much. What a wonderful gift. I will certainly write a review and send to you."

"Sure, I will be most happy." He responded.

"Markus!" he shouted.

"Yes, am right here," came a voice from behind the gate.

"Gil, you may want to step out and greet a young friend of mine. He speaks your language." I stepped out. I did not exactly know which one "my language" was.

"Hallo, ich bin Markus."

"Hi Markus, Ich freue mich dich kennenzulernen. Ich bin Gil aus Kamerun."

"Cool, ich komme aus Deutschland und ich bin hier für meinen Ausensemester an der Universidad Nacional de San Agustin hier in Arequipa."

"Interesant, und wie lange bist du hier?"

"Seit schon einem Monat. Ich bleibe für drei weitere Monate und dann bin ich zürück an meiner Univerisität in Deutschland. Die Uni Magdeburg."

"Super, ich kehre in drei Wochen zurück nach Bayreuth, wo ich promoviert habe. Dort mache ich gerade eine Post-doc Forschung."

"Ok, super. Wir bleiben im Kontakt."

"Ja, sicherlich."

"Ich wünsche dir eine schöne Reise."

"Danke, Tschüs."[6]

I entered back into the car and we drove to Terminal 1 of the bus station. We arrived 30 minutes before departure. Mariana's dad left us at the check-in gate and promised to be back in a few seconds. Indeed,

---

5   Prince Vicunzo.

6   "Hi, am Markus."
"Hi Markus, happy to meet you. Am Gil from Cameroon.
"Great, am from Germany and am here for an external semester in the St. Augustine National University of Arequipa."
"That sounds interesting. For how long have you been here."
"For a month now. Am left with three more months before I go back to my home university. The University of Magdeburg."
"Great. In about three weeks I will be returning to Bayreuth, where I did my doctorate and where am presently doing a postdoc."
"Ok, that is great. We stay in contact then."
"For sure."
"I wish you a great trip."
"Thanks, bye."

he came back in a jiffy with a plastic paper in his hand.

"Gil, this is for you."

I opened it and found a packet of biscuits and a bottle of *chicha morada*.

"This is a very rich type of chocolate, made in Arequipa. You will surely enjoy it."

"Thank you so much! I lack words. In so short a time, you have crowned me with so many good gestures."

"It is ok; we wish you a safe trip."

"We have to go now because Mark, a few other friends and I are going to a concert tonight and dad has promised to take us there," Mariana said.

"Sure, I have no choice. I am their driver, of course," her dad, ironic.

I was amazed by the conviviality between father and daughter. I hugged them and thanked them for their warm welcome.

"You have been so kind to me. With this kind of reception, I won't fail to come back to Arequipa. I will let you guys know immediately I arrive in Lima."

"We will be waiting to hear from you."

They went off. I sat back on the seat, waiting for the check-in to be announced. Watching them leave, I was again marvelled at the racial mixture of Peru. On our way to the station, Mariana's dad explained to me that her paternal forefathers were of indigenous/Spanish origin while her maternal grandmother had African roots. It was quite complex. Mariana evidently had African features, her hair, colour, nose, and so on. Her dad indeed had very short hair, crispy. But these African physical features were not very evident in him, not to talk of his other daughter in Germany, Camila. In Peru, I started learning the trick of detailed facial description. Peruvians knew how to link features and racial provenance.

One girl came close and sat by me, asking what time it was by my watch.

"It is exactly 9 P.M. Are you travelling to Lima?"

"Yes, and you too?"

"Yes."

"That is great. My boyfriend is supposed to meet me here before I leave. He said he will be here before 9:00 P.M. But I cannot see him anywhere. They stole my phone two days ago at the supermarket, so I can't even get in touch with him."

"Oh really? How I wish I could help you. Mine was also stolen yesterday."

"Oh, what a damn coincidence! These guys are terrible!"

As we were exchanging sympathies for our mishaps, her boyfriend came. It seemed like the end of the world for her. At least, there and then, she had something to hang on. She forgot that I was there. It is time to check-in. They are still locked into one another's arms. The journey ends when lovers meet.

My seat was in the second cabin. It seemed quite comfortable. I thought of the taxi driver's disparaging comments about the *Jalsa* agency. Perhaps he took his condemnation too far. Anyway, I could only attempt a judgment when I safely arrived in Lima. This trip had caused me some apprehension the previous day in Puno. Vladimir, my Russian friend read a text message from his acquaintance in Arequipa informing him the highway linking Arequipa and Lima was covered by a huge block, fallen off from a cliff. That was on the outskirts of Pisco. No one had died but it badly obstructed the traffic. I did not want to think much about that. I just hoped the situation had been cleared. From my encounter with the Peruvian landscape, I could imagine that was a permanent risk. My mind went straight to the road along the shores of Miraflores and Barranco districts in Lima. Huge cliffs are suspended over the passing vehicles like the Sword of Damocles. It constitutes a real danger to the security of the vehicles passing under. The city council has developed a security technology to hold the rocks together and prevent them from falling off. The cliffs are wrapped with some form of black tarpaulin wires or nets pitched at safe points of the area. That was a nice attempt but it did not diffuse the danger of that landscape. As I walked under them with Elena on my first visit to Miraflores beach, I felt utterly insecure under those rocks. Suspended in-between the beauty and enchantment of the Pacific coast and the cliffs across the road, they kept me in a sort of limbo. Danger and Pleasure lie side by side in these parts. I imagined how much activity and history that coast has witnessed and/or played host to. Exploration, trade, piracy, fishing, love vows, separation, drowning, wars, etc.

I arrested my thoughts back to the trip before me. I slipped my two bags under the foot stretcher and set ready for the way. I was in no illusion to pull out any book. I tried to put myself in the mental state of someone who would be on the road for close to 12 hours.

As I sat on the bus, in-between sleep and wakefulness, several images streamed through my mind, the embrace of the Uruguayan ambassador after the presentation in honour of Eduardo Galeano at the Book Fair in Lima, when I told him *Las Venas Abiertas de America Latina* (The Open Wounds of Latin America) is the first book I read in Spanish from cover to cover; I remembered the image of the cathedral on top of the Sun Temple in Vilcashuaman, I re-envisioned the face of the Indian child with his meek and serene lamb, looking curiously at me, wanting to understand the marvels of the world through my face; the jovial teenagers I met in Machu Picchu, taking pictures with me in my traditional Bamenda attire; the human beehive moving up and down the Babel of the Inca Kingdom, speaking in different tongues; the lions and tigers in the Mama Africa night club in Cusco; etc. Perhaps, had I not lost my phone, these images won't have flooded, invaded, ambushed my mind in this way. They won't have entered my consciousness with such symbolic force. It is at the point of loss that certain things and people accompany us more closely. In Arequipa, I had lost everything and gained everything. The warmth of the Febres family, the empathy of the woman who offered me a CD of her Machu Picchu images. I checked in my pocket and my new passport was still there, with the *characota de oro*.

When I woke up, it was getting to 2 A.M. but I was still feeling dizzy. My mind and body were in a liminal state. I was neither asleep nor awake, neither thinking nor dreaming. When I, later on, sat up, gaining full consciousness at about 5:00 A.M., I was amazed at how time flies. I have experienced this several times in my game with my alarm clock. Whenever it rings, I wake up and check the time, telling myself some five minutes of sleep is still acceptable. Usually, when I wake up, sometimes it is 60 minutes past, like the wind. Time. I put on my recorder to listen to some of the interviews I carried out in Lima. It could be a useful way of spending my time.

The guy seated close to me is the one who woke me up for coffee. When I opened my eyes, the waiter stood with a kettle of coffee and a plastic cup pointing at me. He also handed me a piece of bread with cheese. It was 8:10 A.M. My neighbour was quite cosy, engaging me constantly in small talk. I felt renewed strength. Chatting with Willy kept me fully awake. He is so natural in his humour and willing to share his opinions on every aspect of Peruvian society. At some point, we had to alight because some passengers had to relieve themselves. But the space was quite bare, no undergrowth cover or shrubs to obstruct visibility. We did the women a favour. We stood and faced one side of the road while they crossed to the other side, shaded by the bus. In the end, everyone eased themselves satisfactorily. I requested Willy, my friend, to take some photos of me with the bus in the background. These were hopefully my "very first" photos in Peru. I kidded with Willy while feeling the loss deep inside me. He sympathised so much with me when I told him about the loss of my phone. He suggested that I block the phone on my arrival in Lima so that the culprit or whosoever buys the phone would not be able to use it. I found the effort not worth the while but merely acquiesced to please him. I accepted the loss.

When we passed at Nazca and Ica, Willy told me Chincha was close.

"I told him I wanted to go to Chincha the following week."

"Oh yes, there you will meet so many Afro-Peruvians."

"That is what I heard. I also intend to visit a district there called El Carmen where I hear there is a very reputable Afro-Peruvian family.

"Los Ballumbrosio, if I am not mistaken."

"Yes, yes, that is the name. I met a member of that family in Lima and she gave me the family's contact. I won't fail to visit them."

We gradually approached Chincha. It was quite a big city. But, at first sight, I did not see black people there. I thought they would be there in their numbers given the impression I had of Chincha as a black hub. What I saw was a figure that caught my attention. It was the image of a straw man, or straw woman, standing in front of some restaurants by the roadside like the Richard Wagner statue which you would find in front of every commercial structure in my German hometown of Bayreuth. Willy told me that such restaurants offered Afro-Peruvian cuisine. I guessed as well. It was written on the wall, but that did not solve the conundrum in my mind.

How could they put such a grotesque image as an advertisement? I thought I was speaking to myself but Willy responded.

"Well, it is just the way it is."

I felt sorry that Willy should have felt compelled to respond. In the course of the trip, that image came back again and again to my mind in full force. Some of the straw figures looked brownish, like the colour of the rain-battered thatched roof you would find in some rural communities in Cameroon and Peru. Others looked more whitish, perhaps more recently erected. Apart from their grotesque qualities, those figures shocked me by their derogatory power. The feeling of visiting Chincha with feelings of solidarity began to wane away. However, I did not renounce my intentions altogether. I had already planned that with Elena. Perhaps there was more to discover.

CHAPTER 26

Back Home in Lima

We arrived in Lima at about 2:30 P.M. When we alighted, as usual, several taxi drivers were scrambling for customers. One old man, certainly in his 70s, came to me talking in a raspy voice.

"Welcome, my friend. I have a taxi and I can take you to wherever you want. Where are you from?"

"I am from Peru," I said.

"No, you are not from Peru, perhaps from Brazil, Colombia or Ecuador."

"Why do you say so?"

"Just your manners and way of being."

"How? I don't understand."

"I cannot say exactly why, but you are not from Peru."

"I am from Cameroon, I am visiting Peru."

Immediately I said this, one girl, a metis, came to me and said:

"I am also from Cameroon. I live in France with my boyfriend." She pointed to a white guy in dreadlocks. We greeted each other, leaving the driver standing there with Willy. After chatting briefly with the couple about our trips, I came back to Willy and the taxi driver.

"He has a car and wants to take you to your destination. What is your street called?"

"*Avenida Petit-Thouars 26, Jirón Soledad 565.*"

"Ok fine, come let us go. S/20 since you are my friend."

"Is it that far?" Willy asked.

"I do not know the distance from here. I have never been to this agency before."

"It is very far, about 20 minutes from here, said the driver, trying to exaggerate the distance to justify his fare."

"But please, take 15." I bargained.

After hesitating, the old man acquiesced and told me to follow him to his taxi parked at the entrance. I bade farewell to Willy. We promised to keep in contact. I was not comfortable being driven by such an old and frail-looking man. I just felt that he should be at home living a quiet life. The car itself was an eyesore and I wondered by what magic of technology it still breathed. It was a tiny starlet, apparently smaller than a normal starlet, almost the size of the two passenger-carrier known in Peru as moto-taxi or taxi-cholo, powered by a motorcycle engine. It is a constant feature in the cityscape of Puno and Ayacucho, amongst the towns I had visited in Peru thus far. I was still to inquire why it is called *taxi cholo*, perhaps something to do with the background of its drivers or the class of passengers likely to board it. *Cholo* meant so many things in Peru, overloaded to the point of semantic emptiness like many popular signifiers. But it is first and foremost a race and class category referring to people of indigenous background who have spent considerable time in the city and have adopted "modern" ways of life.

I was still marvelled by the state of the taxi, a masterpiece of welding and panel beating. Its entrails were all outside, covered with dust. The old man kept veering off when I asked him questions about his car. The outer surface was cossetted together to make the car look at least acceptable to the view. Not before long, we got to the Avenida Brasil. I had been to Breña at Avenida Brasil before to interview the history teacher. That meant that we were not very far from *Jirón Soledad*. But the old man still claimed it was very far. In less than ten minutes from Avenida Brasil, we were at Petit Thouars 26. He arrived at the avenue but took a rather long and tortuous road, crossing several streets and circling before finally settling at my building. I offered to orientate him, to no avail.

"Yes, S/15."

"I know, I offered him a S/10 banknote and was searching in my wallet for a S/5 coin."

"Here we go."

"Thank you, my friend. Have a great stay in Peru."

Of course, his voice sounded better this time around.

Elena and her daughter were in the kitchen. They welcomed me enthusiastically.

She asked if I would like to join them soon at the table. The food was ready. I had just come at the appointed time.

"Thanks, Elena. I will eat later."

"I am sure you need some rest. You look exhausted. I will go out in a while and it is when I come back at around 8 P.M. that you will tell me more about your trip. But I will leave you rice with fried plantains in the refrigerator, ok?"

"Thanks, Elena, thanks very much. We will talk later."

I was glad she understood. I was not in any talking mood. I took my bath and lay on my bed to check my emails and Facebook. I had so many messages. I perused through them but did not fall into the temptation of responding to any.

CHAPTER 27

New Phone

15 August 2015

This morning Elena and I went to the central business district of Lima to find a solution to my breach of communication suffered in Arequipa. Since I was using the Claro sim card, we went to the headquarters of the Claro mobile company to inquire if there could be any solution to my catch 22 situation. We wanted to block the stolen telephone but we were told this could only be done in the country where the phone was registered. I gave up trying to be hard on the lucky owner of my Alcatel One Touch. I resolved to buy a new phone and forget about the mishap. But how could I forget the pictures taken some weeks before at the former concentration camp in Flossenburg, Bavaria-Germany, or those taken at Machu Picchu and the Lima Book Fair weeks before? We inquired from the technicians of Claro mobile company if there was any way of recovering data from the old phone. No, not possible. If I had activated my google+ account there would have been an automatic backup anytime the phone was connected to the Internet. Unfortunately, I did not connect the phone to the Internet for all my time in Peru. I had always resisted subscribing to a roving Internet connection on my cell phone. I thought I needed some puff of air from the sometimes-suffocating cyber world, especially when on such a long trip. But that cost me dearly. I finally bought a Sony Xperia phone on promotion by Claro for nearly S/300, the equivalent of about €100. Given that my Cameroonian, German and Peruvian contacts were now down the drain, I needed to scan my email and Facebook message boxes for any urgently needed contacts, especially those of my Peruvian friends and experts that I needed to meet before leaving that country. Certainly, some would try to call me in vain!!

CHAPTER 28

Back to my Routes

17 August 2015

Three days after my return from Arequipa, I was on my way to Chincha. I woke up quite early, before 7:00 A.M. Elena prepared some tea and scrambled eggs for breakfast before we set out for Chincha. On the eve of our trip, I checked the official fare online and it said S/33. I suggested to Elena the previous evening to consult some of her friends who travel to Chincha more frequently. It is then that she called her friend Maria, originally from Chincha. She advised us to take a mini-bus to the highway and there and then we would find buses to Chincha for only S/10 as fare per person.

Like most of the Peruvian long-distance buses I had boarded before, *Soyuz Bus* was quite comfortable. Since I had not slept adequately the night before, I was threatened by sleep. But I resisted for some time, astonished by another face of Lima that I witnessed as the bus came out of the main city. During my trip from Lima to Ayacucho, I could not see much in the night. Now the outskirts of the city lay bare before my eyes. Lima is big as big can be. With a population of close to ten million, it is ten times bigger than Peru's second-largest city Arequipa, down South. So, like the case with the dancing masquerade of Achebe's *Things Fall Apart*, to know Lima you have to stand at different points. When you approach it from the Pacific shores, La Costa Verde, you are welcomed by the soaring shadows of the skyline of a Pizarresque Manhattan: Miraflores. Same with San Isidro, La Molina, San Borja. But, tarry longer, turn around the Leviathan and visit its backyard and you will find sardine-tin houses perched precariously against the currents of strong modernist winds, along the slopes of La Victoria, Villa El Salvador... You would think some of these are temporary habitation zones for refugees. These tin-houses are habitations for life, nothing temporary about them, except you are amongst those who consider life itself as a temporary condition. Through centuries, peasant families have been blown by waves of poverty from the Andean hinterlands and deposited on the banks of the Rimac, forced to survive in a commensalic relationship with mainstream Lima. Nothing symbolises the iron curtain between the rich and the poor here better than the cement block wall that separates the suburb of Vista Hermosa in San Juan de Miraflores from the opulence of Barrio de Las Casuarinas in Surco. Of course, there are many grey areas, with pockets of poverty in some posh districts while the putatively poor districts on their parts have got some silver linen.

The bus continued its course. Gradually, I fell asleep. Elena resisted much longer, attempting to peruse through a book that she had bought at the Lima Book Fair a couple of weeks ago. But the truth is that when I woke up just a few minutes before we reached Chincha, I found the book under her seat, some pages thoroughly twisted and Elena unrepentantly asleep. I carefully moved her leg off the book under her feet. This gesture woke her up, she sighed, yawned and asked me in her dizziness:

"Are we already in Chincha?"

"I do not know, it seems we are arriving soon. We have been driving for more than two hours now."

Elena took her book and carefully folded it back into her bag.

"That is what it means to read while sleep." I teased her.

"I am damn tired. I do not know why. But you know after we separated last night I still spent many hours on my computer."

"Me too. I finally slept at close to 3 A.M."

"Yes, I understand. Do you know that thanks to you I have sought to know more about Peru? I would not have been going to the Bookfair every day. Just look at the number of friends and intellectuals you have loaded me with in Lima!!"

Soon we were in Chincha. It seemed to be a very lively town. The streets seemed much wider than in most of the towns I had visited previously. Hawkers scrambled for attention while along the alleys, smartly dressed waiters and waitresses smiled commercially as they beckoned on customers to get into their restaurants. They were, however, less abrasive than the ones in the touristic resorts of Cusco and Aguas Calientes. I was immediately attracted to an androgynous straw figure. Elena confirmed to me that it was a symbol to indicate there was a restaurant for Afro-Peruvian cuisine around. As we moved further, close to the car park, one of the straw figures was female. It had cursorily red-painted lips, charcoal black face and a black crunchy wig, hanging on its head.

The red lips reminded me of some childhood images. When we were young, our female counterparts used to harvest the seeds of a tree which, when smashed, produced a deep red colour. This was their first beauty product which they used to paint their lips, fingernails, and toenails. The end result was always theatrical and grotesque. That was the closest comparison I could make in my mind with the black straw figures. The figures were ubiquitous, a key feature of the Chincha scape, but to me, they were eyesores in a city that turned out to be more beautiful than I had imagined.

We did not spend much time in Chincha. I accompanied Elena to buy some fried corn and roasted cereals. In Peru, not only are there a thousand and one types of foodstuffs, but the gastronomic creativity of the people enables them to device myriad ways of transforming food-stuffs for consumption. Maize alone has got tens of forms in which it is transformed. The diversity of food crops on sale in Chincha, reminded me of the authoritative voice of Guaman Poma de Ayala, one of Peru's first writers, asking the people to diversify their farm products, against the monoculture and scarcity imposed by the Spanish colonial regime:

> Let much maize and potato be sown, likewise okra, and let there be
> caui, caya, chuño, tamos [various root crops], chochoca [ground up dry
> maize], quinua, ulluco, masua and every food even including herbs so
> that they can be dried and eaten all year round and let there be sown
> as commons and sapsi maize, potatoes, chili, magno, cotton . . . And
> every year let them be accounted for.[1]

We took a minibus to El Carmen. It looked quite modest from the outside but the interior was a sorry sight. The flesh of the steering wheel was completely petered out and what remained was a threadbare iron bar. It looked more like a wooden steering wheel. When the number of passengers was sufficient, the driver entered and kickstarted the car. My little faith in the near wooden steering was compensated by the serene

---

1   *Nueva Cronica del buen Gobierno* (New Chronicles of Good Governance) is a critique of
    the colonial government in Peru. With Inca Garcilaso de la Vega, Felipe Guaman Poma
    de Ayala (ca. 1535 – 1616) was one of the first indigenous writers to question the logic of
    the colonial regime and to propose alternative approaches to governance. His manuscript of
    the above text, full of drawings and illustrations, was re-discovered by the scholar Richard
    Pietschmann in the Royal Danish Library in Copenhagen in 1911 in a library in Holland,
    almost four centuries since it was written.

and composed demeanour of the driver, a slim Afro-Peruvian in tight jeans. As we approached El Carmen, I saw affixed to the electric poles a very beautiful image of a black woman in white/red apron bearing the word ANITA. I attempted twice in vain to take a zoomed shot of the woman. The third attempt was successful. The camera captured the gleaming smile and I had it there with me on the bus. The caption read MAMAINE. The driver told us she is a very important cultural personality in that locality thanks to her delicious Afro-Peruvian cuisine that has earned her nation-wide fame. Her restaurant is at the same time a cultural centre, we were told. Elena and I resolved there and then to visit her foyer when we get to El Carmen. The trip was quite brief, roughly fifteen minutes. We paid just S/2 each.

Upon alighting, we inquired from the driver where the family compound of the Ballumbrosio was. We followed the description and got straight to the compound. There were two ladies in front of the compound, plaiting their hair while two kids, a boy and a girl, were playing around, one running after the other to dispossess her of what seemed like a small ball. There was a restaurant on our left, opposite the road to the Ballumbrosios. Elena wanted us to go eat something before going to the compound.

"Mind you, we are now in Africa. How can you say we should eat before going to visit a family of this stature? In Cameroon, for example, when you visit someone, they cannot let you go without offering you something to eat."

Elena laughed and retorted,

"This is Peru."

"Well, African culture never dies, it lives on in our veins," I said.

As we approached the compound, the scenery of women plaiting their hair and children playing in front of the compound reminded me of home. We moved closer and greeted.

"Hello, is this the family compound of the Ballumbrosio?"

"Oh yes, you are right there, welcome." Said the lady whose hair was being platted. "Thank you. We are coming from Lima. I am Gil Ndi-Shang from Cameroon, but I live in Germany."

Elena introduced herself and continued: "We came to learn about the family of the Ballumbrosio and their contribution to the musical culture of Peru."

"Once more you are welcome. Please feel at home, you can get into the house. Luanda! Luanda! Please go and call your mom to come and talk to the visitors."

Luanda stopped playing and dashed into the parlour.

"It is my sister Lucia who usually explains things to visitors. She is in the kitchen and will be here very soon."

Soon Lucia arrived. She was all smiles. After another round of self-introduction, she took us into the parlour.

"I met your sister-in-law, Giancarla in the Book Fair in Lima and she said if I go to El Carmen I should not fail to visit her family there," I said to Lucia.

She was so happy to hear the name of Giancarla, her sister-in-law. She called her sisters who were plaiting outside to inform them that I knew Giancarla. They all responded with amazement.

"Look on the wall, here is Giancarla with my elder brother, Miguel."

"Oh, I see!" Giancarla, seemingly in her teens, with a gleeful face, at the feet of a mid-aged man, both smiling, with hands on the Peruvian cajon, the drum. It was a nice shot and the bliss on the faces repre-sented this kind of a happy life only capturable through pictures. The black-white background added to its romantic intensity. It seems the rhythm she produced with Miguel together connected their souls in non-detachable ways.

Lucia went briefly to the kitchen to take care of her pot on the fire before coming back to take us through the family's musical heritage with the aid of the images on the wall.

"The Ballumbrosio family is very well known in Peru and beyond thanks to the talent and openness of our dad, Amador Ballumbrosio. He was an Afro-folklore musician that won many prizes throughout Peru and abroad for the quality and originality of his music. We are twelve siblings. Some of my siblings now live in other parts of Peru while others are in the USA, France and Dubai, etc. Some have chosen the intellec-tual field, while others have continued with the musical heritage of my dad. This house receives a lot of visitors from many parts of the world, USA, Spain, Brazil, Cuba, and recently France, ever since my brother emigrated there. And now from Germany and, which African country did you say you are from originally?"

"Cameroon", I reminded her.

"Yes, from Cameroon."

"Did your dad ever travel with his music to Africa? Or, do you know if he had any contacts in any African country thanks to his art?"

"No, he did not know much about Africa. It was in his imagination. It was poetry for his text. He was not even clear about what part of Africa we came from. He always made us think that we are from Ethiopia. But my sister who is plaiting her hair outside always argued him out. She did not believe my dad's suppositions."

"That is quite curious! I would have thought of perhaps from somewhere around the West African coast. But again, the slave routes were very complex in Africa and it is possible that some enslaved persons came from parts of Africa far removed from the Atlantic coasts. The history of slavery is not yet fully written."

"You know what? My son, the one you sent to call me, is called Luanda. A town in Angola."

"Oh yes, it is the capital city. I heard the name and was very intrigued by it. Are there other people in the family with such names that are related to Africa?"

"My niece, the little girl playing outside, is called Kernes. It is meant to sound like Kenya, the African country."

"What a beautiful name. I hope he grows up to visit Kenya!"

"Haha. I hope so too! There is a woman very well known here. As for her, she believes firmly that her family came from Angola. You heard of Mamainé before?"

"Oh, it is this woman on publicity boards on the road from Chincha. The one whose images I took on the way." I recalled.

"Oh yes, she owns the restaurant by her name."

"Yes, we resolved to go there when the bus driver told us she owns one of the best restaurants around here," Elena said.

"Yes, it is just the best place to eat here. When you go there, tell her I recommended her restaurant to you. She is a good friend."

"Yes, we will. But I think we shall also go to one museum. Someone told us there is an interesting Afro-Peruvian museum around here. Elena insinuated.

"Do you mean Hacienda San José?"

"Yes, certainly!" Elena and I responded.

"It is also a museum, hotel and cultural centre. There you will get invaluable information about the slave history of this place.

"At what time does the museum close?"

"I think it closes at 5 P.M."

"So, it is better to go there before you get to Mamainé."

Before we left the family, Lucia called the two kids to demonstrate to us the *el festejo*.

The little boy, Luanda, sat on the drum and began beating it rhythmically while Kernes was on the dance floor.

As Luanda began to drum, Kernes started twisting her heaps with incredible suppleness and sprightliness. The dance is called *el festejo*. There was much synchrony in their craft. I guess they do that quite regularly. When they grow up, they will certainly be great performers. Luanda stopped drumming and moved to the floor. *Danza de zapateos, tap dance*. In dexterous cadence, he tapped the soles of his shoes on the floor, producing beautiful rhythm. In the climax, he clapped his hands in between his legs and behind his back alternatingly while the soles stamping produced more and more complex rhythms. The dexterity of the two kids beat my imagination.

I requested Luanda to continue drumming while I tried to imitate the young *zapateador* but my movements were bereft of rhythm and I quickly resigned. I placed 2 *solitos* on the forehead of each of the kids and we took our leave.

As we stepped out, Elena reminded me that we had not taken a photo with the entire family. As usual, she offered to play the camerawoman and took a series of shots of me with the Ballumbrosio family. Later, one of the ladies took one shot with Elena, myself, Lucia and the two kids, the performers of the day. We took our leave and went straight to the *Plaza de Armas* where we took a taxi to the *San José* museum.

CHAPTER 29

Colour of Life, Colour of Death

We paid an entrance fee of S/20 per person. It was a large land surface, acting as a museum, a hotel, a cultural centre with a large orchard and a vast space with beautifully pruned flowers. There was a cathedral on the left flank of the building. At the entrance to the main building, two smartly dressed ladies came to welcome us.

"You are welcome to the Museo *San José*. In a few minutes, the tour will begin. It will take about one hour.

Noticing her difficulties, Elena told her to do the tour in Spanish, that although I was not Peruvian, I had no problems following her in Spanish. The girl conceded, with an evident sense of relief. She asked us to wait on the veranda as she dashed into the big building. There was a large table stuffed with handicraft products. Most of them were baskets of various shapes. On one part of the table were objects portraying the black identity of El Carmen. I also found what looked like what we call *maramnuh* in my language, Limbum, made of boiled maize paste wrapped in plantains or banana leaves. We bought two loaves.

After close to ten minutes, the guide came out for us to start the tour.

"You are right here in the *hacienda* San José which has been converted into a museum and a hotel. This structure contained thousands of enslaved Africans who worked on the sugar and cotton farms of the Jesuit priests. With the expulsion of the Jesuit priests from the Americas in 1767 by the Spanish Bourbon monarchy, the property passed through many hands, including at some point, President Augusto Leguia. Its current owner is a business lady from the Benevides family. A violent earthquake hit El Carmen in 2007 and destroyed part of the structure. The destroyed section was however reconstructed by 2010."

She took us into the house, showing us old farm tools that were used by the enslaved persons for shredding sugar cane stems. Then she moved to one of the tools, quite similar to the ones she had shown us before.

"The instrument over there. Can you guess what it was used for?"

163

"For welding, or let's say bursting holes in wood or something similar," Elena suggested.

Meanwhile, I was still figuring out the intrigue embedded in the girl's question.

"It was what they used for engraving the slave master's name on the bodies of the enslaved".

My blood chilled as the lady explained this. Abjection in the slave plantation and concentration camp takes its most virulent dimension in the nature of the relationship between apparatus and use. Under these conditions, the abuse of otherwise useful tools has agonising effects on the subject's body. Think of the oven in Auschwitz. The same oven that was used to burn debris and animal carcasses was slightly modified by the Kori and Topf & Sons Company to bake the human flesh. Ernst-Wolfgang Topf, the brother of the company's chief engineer Ludwig Topf, swore that the crematoria were innocent.

Coming back to the slave industry, I remember having read somewhere how the acronym "RAC" was inscribed into the skins of many enslaved people from Africa. It is read as an acronym but when instilled into the human book, it is painfully abbreviated letter by letter, with the skin feeling the full thrust of the contours of every letter. RAC stood for the Royal African Company that was a key slave-trading firm. The most disturbing aspect of it is not even the fact that it was "royal" but rather that John Locke, that venerated 17th century liberal philosopher, was one of its shareholders. I also recalled a fact I came across in a volume of Alistair Cooke's *Letter from America* that the English transported the first blacks from Africa to Virginia, the USA, on a ship bearing the ironical name of the "Jesus of Lübeck", owned by John Hawkins, a trade partner of Queen Elizabeth I[1]. I also remembered the numbering process in Nazi concentration camps. The act of appropriating and thingifying the prisoners through numbers, the industrial process of dehumanization. With that instrument, the slave got a new name, that of his/her owner. The slave, the camp inmate lost its name, and the new name-number was instilled in pain on its body, its mindless mind and selfless self. Both the Nazi inmate of the labour Camp of Auschwitz III and the black slave of the hacienda were given the illusory promise that hard work was the route to freedom.

From there, we moved downstairs to an underground chamber, a

---

1   This was in 1564 and the ship contained 400 enslaved Africans.

dome-shaped compartment. Half-lit, with rough concrete walls. The floor was not cemented. It was a rugged slab of concrete gravel. I guessed it would be hell walking on it barefooted. On the floor, there was a long iron bar, stretching on two pillars strapping it to the ground. The bar contained about six iron buckles, meant for human palms and feet.

This was a correctional facility. Enslaved persons accused of any kind of crimes were tortured here. At times a group of the enslaved could be brought into the room to witness the exemplary punishment meted on their kind as a forewarning against any potential criminal. At times the master commissioned the capo, the head slave, to do the torturing. Here, Negro was culprit, Negro was victim, Negro was witness. Auschwitz flashed across my mind again. It also saved like a detention facility. Someone could be locked in this place without enough light for weeks. Sometimes, after torture, many came out of this place seriously incapacitated for life. Some died shortly afterwards. For some, it was a purgatory of no return. Corrected for life.

From the underground cavity, we moved into the Cathedral nearby. It was a church meant for the aristocratic Jesuit priests. The wall behind the altar was made of fine wood and with edges of gold. We were told that it was shipped from Spain, dismantled into three different parts. On the altar were dozens of statues of the Cristo, Santa Maria, San Pedro, Santa Rosa, San Juan, etc. primarily in gold and diamond. If our wooden gods could not speak in the face of anomy, couldn't the golden and silvery gods peering at me from these lustrous walls at least feel the bitter tears on the cheeks of enslaved Africans and lend them some transatlantic wings? Why then rob the Indian of their metal if these gods never had powers beyond the decorative? Why force them to unearth their *huacas* to desecrate the memories of their ancestors just to adorn dormant ancestors of foreign fields?

"Where was the place or the column of the enslaved in this cathedral? I guess the ones behind or at the edges." I asked.

"Oh, I forgot to tell you that aspect. They were not allowed in this church. This is because they were not considered to have souls. They were not worthy of God's grace." I could not reconcile the fact that the slaves were not allowed in the chapel meanwhile religion was used to capture their minds and to make them malleable and docile.

"Nowadays, the cathedral is not used for regular church service. It is used in a few cases for weddings and other very special and solemn occasions. It is more of a museum too." I was amazed at the very short distance between the door into the underground cell and the precincts of the church. I stood at the altar of the church. Elena took the phone and took two shots of me. As the camera flashed in my eyes, with the instant recognition of these past centuries, part of me could not enter this space, that part of me shouted out for a change of fate, that here, on this very spot, a voice propelled from the torture chamber, charged with pain. The gods of Africa were deaf to his/her cries, the gods of the Indians turned their eyes away, not able to save their very own species, how could they rescue foreigners? The Almighty God, the god of Europe, hence the gods of the world, failed to listen to this voice.

From the church, we went down to the underground. At the entrance was a basket containing torches.

"Please take a torch because it is quite dark inside there. Does anyone of you have claustrophobia?"

"It is ok; I have no problem with that."

Elena equally shrugged her shoulders in denial.

"That is fine. Please, follow me. The guide told us."

I enjoyed the style of our tour guide. She guided by innuendos. She would let us step on the threshold; occupy the space, allowing our imagination to wander, to guess its rationale before she goes ahead to explain to us what the ground on which we stood meant. This was a creative tour guiding method.

"This tunnel is only meant for Peruvians, Elena. It is not for tall Cameroonians like myself. You see, I almost knocked my head on the roof."

Elena and the tour guide giggled at my statement. Then the tour guide went ahead to explain where we were.

"This was the underground route used to smuggle enslaved persons into the *hacienda* from the dockyard of Tambo de Mora, roughly 40 kilometres away from here. When the victims arrived in ships at the dockyard, the slave owners declared just a few "goods" to the customs officials meanwhile a majority of them were smuggled through this channel. This route runs right from the port of Chincha right into this place. Many died here due to congestion and lack of oxygen."

"So, the tunnel was actually for me". I thought to myself. This was no more a cause for fun.

We continued sneaking through the tunnel, knock-kneed, converted into some rodents sneaking in and out of their burrows.

At one point, the guide pointed at one of the tunnels that branched upward.

"Over here is an escape route used by the slave merchants whenever they came under threat. This road led to the bedroom, directly under the wardrobe of the slave master. The enslaved were forbidden from using them."

We finally came out of the underground tunnel and found ourselves at the other side of the building. That was the end of the tour. What an end!!!

After a few minutes, the guide came back and told us:

"Sorry, I forgot to show you guys something. Do you see that tree standing over there?"

"You mean that big tree with soaring branches?" I asked.

"Yes. That tree was brought in from Africa in the first quarter of the 19th century."

"Really? Can we go closer to it?"

"It is not possible because the lawn is undergoing some treatment. People are not allowed to walk on it."

The tree was standing there, with wide branches. Some of the branches were dead, while others were fresh and very leafy. The roots were all buried underground, not like those trees with roots splayed some metres above ground level. I tried to connect it with any tree type I know at home in Cameroon but could not. But, then, I felt that tree rebuking me vehemently,

Impetuous child that tree, young and strong
That tree over there
Splendidly alone amidst white and faded flowers
That is your Africa springing up anew
springing up patiently, obstinately
Whose fruit bit by bit acquires
The bitter taste of liberty.
(*David Diop*)

We left the museum at almost 5:20 P.M. I took a last look at the structure, this time around, focusing on what lies under its bristling three stars: the human burrows underneath. But the towering tree again brought consolation to my soul. Luckily, we found a car outside *hacienda*. But it was taking a passenger to a different direction. We pleaded with the taxi driver to take us to the *Plaza de Armas*. He asked us to talk with the lady who hired him. The lady quickly consented. In the car, we made them understand that our final destination was Foyer Mamainé in *El Guayabo*. The lady was so kind as to ask the driver to drive us right there.

CHAPTER 30

Swing Low, Sweet Chariot

Soon we alighted in front of Foyer Mamainé. We thanked the driver and the lady as they drove off. The restaurant was a large complex. When we came in, we saw that the stage was set with microphones and speakers, but there was no one on stage. A group of children were crowded around a laptop in front of the cashier's counter. They were all dressed in colourful uniforms. Either they had already performed or they were still gearing up for it. One of the waitresses came up to us.

"Good day lady and gentleman. You are very welcome. Here is the menu."

"Thank you, please. Will there be a performance tonight?" I inquired.

"They just finished about 30 minutes before you came in."

"What a pity! Will they play again sometimes later today?"

"I am not sure, we close here at 7:00 P.M."

We gave our order, a plate of rice, chicken, with a special blackish soup. As the waitress went into the kitchen, we roamed our eyes around the place. My eyes fell on the numerous family pictures of Mamainé and family, Mamainé in her teens, the restaurant in its early days, Mamainé's various awards, Mamainé, her husband and three young kids; etc. The pictures ranged from black and white unto the present colour photos. In short, it was an efficient tracing of the evolution of photography altogether. I fell in love with the Afro hairstyle of Mamainé's teenage days. These pictures took me back to my own family albums framed on the walls of our parlour. I remembered the mythic photo of my paternal granddad, Shang, who died before my birth; my dad and mom as young couples; my mom in her miniskirt; my dad in trousers that were tight-fitting at the levels of the thighs but trumpeting progressively down and splaying over his shoes, etc. My mother liked commenting on her photos. In a defensive mood, she would tell us that in their days they wore miniskirts but were not as frivolous as 'modern' girls. My sisters always wanted to put her to task on this point. We the boys sat back and watched them debate. I have not been home for long. I wonder if those photos are still on the walls now that Facebook has replaced our walls with new walls.

The waitress brought in the cutlery. The food was on the way. I was damn hungry. Soon, one of the young girls manipulating the laptop with her peers left her seat and moved quite close to Elena' shoulder, looking at me steadily. I greeted her and she responded confidently. It seemed like she wanted to talk to me but did not know where to start.

"What is your name, by the way?"

"Mya Zuleyka Oliviero Rivadeneyra…"

"Oh really, all these are your names? How do you spell it?"

Mya came closer to me and I provided her with a pen and paper and she carefully carved her name in beautiful handwriting.

"Wow, how beautifully you write! Do you have a Facebook account? I want you to be my friend." I asked, just out of curiosity, silently thinking that she was rather too young to possess a Facebook account.

"Oh yes, I have one."

She took my phone and after some false start, she got used to the keyboard. She accessed her Facebook account and invited herself. In dexterous calligraphy, Mya carved her names on my phone. Our table was now fully set. I invited Mya to have a taste of our food.

"I have already eaten. Thanks"

"Mya, you are from Africa."

"No, I am from here."

"I know, but you are from Africa."

Mya again shook her head emphatically.

"Yes, you are from Africa and from here."

"Ok. I have heard." She smiled at me and went back to her friends as we started savouring our food. It was quite delicious, and with the accumulated hunger, Elena and I finished it within very few minutes. The body language said it all. I burst out laughing.

"We need a second one, right?"

"Yes, of course, there is an implicit consensus."

We called the lady and ordered a second plate. This time around, we went for *carapulcra*. It is a stew of pork and dehydrated potatoes with peanuts, garlic and other spices. It is a modern adaptation of a traditional Andean dish. It is usually eaten with rice and boiled potatoes. On passing our order, I asked if we could get to talk with the chef, Mamainé, herself. The lady promised to call in Mamainé when we finished eating. A young man came in and greeted us with a very friendly smile and took a seat near the girls. He kept looking at me with much attentiveness. With food in my mouth, I only returned his gaze by casting a smile of recognition. In many cases, when I meet a Black person in the diaspora, I always test the waters with a cosy smile. Sometimes the smile goes unnoticed; or rather the offer gets ignored or utterly rejected. But in many cases, I receive a return smile and brief words of greetings. It is a way of testing opportunities for the expression of brotherhood.

When we finished eating, the waitress called in Mamainé. The lady came smiling. Some people look alike in their pictures and in reality, whose smile on pictures is not an identity prop marshalled to catch the transient glaze of the camera lens. A smile that prompts from the heart, lighting up other faces in a near-domino effect. She embraced us.

"Welcome my friends, how are you? Where are you from?"

"I am from Cameroon, but I reside in Germany where I study." Elena introduced herself.

"Oh, that is so nice to hear. So, you are right from Africa! I like your dress so much. When next you are coming, please bring me just one piece of this. It is just wonderful." I promised, though not very sure of when I would be back in Peru again.

As we were discussing, her husband came in. A very composed and reflective man endowed with a profound smile. He looked like someone I knew before. These faces reflected other faces from home, not just by their blackness. Not before long, two other men came in through the door leading to the kitchen.

"*Familia, familia.*" Shouted one of them, seemingly the most advanced in age, joining what was turning into a euphoric family meeting.

"*Bienvenida familia.* Welcome to Peru."

"He is from Cameroon," Mamainé informed him beforehand.

"Oh, from Cameroon. Do you play football too?"

"Oh yes, I do."

"Yes, Cameroon is a great football nation", he exclaimed. At this point, the guy who had been looking at me courteously also joined in. A round of embraces and family photos. Again, Elena was on point.

"I am so happy with all of you. I feel very much at home in Peru, but most importantly I am very happy to be in El Carmen. When I came people associated me with different identities. Brazil, Colombia, Ecuador, etc. But those who thought I could be from Peru assumed that I am likely from Chincha. Thus, my main intention was to visit Chincha. But

I was told that it is specifically in El Carmen that there is a dominant African community. So that is why I came right here. We were at the Ballumbrosio this afternoon and Lucia told us about Mamainé. I am very happy to be here my brothers, my uncle, my mother, my sisters. History worked against this reunion for centuries. But here we are today. When I see you, I see hope. I met my friend Mya here today. The young girl, there she is over there. Who is Mya's dad?" They pointed to one mid-aged black man standing at the door with the watchman. On hearing his name, he moved close and joined the group.

"We then formed a circle and each one of them gave a share of the story of the black community in *El Guayabo*."

In the middle of his narrative, the elderly man stopped and asked me.

"Have you been to the Catacumbas yet?"

"Yes, I have been there and I went right into the underground tunnels. Horrible!" I said, almost feeling guilty for having initiated a meeting that led these people to remember such a bitter history. After commenting on Cameroon football stars Roger Milla and Thomas Nkono and how popular they still are in Peru, the young man went on to tell his part of the story of Guayabo.

"This place suffered a lot. You know what? Because we were unlucky to have just the cruellest European colonial masters here: Spaniards and Italians. The cruellest of them all, I tell you." I was intrigued by his mention of Italians concerning Peruvian colonial history until he explained to me that in the 19th century many Italians bought landed property in many parts of Chincha. I was left with his sense of categorising the Italians and Spaniards as the cruellest colonialists. I remember that someone had told me some weeks before that the imprints of Italian cuisine are also very present in Chincha. I did not know that they left other imprints on these parts.

Soy del Guayabo
Desde niño yo tenía que cuidar
Los frejoles en el campo a sembrar
Para que mi buena madre los pudiera cocinar.

Me dormía al costa'o del algodón
Me tapaba con mantita a veces con mantón

Los frejoles que en la olla hirviendo están
 Con la leña del Huarango que corto el negro Batan

Soy del Guayabo del Carmen
La tierra 'onde están los negros de buena sangre
Soy del Guayabo si señor
Soy del Guayabo, como no
Donde derramo bendiciones el niño Dios

Mis hermanos sin zapato
Las espinas le abren paso
Por que saben que ellos van a trabajar

Del Guayabo soy señores,
Son mis padres son mis hijos
 Del Guayabo, Chincha, El Carmen soy yo

(English translation)

I am from El Guayabo
From Guayabo Chincha El Carmen I am.
and my parents, and my sons
I am from El Guayabo

because they know they go to work
they clear the thorns away with their feet
my brothers barefoot

the land where baby Jesus spread blessings
I am from El Guayabo of course
I am from El Guayabo yes sir
The land where the blacks are of good blood
I am from El Guayabo from El Carmen

with the firewood the black men Batan cut
the beans are boiling in the pot
sometimes with a big blanket
I was covered with a little blanket,

I used to sleep by the side of cotton

for my good mother could cook them
of the beans in the land to sow
since I was a kid I had to take care

It was getting dark and the restaurant's closing time was approaching. But we did not want to separate. Embrace upon embrace and repeated farewells. I promised to bring them the fabric of my Cameroonian jumper when next I visit. We took a taxi from the restaurant straight to Chincha. It cost us roughly S/30 but it was the best choice. We easily found a bus going to Lima. We got to Lima at close to 11 P.M. exhausted. As I went to bed, I was still haunted by the images of torture in the underground cells of the hacienda San José. Its pornography was unbearable. Jesuit priests/slave trade/torture chambers? How could that be possible? How could that be compatible? But in spite of my drowsiness, half-awake, half-thinking, one thing was clear to me: When it comes to sharing instruments of torture, the universal transfer of technology has been at its best. From feudalism to caudillismo, from monarchism to Enlighten-ment and post-Enlightenment, from colonialism to post-colonialism, from Inquisition to plantation economy, what Homi K Bhabha refers to as the barbaric transmission of culture has been unmistakable. Guil-lotine & Co are global trotters, scaping freely across borders, a perfect dimension of globalisation. When it comes to sharing technologies of pain, there is no clash of civilisations, only (in)human fraternity amongst Moslems, Christians, Buddhists, atheists, confessionists etc. I remembered the long list of medieval torture instruments that I once saw during an exhibition in Prague some years before. The names of the instruments depicted the part of the body that they targeted and the crimes for which the victims were convicted:

> Mask of infamy, mask of shame, violin of disgrace, Godmother, impale-ment, the virgin of Nuremberg, the iron cage, the head crusher, frocks of penance, beheading, defenestration, the prayer Cross, the chastity belt, the street sweeper's daughter, water torture, the spiked collar, the break-knee, the breaking wheel, the wheel, the two-legged cage, the kneeler, the vigil or guided cradle, the Falbrett (harbinger of guillotine) the pillory, the witch's chair, the noise-maker pipe, the thumbscrews, the anchor, the Rack, the handsaw, the iron boot, the iron brand, hot

pliers and pincers, the staircase of stretching, the oral, rectal and vaginal
pear, the iron shoe, the hangman...

Some of the names sound ridiculous, sarcastic and absurd, but that
only reminds one of how many lives they have squashed, smashed,
squeezed, ground, severed, suffocated, asphyxiated, erased, garrotted,
snuffed, strangulated, immolated, liquidated... As imperial powers spread
their course and curse across continents, these instruments travelled along
with them and became part and parcel of the macabre system of the
Inquisition, the plantation economies and colonial regimes. They are still
used today by many pseudo-democratic regimes of death that flourish
in parts of the world, including Africa and Latin America. When and
where the specific technologies cannot be exactly replicated, they are
improvised. And you know what improvisation means when it comes
to technologies of pain. The improvised, the circumstantial, turns out to
be more efficient than the original.

When I woke up the following morning, I tried to forget about the
depressing images of torture and suffering and focus on Mamainé, Mya,
the tree, the tree from Africa, spreading its leaves on the orchard, splayed
to the rays of the sun, the American sun. I felt lighter, not like some days
before when I felt exhausted, as disinterested as a wet blanket.

CHAPTER 31

Avenida Berlin - Miraflores, Lima

20 August 2015

I went to Miraflores to meet José, the son of the history teacher whom I interviewed. He had come for his father's book launch. After the event, he got to learn that I am from Cameroon and engaged me in an interesting discussion on Cameroonian football. We exchanged email addresses and agreed to meet on my return from my trips in the southern part of Peru. While waiting for him, a man approached me, smiling:

"Hello, how are you?"

"I am fine."

"You are not Peruvian, are you?"

"I am Peruvian, and you."

"No.

"How do you know?"

"From your accent."

I was shocked. Had he listened to me speak for some moments, I would have believed him, except he meant the accent of my body, my colour.

"I was just kidding. I am from Cameroon but I live in Germany." I said to him.

"My maternal grandmother was a *metis* of African origin while my maternal grandfather was from Spain. I live in France and I have many African friends, including Cameroonians."

"So you are African. I thought I was the only African on this spot," I joked.

"Hahaha. The man laughed. Not in Peru, my friend."

"What are you doing here?"

"I have to meet someone here at 6:30 P.M. It is two minutes past."

"I am also waiting for someone. He was supposed to come at 6 P.M. but he has not even called. I guess you have noticed how unpunctual we

176

Peruvians are."

"I have had some experiences with lateness here and it wasn't fun at all. But some friends I have met in Lima are very punctual."

As we were discussing, José arrived. He apologized for being a bit late. He said he had difficulty finding a place to park. I introduced him to my newfound friend and we left to a bar near Avenida Berlin, Miraflores. The bar is located on a very busy street known as *Calle Pizzaria*. The alley, measuring just about two hundred metres, is a hub for discotheques of all types and some of the most luxurious restaurants in town. I was told it is a popular spot for tourists and that it could sometimes be dangerous in spite of the massive police presence in the place.

As José and I passed by, restaurant agents trying to sweet talk us with all kinds of menus and offers assailed us from one side of the road to the other.

One of them followed us for close to 10 metres at which point José had to make him realize the futility of his efforts.

"If we want to eat we will tell you, we are not eating now, my friend."

"But you can come and have just a drink, it's ok." The waiter suggested.

We simply entered the next bar, *Rustica*. It is a well-established bar with several annexes in many parts of Lima.

No sooner did we settle down that a guy in a black suit, cornered us and in a very soft and gentle tone, made his proposal. Dazzling a photo in front of our eyes, he said:

"It is called Eclipses. In San Isidro, not far from here. I can take you there in my car free of charge. The entry is just S/100. The girls are Colombians, Brazilians, Mexicans, Ecuadorians, and Peruvians. I bet you."

"Please, we have just come here to drink, nothing else."

"Ok, or if you just want to have some nice time, I have some contacts. I can... José interrupted him.

"Please, it's ok. Won't you leave us in peace? I don't want to talk too much." José became impatient from his tone and the gentleman simply made way, joining other colleagues standing with him at the entrance of the street, targeting every "responsible" passers-by.

"Usually, they just stand at the entrance. Now they are becoming much more intrusive. I don't know why this society has deteriorated to this extent." José said, embittered. I narrated my experience on that alley which I visited with Elena close to a month ago.

"They are very pushy. The first time I came to Miraflores we passed here and one gentleman came asking me if I wanted some weed. I could least expect that in broad daylight."

"Ya, that is very common, especially at night. They have the key to all forms of devilish desires. That is *Calle Pizzeria* for you." Jose said.

We ordered drinks. I took just a small bottle of Inka Cola. José took soda water. It was getting dark and I wanted to be in full control of my reasoning faculties on my way back. I had learned the hard way in Arequipa. José too was not a heavy drinker, he confessed to me. He still had to sign some papers at the university before going back home. He just wanted us to share a drink after our brief meeting at his father's book presentation. We talked about almost everything within the limited time we had. Football, family life, the history of Peru, the geopolitics of Latin America, etc. I was amazed by the analytical acuity of José. He had a very deep sense of perception and even though a medical doctor, his reading of political affairs and international relations was very profound. I think the medical field invests some of its practitioners with immense insight, the ability to rationally dissect socio-economic reality in the same way as they probe with syringes into an ailing human body. Perhaps the intimate moments they spend with their patients give them access to the psychic refractions of the issues that inhibit the social body. Think of some of the greatest politicians in world history. You will find behind them many a student of medical sciences: Che Guevara, Amilcar Cabral, Frantz Fanon, Samora Machel, Agostinho Neto, José Rizal, etc.

We separated at about 8 P.M. He went to where he had parked his car while I crossed over to Kennedy Parking to board the bus to Lince on the other side of the road. I was attracted by an open-air concert at the hemicycle of the Park. There was a relatively huge crowd there. In the middle stood a young solo guitarist. It was sweet romantic music, sung in a beautiful voice in an almost mournful tone. I lingered around for a few moments. A young boy stood close to me and I wanted to inquire more about the singer.

"Hello my friend, how are you?"

"I am fine and you?"

"Am fine, thank you. Now, tell me, is this guy very well known in Peru?"

"No idea. I am new here."

"Oh, I see, me too. Where are you from?"

"Mexico. And you?"

"From Cameroon. Have you come for business, exchange programme, or something?

"No, I am already working. I am an engineer. I just came for a one-week visit. I was in Machu Picchu two days ago and I will be leaving for Mexico tomorrow."

"Oh really. I was also in Machu Picchu last week."

As we were discussing, a young girl, who was sitting on the edge of the hemicycle just a metre away, stood up and moved close to us. I had noticed her playing graciously with a cat in her arms and that sent chills down my spine.

"Hey guys, I am Genesis from Venezuela. Nice to know that you guys are also from different countries. That means I am not alone."

She sounded very carefree. We introduced ourselves in return.

"O that is right. Are you also here for tourism?" I asked her.

"No, I am here as a voluntary medical assistant under a World Health Organisation programme. I have been here for one month now. I am leaving next month."

She requested for our Facebook names and instantly invited us since she was connected.

"I am hurrying to meet a friend but we can keep in touch." She said and left.

Few minutes after, the Mexican guy also took his leave, saying he had to arrange his bags on time for his flight the following day. I hung around for more minutes till the guitarist stopped singing and the MC was introducing another band on stage. That is when I realised that behind me were dozens of cats playing around and chasing one another. When I threw my eyes further afield, behold! Cats everywhere. Various colours! I made haste to the bus stop. I later learned that another name for the park is *Parque de Los Gatos*.

CHAPTER 32

Columbus, Close the Door of your Seas!!

26 August 2015

Second trip to Chincha and El Carmen. Elena and I arrived in Chincha close to midday and took a *taxi cholo* to Tambo de Mora. We met an old couple in front of a house at the entrance to the dockyard. We asked her if it was safe to go down there.

At night, it is a bit dangerous but not during the daytime.

I took the lead, moving down the wharf. I moved towards the fisherman ahead of me. There were two ships further asea, partially covered by the fog in the firmament. Certainly, they were carrying *real* goods, I conjectured.

I moved past the fisherman. I doubt if there was any fish in his net even though the fisherman shook and peered into his net with missionary zeal. He looked at me briefly and went on examining his net with slightly hopeless expectation. He reminded me of the biblical fisherman whom Jesus summoned to follow Him so he would make them fishers of men. Unfortunately, I was no Jesus, unable to promise the man better and more worthy tidings. I had no vision. No miracles. Only the Ocean, the Ocean, with memories of Numbers shoved into the sea. I moved closer to the sea, this time with slightly faster steps.

"Gil! Gil! Gil! …" A voice echoed from afar, mixed with the flushing waves. It came as if from the Ocean. Elena calling. I moved on, undeterred. There was a distance between us. She was close to thirty meters from me. I was approaching the tip of the wharf. I looked at my hands. Black. I looked at the waves flushing against the edges of the wharf, cold drops splashing on my body. I was closer to the sea as if to embrace it. She was standing there, on safe ground, certainly concerned I was playing with danger.

"Gil... Gil... Gil… It is dangerous...."

I moved closer and closer to the ocean, part of the quay was broken but had been replaced by two tree trunks, like a wooden bridge, I tight-walked on the Pacific *Rampe*, to the precipice where a swarm of blackbirds had assembled. The closer I got, the further they moved to the tip of the wharf, and in their team slowly, graciously flew off. I stood there, admiring their freedom, the freedom of the black albatrosses. I watched them flapping their wings above the sea, mixing with other birds flying from the Southern sky. The men, women and children who came here were bereft of wings, feet chained to the ground, facing reality, human reality, the reality of men over men, the reality of my race, the reality of modern capital.

Albatroz! Albatroz! águia do oceano,
Tu que dormes das nuvens entre as gazas,
Sacode as penas, Leviathan do espaço,
Albatroz! Albatroz! dá-me estas asas.
(Castro Alves – O Navio Neigro)

(English translation)

Albatross! Albatross! Eagle of the ocean,
You who sleep in the mist of the clouds,
Shake your feathers, leviathan of space
Albatross! Albatross! give me those wings.
(Castro Alves – The Slave Ship)

Nothing pacific about this place, I thought, as my mind swam in the waves of the Pacific; a crucial space in the atlas of a difficult world. Centuries back, shackled hands were brought to a strange shore. The distress, the anguish, the hunger, a journey of no return, severed from their history, their culture, the pain of separation, mother from child, brother from sister, grief answers grief, mourning the loss of those who did not make it, those thrown at sea to evade the British squadron, those counted only as numbers, only as material wealth, those counted only as hands for the hectares, those counted as the pride of the master, as a symbol of social status, those ones who were counted but did not count. Here was a public space, a space of distinction, a space of separation and strange unions. I look at the waves; they are calm but at times they would come with renewed velocity, splashing me with jerks of water, the currents retreat, gather more force, summon new strength, then instantly invade the coast, and then retreat to the gigantic mass. Wilful pain on man by man, man using man to enrich himself and impoverish his humanity, a world built on injustice, wealth built on the other's sweat, masters of the world, trade of exploitation, the blood of the wretched of the earth. I thought of Mya, Mamainé, Nicomedes, Ballumbrosio, and those others who never became great, who could not go further, who finished too soon, whose seeds ended, scattered on the seas, eaten by crows on the sugar and cotton fields, those who quenched under the tunnels, those voices that yelled and I was not there, you were not there, we were not there. I look at myself, look at Elena, at the bus driver, at the sky, at the sea. If life is a stage, why do some people die on stage, why do some people die at sea, denied a burial, denied proper tears, no reed on their tombs. Yes, centuries have passed, some have forgotten, some do not care, but for others, memory refuses to go away, it lives with us, in our language, in our veins. Oh God, close down this stage!!

We left the shore, went past the young men playing cards. Certainly, they must have been wondering what we came to do there; the question was visible on their faces. We waited for the car to take us to Tambo de Mora. We were told it was better to move to a closer and more accessible junction. The distance would take us roughly 15 minutes on foot. Since we were short of time, we pleaded with one young man driving a carriage to transport us to the junction. It was a short van pulled by a motorcycle engine, apparently used to transport sheep and, perhaps, fodder. We hopped into the carriage. It was fun, though. It took us about five minutes to the junction from where we got a vehicle to the central park of Chincha. From there we found a mini-bus to El Carmen.

We arrived in El Carmen some few minutes to 4 P.M. We entered a restaurant along the Plaza de Armas. It was a late lunch. Too eager to visit the slave wharf, we did not have time at all to eat. This always happened every time we got to Chincha and El Carmen. While Elena sat down, looking at the menu, I was busy taking pictures of beautiful statues of black women lined up at the entrance.

"Elena, I guess you see the differences between these statuettes and the straw figures in Chincha."

She came out to look at them. She must have been wondering what I was still doing outside when I was the one complaining of hunger.

"They are so cute!" she confirmed.

"Yes, they are ingenious." Images of black women in nicely coloured loins, with cowries around their necks, pieces of cloth tied around their breasts and waist. This is black."

Elena went back and I followed. Just as I sat down with her, a brainwave occurred to me and I opined to Elena:

"You know what? I guess they said the Afro-dance museum closes at about 5:00 P.M. I suggest that since it is getting late, we go there first and come back to eat here later."

"I see. Lucia said the last time that the museum closes at 5 P.M. That is a nice idea. If we delay we may not meet him. We will ask those guys around the park where the museum is exactly."

We explained the situation to the waiter, promising to come back as soon as we are through with our visit to the dance museum. It was a hard choice for us to suspend the very promising menu made of chicharrones, (pan-fried chunks of pork with yuca), *arroz con pato* (rice with duck meat), and the *Carapulcra Chinchana* (dried potatoes in a peanuty sauce over pasta).

We inquired from some boys selling statuettes of Afro-Peruvian iconography at the *Plaza de Armas*, in front of the Cathedral. One happened to be the son of the museum proprietor, Maestro Guillermo Santa Cruz. He accompanied us to the house-museum, just five minutes' walk from the Plaza de Armas. Before we left, I looked at the makeshift signboard placed near a black woman who was selling products packed on what seemed like a movable cart. On the signboard, I could read:

Tutuma
Licor
Afrodisiaco
Del Tio Mandingo

(English translation)

Tutuma
Aphrodisiac
Liquor
By Uncle Mandingo

Maestro Santa Cruz welcomed us into his parlour cum museum. He is a short stout man, probably in his mid-fifties, though my guess of people's age always proved wrong in Peru. In my view, many of them look much younger than their ages. Maestro speaks in a strong, firm voice. He bade us take a seat and he went into the inner room to collect his violin.

The parlour is divided into two sections separated by a broad curtain: the hind section is used as conventional sitting room, with dining set, reading table and a set of chairs, while the anterior is the museum with a set of chairs for visitors, with an assemblage of statuettes of Afro-Peruvian iconography on the windowsill. The wall was lined with an array of photos, newspaper cuts, framed and laminated awards and distinctions. The photos seized my attention. I stood there scanning through them. Many of them were in black and white. They depicted various generations of Afro-Peruvian life in El Carmen and other parts of Peru. There was also the picture of popular Afro-Peruvian bands, some of them as far back as the early 20th century, Maestro Guillermo later explained to us. There was the photo of the maestro himself, performing with the great Ballumbrosio.

Maestro Santa Cruz came out with his violin in his hand. But before he began playing, he narrated to us the history of the black presence in El Carmen, plantation life, the phenomenon of *cimarronaje* whereby enslaved persons rebelled against bondage and established outlaying independent settlements, the anecdote of the black Christ of El Carmen, the dance culture and its influences, etc. He seemed to have a broad mastery of history. He promised to let me photocopy some of the history books he had on the subject.

It is then that he made recourse to the violin. Before playing, he explained that the violin is more of an Andean than an Afro-Peruvian musical instrument. It is one of the cultural confluences and metissage that developed from the coexistence of these two races amongst others. But they have a different way of holding the violin when playing it. The indigenes hold it closer to their shoulder than the Afro-Peruvians who lean it against their forearm. The maestro began playing. The pitch was high, the tone sharp, but very synchronic and beautiful. He sang along...

Ya salió mi caporal
Con su chicote en la mano
Panalivio malivio san.

Se parece al mal ladrón
Capitán de bandoleros
Panalivio malivio san.

Yo me corté con la hoz

Ya me sale mucha sangre
Panalivio malivio san.

No es la sangre que me sale
Sino que me mata el hambre
Panalivio malivio san.

Zancudito me picó
(salamanqueja me mordió)

Malhaya sea ese zancudo
(malhaya sea que me pico)

Zancudito por aquí
(zancudito por allá)

Malhaya sea este zancudo
(malhaya sea que me picó)

Que me picó, que me picó
(en la punta el corazón)

(English translation)

Here comes the slave driver
With a whip in his hand
Panalivio malivio san

He looks like a thief
Captain of bandits
Panalivio malivio san

I've cut myself with a sickle
And I'm bleeding profusely
Panalivio malivio san

It's not blood that pours out of me
It's the hunger that's killing me
Panalivio malivio san

The mosquito stung me
(the salamander bit me)

Cursed be that mosquito
(cursed for biting me)

Mosquito over here
(mosquito over there)

Cursed be that mosquito (cursed for biting me)

It stung me
(on the tip of my heart)

The song is an exchange between the plantation white master and the capo, the chief slave in charge of taking the slave workers to the field and reporting to the master on their conduct. The song has become one of the most popular hit songs of Afro-Peruvian musical scene. The Afro-Peruvian Grammy Award winner Susanna Bacca has a beautiful rendition of it. After singing, Maestro Santa Cruz went to the other compartment of the parlour and turned the computer on. He inserted the CD of the playback and began demonstrating. He did it with dexterity. Then he asked me to join. *danza de zapateos.* Elena was taking the footage. It was not as easy as it seemed. My steps did not produce the same effect as those of *El Maestro.* I could also complain I did not wear proper shoes for the zapateos. The soles of my Inca-designed canvas were not suited for a dance that depended on the hard and systematic knock of the soles on the cement floor for its musicality. I promised to come back sometime with the proper pair of shoes to continue the lessons.

It was getting dark. The maestro proposed to accompany us to Chincha with the documents I needed to photocopy. That was kind of him but since it was on a Sunday, the two photocopy shops in El Carmen were closed. We hinted him that we had not eaten the whole day and would go find some food before we get on the bus to Chincha. He recommended to us a restaurant just two alleys away from his house; an alley after that of the Ballumbrosios. Then, when we are through we can come back to his house so we take the bus to Chincha at the Plaza de Armas. He insisted we tell the lady at the restaurant that we came there upon his recommendation. It is the restaurant where, during our previous visit, Elena had suggested we have a meal before going to the Ballumbrosios although we ended up going to Mamainé upon Lucia's recommendation. Now we were coming back there on maestro's counsel. It seems every museum here is connected to a restaurant. It is a chain. This is America. I remember my time in Santa Ana, California, some four years back. The hotel waitress continuously recommended specific restaurants around to us, handing us discount cards for that matter. Not to mention her insisting that we enjoy the nice beaches around, steadfast to call the taxi-driver for us upon our slightest show of interest.

After a delicious plate of *Carapulcra*[1], we paid a brief courtesy visit to the Ballumbrosios. Lucia was very impressed by our gesture. When we went back, the Masetro was already waiting for us. We moved down to the Plaza de Armas and within a short while we were on our way to Chincha. But before taking the taxi, we were detained by a group of children, black and metis, offering to dance the *zapateo* for us of course in expectation of their tips, a *solitito*. We told them we were in haste. On the other side, one young guy came near us with a black wig, asking us to wear it and take a picture with it while sitting on the *cajon*, the drum. Elena was rather enthusiastic. I showed my disinterest and followed the Maestro down to where we had to take the bus. After wearing the black wig and having me take a snapshot of her, Elena scampered through her purse to get the tip for the young owner of the paraphernalia for the performance of Afro-Peruvian identity.

On the way to Chincha, luckily, there were photocopy shops close to the bus station. Maestro Santa Cruz and I stood there for the photocopies to be produced while Elena proceeded to the agency for our tickets. It is then that the maestro narrated to me his complex genealogy. His paternal grandfather was a *zambo (a child born of a relationship between black and indigenous parents)* while his maternal grandmother was of Spanish-Chinese metissage. Physically, he was quite light-skinned. Elena came just when we were through with the photocopies. After that, we bade the Maestro farewell and boarded our bus back to Lima. Elena and I talked all along, uninterested in the violent film on the TV screen onboard. I wondered if such a film was appropriate for passengers,

---

1   It can be described as dried potato stew, with peanuts, pepper, garlic and other spices. The name "carapulcra" is derived from the words 'cala' which means 'caliente' (hot) and 'purka' which refers to the door of the barbecue furnace.

perhaps after a long day of work. The film was as long as the length of the trip. I remember asking Elena at the beginning of the trip why she always refers to her friend, the man with whom she welcomed me upon my arrival in Lima as *el chino (the Chinese)*.

"Don't you see the shape of his nose?" She asked me. The facial signs of Peru were too complex. I was still learning the art of describing people's faces and types of hair in Peru. It was a difficult assignment. Elena made me believe the name *chino* did not offend her friend in any way; most of his friends refer to him by the same name. I remembered my own experience in *Hydro-electrico* with the word *morenito*.

When we alighted at the bus station, several taxi drivers were looking for passengers. A young female driver took us to *Jirón Soledad*. It was almost 11:00 P.M. I went straight to my room, not wanting to open Facebook or check my mails after such a long and exhausting day. It was a day of mixed feelings, with the fun of the *danza de zapateos* after the memory-laden visit to the dockyard of Tambo de Mora. But even as I danced with the maestro that evening, I did not lose track of the grim reality from which the dance and the songs emerged. As I went to bed that night, Castro Alves' verses revisited me:

Fatalidade atroz que a mente esmaga!
Extingue nesta hora o brigue imundo
O trilho que Colombo abriu nas vagas,
Como um iris no pélago profundo!
Mas é infâmia demais!… Da etérea plaga
Levantai-vos, heróis do Novo Mundo!
Andrada! arranca esse pendao dos ares!
Colombo! fecha a porta dos teus mares!
(O Navio Neigro – Castro alves)

(English translation)

Atrocious fatality that the mind crushes!
Extinguish now the dirt brig,
The track that Columbus opened in the waves,
Like an iris in the deep abyss!
But this is too much infamy!...of the ethereal land
Rise, heroes of the New World!
Andrada, rip that flag of the air!

Columbus, close the door of your seas!

(The Black Ship —Castro Alves)

CHAPTER 33

Black Saint, Black Christ

26 August 2015

I visited the Nature Museum in the morning. Elena went to her dentist and promised to meet me at the Nature Museum so that we could later continue to the *Museo de la Nacion (National Museum)*. However, she spent much more time than foreseen and I proceeded to the Museo de la Nacion alone. Behold, the museum was closed down due to renovation work. I informed Elena and we agreed to meet in front of the Inquisition Museum. During our previous visit, I was psychologically ill-prepared to face the horror of the Inquisition. Thus, a second visit was necessary. I had the impression that this time the tour guide was more patient and spoke more clearly. After that, Elena and I proceeded to the Afro-Peruvian Museum. It exhibited black slave experiences in Peru, through the abolition up to the present period. I took every image; leaving out any face was like side-lining, neglecting a soul that deserved my empathy, a voice that needed to be heeded.

Looking at the wall, I was intrigued by the name San Martin de Porres as one of the many black icons in Peru. In Chincha, I was amazed at hearing that they celebrate a feast for the Black Christ, *el Cristo Negro*. One thing you notice in Peru is the proliferation of saints in that part of the world. Every city, village and even quarter has their patron saint. Several shrines and ritual activities are organised in their honour. But whenever you visit Lima, you won't leave without hearing about the Black Saint Martin de Porres, the miraculous healer. He was the illegitimate son of a Spanish noble and a Panamanian slave woman. His mother had to resort to laundry and several menial jobs to ensure his upbringing. His father, not very keen on acknowledging his mulatto son, handed him to a master on the Malambo Street of Lima to learn the trade of shaving and later on surgery. But young Martin preferred the cloak. Since Blacks were only allowed to occupy the lower rungs of the clergy,

Martin suffered a lot of denigration and insult, being referred to with derogatory remarks due to his being an 'illegitimate' son. He dedicated most of his time to prayer and meditation. Ricardo Palma,[1] the famous Afro-Peruvian historian recounts, with his characteristically laconic and humorous tonality, some of the various ways that Martin used to "miraclify": suspending a falling bricklayer in mid-air and saving his life through prayer and successfully washing a cube of murky sugar in water and making it clean and refined. Martin also had a passion and compassion for mice, these rodents, "honourable guests" that first arrived Peru on the ships of the conquistadors in 1552. Soon the mice became pests in Lima. Nevertheless, Martin stressed his love for them by insinuating: "When God was wasting time on me, He might have created a mouse or two." A keen diplomat, Martin succeeded in keeping under the same roof three incompatible divine creatures: a cat, mouse and dog, intervening in his commanding pacifism, each time any of these creatures broke the rules. Martin's miraclifying force was so astounding that his name became a saga in the entire Peru and beyond. Till this day, his name is honoured in every altar from Lima to Scarborough, from Santiago to Oxford. There is a district in Lima to his name. He was canonized in 1962. It is believed that several years after his burial his body remained intact, enhancing the myth around the saint's miraculous identity. Why did it take that long for Martin de Porres to be canonized? Well, some critics like Nicomedes Santa Cruz claim race had a role in it. The latter states, with a sense of sarcasm, that:

> Now in 1959, 320 years after his presence before God, the Vatican asked for three more miracles from the Dominican Order, the same hierarchy which had prohibited him from performing more miracles during his lifetime.[2]

After his canonization, Cathedrals have been erected in his honour in places like Lima, Ayacucho, in Peru, Paysandú in Uruguay, New York, Chicago, Queens in the USA, Colombia, Mexico, Argentina, Venezuela and Italy. In the central Basilica of Lima, mass is celebrated in his honour

---

1 Ricardo Palma (1833-1919) is one of the best narrators of Peruvian colonial and Republican history. He was partially of African ancestry. His major work *Tradiciones Peruanas* (Peruvian Traditions) is characterised by irony, sarcasm and a thirst for paradox and the contradictions of a class and race-based society.

2 *Nicomedes Santa Cruz, Complete Works II* Research (1958-1991), p. 223.

on the 4th of every month.

Then finally I came to the image of the Black Christ, known as *El Señor de los Milagros (The Lord of Miracles)*. I did not bother to go through the text apposed to it because many a Peruvian had recounted to me the story. Each account had its modulation and tone. But the account I read in Ricardo Palma's *Tradiciones Peruanas* (Peruvian Tradition) is one of the most widely accepted. The story goes that on 13 November 1655 at 2 P.M. a strong earthquake hit Lima and its environs, destroying many lives and property. But then, a miracle occurred in a suburb called Pachacamilla. The wall bearing the painting of a Black Christ remained unscathed, undamaged while all around it was in ruin. This image was painted by an enslaved African from Angola, Pedro Dalcon o Benito. The wall soon became a point of pilgrimage. The first person to discover the Christ on the Wall was Antonio Leon. He testified that praying to the image of Christ cured him of severe frontal headache which defied all doctors in town! The news spread like wildfire and since the tears of this world are in abundant quantity, many people started trooping around the image of the crucified Christ to pray for relief, depression, provision, forgiveness, prosperity and healing. Many testified their desires were fulfilled!! But the space around the miraculous wall also turned into a space of conscientisation and the raising of awareness about the economic and social conditions at the time, especially amongst the enslaved, the most frequent visitors to the sanctuary of the Black Christ. This alarmed the government which decided to ban any meeting around it and subsequently to undo the painting on the wall. This took effect between the 6 and 13 September 1671. A group of soldiers were sent to dismantle the Black Christ but it had a boomerang effect. The first agent climbed the ladder to undo the image but quickly descended claiming he felt a swathe of pain on his chaste. The second agent came down the ladder with an even more astonishing testimony of the spiritual power of the Black Christ. "As I approached it, the crown on His head turned green and beautiful and I could not fulfil the order. There must be strong powers in this image. It is truly Christ!!" It became clear that the image was a spiritual force. With protests from the people, the government gave up the plan to destroy the Black Christ. But more was still to come. In October 1687, a tsunami destroyed part of Lima where the Christ of Miracles was located. The Black Christ stood strong and firm while everything around it was turned into rubble!! Needless to say, the Christ of Miracles became the patron saint of Lima and Peru and a procession in His honour takes place every 18 and 19 October. Today it is considered the most populous religious procession in the world!!

When we were through with visiting the Afro-Peruvian museum, we met up with Miguel and some colleagues in China Town. They had just finished eating when we arrived. I ordered a plate of *arroz chaufa (fried rice)*. From there, we had the choice of either visiting *museo de oro* (Gold museum) or *museo de antropologia* (Anthropology Museum). We opted for the latter since it was closer. I also had to meet my friend from Venezuela at 6:00 P.M., so we had to make haste. Unfortunately, we got to the Anthropology museum when it had just closed. It was 4:15 P.M. They close at 4:00 P.M. Elena tried to persuade them to let us in, explaining to them that I came from far and that it was my last opportunity to visit the museum. The officer, an Afro-Peruvian kindly told us that though he understood our situation and felt for us, it was against his work ethics to act otherwise. I admired his respect for the law. I did not want Elena to plead further. A bit disappointed, we returned home, having visited neither of the museums.

At exactly 6:00 A.M. I was at *Parque de Aguas,* waiting for my Venezuelan friend, Genesis. The park was a real touristic resort. People, especially couples, came around in their numbers to enjoy the intricate hydro-choreography of the park. Genesis wrote me a message saying she was still in the taxi, enmeshed in heavy traffic. That is Lima. She texted me again saying she had missed her way and would take much longer time to come. She finally came an hour later, full of apologies. We strolled around, marvelling at the waterworks and finally separated at about 8 P.M. after having dined together in a Chinese *chifa* restaurant.

CHAPTER 34

Meeting the Poetess

27 August 2015

Visit to the poet, critic, and lecturer at the Catholic University of Peru, Victoria Guerrero, called *Jorge Chavez 31*. Due to my fear of her cat, I preferred we carry out the interview in a different venue. Victoria's cat is very attractive: clean, healthy-looking and tiger-coloured. But due to my phobia, all these qualities produced a boomerang effect on me. She was astonished by my squeamishness and kept laughing at me as I squeaked like a child in the presence of the cat. We took a stroll while she explained the history of the district of Pueblo Libre to me. The district is called Pueblo Libre because it is the only place that remained outside Chilean control when the Chilean army occupied Lima during the War of the Pacific. We went past the house where San Martin and Simon Bolivar lived. We then went to a bar and ordered juice as we commenced our interview. I left with the impression of having met a deeply committed author and a well-read critic. As a poet, she is postmodernist to the brim. Her poems have such an existentialist depth that one would think she has either experienced too much herself or perhaps is excessively preoccupied with fundamental human problems and injustices.

I left her to prepare for her classes and went to the anthropological museum. It was full of dexterously curated artefacts of the Peruvian civilisations of Chavin, Wari, Nazca, etc. After that, I met up with Daniel Carillo in front of the Inquisition Museum at 4:00 P.M. Daniel was punctual as usual. We went to Amazona book market where I bought a mixture of five Peruvian novels and history texts.

CHAPTER 35

Lima Buscapes

The real life of Lima takes place on the bus; an ambulant book of many pages. When buses reach the bus stop, *paradero*, you cannot ignore the chants of the controller, *cobrador(a)*, singing the destinations of the bus to would-be passengers, beckoning on them to climb on board. The cobrador(a) is the driver's aide, what we call "motor boy" in Cameroon. Curiously, in Lima, most of them are females, "motor girl", you may say. The cobrador(a) lets passengers in and out, collects fares, delivers receipts, advertises bus directions, etc. Some of them carry a bunch of placards in their hands to indicate the trajectories of the bus. Most are dressed in material trousers with a tucked-in shirt. They always bid you climb the bus in haste because buses are always scrambling to be the first to arrive at a bus stop to gather more customers on board. Like taxi drivers in Cameroon, Lima bus drivers are always in haste. As a stranger, you would think accidents certainly occur very often. But by some magic, perchance or thanks to the rosary which many of the bus drivers hang on their steering wheels, Lima seems to be very safe for driving. Chants of *Sube! Sube!* (climb! Climb!) are the most permanent features of Lima's urban soundscapes. When these are chanted, it does not mean the buses have stopped for you to enter. No, you enter while the bus is in motion. Same as when you hear *Baja! (Alight)*, you jump as quickly as you can. On the bus itself, you take your seat if you are lucky enough to find one. I always preferred to stand because the seats are too close to the backrests in front, making my legs cramp, disagreeably. I always joked with Elena that those buses are made specifically for Peruvians. Not for Afro-Yankees like myself. As for Elena, she sat quite comfortably. In most cases, the fare in Lima is very fair: 1 sol for normal distance, 1.5 for long inter-district trips and 50 *cents* for shorter distances. The worse part is when you have to alight. You need to move close to the door as the bus gets nearer to your destination, otherwise, the bus won't wait for you. *Baja*, if you want to alert the driver that you are alighting. After about a week in Lima, I began taking the bus on my own, since Elena had to run her private errands in town. When I asked the *cobradora* if we were arriving Jirón Soledad, she sang to me: *Faltan dos paraderos. Pero no te preocupes, te voy a decir a la llegado.* (We are left with two more stops. But do not bother; I will alert you when we are getting close). Elena and I would never cease laughing at the way the female cobradora in the bus we took to Baranco would chant the destinations: *Salaverry Venezuela Cuba Universitaria... Sube! sube!* At the Cruz del Sur and other travel agencies, I also adored the way arrivals, departures and delays were announced, fashioned into a song: *El bus en proveniencia de Ica llega en 15 minutos. La salida seria la puerta numero cinco. Por favor, queden asentados. Los agentes de seguridad les dirían cuando podrían ponerse en la salida para acoger los suyos.* (The bus from Ica arrives in 15 minutes time. The exit is at gate 5. Please remain seated until security agents tell you when to come to the gate and welcome your loved ones.)

In Lima, buscapes are propitious spaces for the exercise of the profession of mendicancy. On my way back from San Marcos University campus during my first visit, Elena and I had an interesting experience on the bus. At Plaza San Miguel, a seemingly teenage boy and a girl entered the bus. The girl was carrying a child on her back and no sooner than later, they began their synchronic performance. The boy held an instrument that produced a jingling sound while the girl responded with a form of rattling clapper. It was music anyway. After playing for some minutes, the boy explained his fate: he needed money to take care of his wife and their child. More so his wife was pregnant and needed to attend clinics. The wife put on a countenance that could draw empathy from the most stone-heart human being. He removed a long roll of biscuits from his sachet and gave a long treatise on the peculiarity and medical qualities of the biscuits and then passed it around. It reminded me of the mobile bus pastors cum "modern tradi-practitioners" (some people consider them as mere charlatans) on inter-urban transport buses in many parts of Cameroon. Sometimes when they start their preaching cum advertising, you determine to be indifferent, to feel like you are not sick, spiritually or physically (even though we are all patients). But as soon as they begin "to pray for journey mercies", you bend your head and even close your eyes, certainly under the influence of your childhood religious habitus. Of course, the nature of roads and the state of some buses always necessitate some divine intervention for safe arrival. More so, you do not want to appear to your fellow sojourners as the door through which the devil will enter and wreck the trip. Like colonial subjects and colonial priests, as soon as you open your eyes, your five hundred francs note is with them. In return, you are left with God's blessings and a sachet of Chinese panacea that cures gonorrhoea, obesity, indigestion, impotence, low sperm count, rashes, etc. etc. I guess in some few years to come, the Chinese will be doing the sales themselves. They are in all sectors of medium-size trade in Cameroon, some say they now sell roasted fish in the streets of Douala. Anyway, that is another story altogether.

This short boy and his wife drew sympathy from many a passenger as seen from several coins dropping into his straw hat, el sombrero. Some did not care to receive biscuits in return. Elena and I jointly donated S/2. She took two small packets of biscuits. I was not particularly tempted. At the next stop, the couple stepped down, after having made the best out of the ambulant community of sympathy on the bus.

What amazed me was the convivial nature of Limeños[1]. Even those who enter the bus with an air of apartness, nicely ironed and pleated coat, white shirt and well-kempt, office type, are never indifferent to the lot of the wretched. Even though they observe the bus performance with a sense of detachment or partial recognition of their presence, they always end up slotting in one *solito*, at least 50 *centitos* into the *sombrero*. I remember taking the bus from Pueblo Libre to Abancay to meet up with a friend in front of the Congress House. A young boy of about 10 climbed onto the bus and with a bell-like figure began to sing, banging his fingers insistently on his instrument. It produced a strident and almost annoying sound, getting directly into my eardrum since he stood right in front of me. Seemingly, I was the only one who felt disturbed. Life continued on the bus. After his performance, a few persons put coins on his palms and then he alighted. This time, I was not moved. Minutes afterwards, an old man entered the bus with a radio player tied to his waist. He activated it and it produced what sounded like old-time Peruvian hits. The CD player itself was a modern relic. As it played, the mobile disco-man passed his sombrero hat around for tips. During my last trip from San Marcos, two beautiful girls entered the bus. One was playing the guitar as the other sang along. It was a melodious religious tune, though the two dressed more like punk artists. They were quite procedural in their collection. The singer said they animated for fun but anyone moved by the message and the music could make a gesture. Of

---

1   Inhabitants of Lima

course, music is a great ministry. More so, God works in miraculous ways: the bus got stuck in traffic and the melody of these two girls was our only source of comfort in that moment of impatience. Coins rained in the guitar box held by one of the girls as she passed it around after the praise and worship. There seemed to be a tacit arrangement between some of the bus animators and the drivers. Some did not pay for the fare. Perhaps there was a sense of familiarity between them. Perhaps they had their way of settling accounts. These were real machetes! In the streets of Bayreuth, I had always found the music performances in front of supermarkets or at the *Maximilian Strasse* (Maximilian Street) as a very creative form of begging. Lima took this practice further.

One of the performance spaces in the Lima traffic system is on the road, at the zebra crossing. Whenever cars waited for the green light, it was time for the acrobats to begin their displays in front of the stationed cars. This could be within the space of three minutes. But you are entertained to the brim. When the acrobats sense the green light, they move to the drivers with a sombrero, otherwise with bare hands, to collect their tips. I often felt tempted to stand and watch whenever I was lucky enough to encounter such displays. You could not just pass unruffled by the beauty of the scenery. A young boy, manipulating a football in Ronaldinho-style acrobatics, the ball sticking to his body, obeying every command as he performed numerous feats; a young girl, Hula hooping, throwing rings in the air in marionette-style; close to five multi-coloured rings, circling them around her waist and then flinging them into the air in turns. None touched the ground! I found the most dangerous version of these feats on my way to the *Cruz del Sur* agency. A man manipulating close to three machetes, throwing them in the air and catching them in turns; in the same rhythm, he would stand one of the machetes straight on his head with incredible mastery.

CHAPTER 36

Send-off Party

28 August 2015

A few friends spent the evening with us as a send-off for me. They were about seven. Elena, her friend Milli, Miguel, Fernando, Gustavo, Hortensia and Carmen. Elena and I had bought enough beer and wine the previous day for the occasion. She also prepared some Peruvian fries. Her friend Hortensia also brought some special doughnuts. We had fun, drinking, chewing and chatting about Cameroon, Germany and Peru. The most important part of it was the *festejo* dance. Though everyone got to exercise their dance steps at some point, I cannot forget the moment Elena and Carmen took to the floor. Gustavo was playing the *cajon*, the Peruvian drum. Fernando was on the guitar while his friend Miguel played the *cajita*. It is a small box with a lid which opens and closes like a rhythmic valve. It serves to keep up the pace but was originally used as a box to collect money in churches. At first, they gave it to me to play but I could not produce the appropriate rhythm. When the three took control of the instruments, the tempo gained a different momentum. We only lacked the *quijada de burro*, the donkey's jaw, Gustavo lamented. As its name suggests, it is a donkey's jawbone which produces the sound of a rattle. Elena and Carmen swayed with impressive agility. Both were a bit advanced in age but you could not even guess. While Carmen was more energetic, enchanting us with multiple twists of her slim body, Elena took it more graciously, swinging in a way that seemed to flow from the veins. Both mastered the rhythm and reduced us to humble spectators. When the instruments stopped, we removed our hats for them in utter respect.

Upon my instigations, we discussed at length on the history of Latin America. Looking back at history, I imagined the affective conviviality of putative opposites with regard to this continent. Here in Peru, iron-curtained separations are slanted: Church/hanging, abundance/scarcity, pleasure/danger, affection/enslavement, dream/reality. I remember having asked my three female friends Milli, Carmen and Elena what sounded like a naïve but at the same time provocative question: How do you feel so much wrath against the Spaniards when almost everything about you is Spanish even though most of you are mestizos, born of the union between White Spaniards and Indians? Carmen was the first to respond. "When it comes to looking back at the history", she said, "We take sides with the maternal side, involved in an imbalanced relationship with the macho Spaniards. The Spanish men basically raped many of them. It is from that affective maternal side that the wrath is vented to the conquistadors and their destructive heritage." Elena and her friend Milli kept telling me that those who carried out the Conquista were the criminals and the most unscrupulous of the Spanish stock. "Our Spanish forefathers were robbers, prisoners even at home in Spain," I replied to them. "Oh, ladies do not be so harsh to yourselves. Your parents could have been the exceptions". We all laughed and continued drinking our bottles of *chicha morada*[1].

At close to 11 P.M. the ladies left. It is Hortensia who was first to leave. She is Afro-Indian Hispanic. She was informed by Elena of the party and she wanted to come and see her African brother. She brought some cake for the occasion. Thus, it was just four of us talking and listening to Peruvian *huayno*. Though I have always considered huayno more as music to be listened to than a dance rhythm, Elena went on *solo* dancing with renewed energy. From her body movement and her utterances, it was clear that she was losing her sobriety. When the music stopped, she took her seat, emptying the dregs of the wine on the table. We continued discussing but henceforth, Elena damned everything as pure MIERDA (SHIT). Politics, church, life, etc., all was MIERDA. Then she became very quiet and pensive. Suddenly, she burst into tears. Miguel moved close to her and she hung on his shoulders. I was almost moved to laughter by her MIERDA but I suddenly began considering the dramatic nature of the situation. I knew some people cry when they are drunk, but I felt for Elena. Certainly, the crying was an expression of pent-up emotions that had welled up in her for years.

"Why, why, why can't we accept everyone in our society and live together as human beings?" Elena lamented. No one could guess what

---

1   Sweet juice made from maize.

the question was aimed at. But she persisted in near monologue and then broke the narrative. Miguel moved closer to her and made her lean on him again.

"What is the problem, Elena? Why? What is the issue, please tell me." Elena could hardly speak. She was sobbing continuously.

"I am thinking about all what my son has gone through here. My son, presently in the United States. Ricardo suffered a lot in Peru, with his dark skin. Even his schoolmates and friends discriminated against him. He could hardly make friends when at school here. I wonder how that has affected him I wonder what life is like for him in North America." It is then that we understood the cause of Elena' anguish.

"Elena, all will be fine. Please, stop crying, it is ok. They do not accept him but you have accepted him; that is the key thing. The mother's acceptance is all we need in life. Your son is ok where he is, ok? Miguel assured her. Elena remained silent and pensive, still sobbing. And then she spoke in a serene voice.

"I am a very liberal person. I believe in the equality of every human being. The rest is MIERDA. I do not know why they should discriminate against my son based on his colour. Why, why, why?"

The three of us were taken aback by this outburst of emotions. Miguel, on whose shoulder she laid her head, acted with impressive equanimity. He tried to calm her and to assure her everything will be fine.

Her outburst affected my mood that night. An evening that began in revelry was ending on a doleful mood. She had never really opened up to me on that topic. She merely told me her son was dark-skinned because his father, her former husband, was of African descent. But she had not really narrated to me the travails and the racism suffered by Ricardo. When the others left, Elena and I simply went into our respective rooms. The following morning, she was quite upbeat, surprisingly. I did not want to make any mention of the night before. She is the one who opened the topic.

"We had a nice time Gil!"

"Oh yes, it was a great night we had. All thanks to you, Elena!"

CHAPTER 37

See You Next Time

29 August 2015

I attended the birthday party of Oswaldo Reynoso's friend. She turned eighty-six. Miguel Cannavaro had promised to create an occasion for me to meet Oswaldo Reynoso, a literary mogul who could tell me much about the literature/history of Peru and also about the rebel movement since he was a lecturer in the University of Ayacucho in those difficult years. In the ensuing hours, we moved from discussions about *Sendero*[1] to different cultures of Africa. The other guests present were: an old investigative journalist who had once interviewed the leader of *Sendero*, Abimael Guzman, in prison; a younger female journalist and her friend, not forgetting the housemaid and another girl in a miniskirt who were silent throughout the party.

After the cutting of the cake to the tunes of "Happy birthday to you" (in English), the housemaid served us a sumptuous meal. It was quite delicious. The celebrant, Clarenda, took the pains to explain the components of the meal before us. Given her age and medical situation, she was almost gasping for breath in the course of speaking. After the meal, we left the dining room for the parlour and were treated to some red wine. Instead of the Africa-meets-Latin America discussions we had before the meal, moving from comparative colonialisms through Che Guevara in the Congo to the Senderos Luminosos of the world, we were now discussing more personal issues in groups of two or three. The female journalist asked me about the nature of insecurity in Cameroon as a result of Boko Haram. It is then I noticed how terrorist attacks in Maroua-Cameroon had affected me in Lima. Weeks before, when I met Reynoso and Miguel in Quirolo, the bar of the "Hora Zero" poets, we had commented that Cameroon was a peaceful country, as compared to

---

1   Shorthand for *Sendero Luminoso, The Shing Path Rebel Movement.*

others that have been recently plunged into civil wars and even chaos like Central African Republic, the Congos, Chad, etc. Miguel knew much about that history. Now, the discourse had changed. News of terrorist attacks in Maroua was reported worldwide. I lost that safe ground, the island of peace was at war, fully at war. I needed other distinctive factors as ways of defining my Cameroon identity.

Miguel brought along the book that he had promised me at our first meeting: *Les Betis du Cameroun*[2]. He said he had bought it thinking he could force himself to read some French. But in the end, he could not make much sense out of it. That notwithstanding, Miguel impressed me with his quest to connect with Africa and particularly with Cameroon. He had astonished me at our first meeting by naming the entire squad of the Cameroonian national team. Being given a book on Cameroon culture by an Afro-Peruvian in Peru was interesting.

I left the birthday party mid-way because I had a presentation on African poetry to some students from San Marcos University. The other participants felt sad that I was left with very few days in Lima.

"You should come back to Peru, my friend", said Oswaldo.

I said I hoped to come back. That did not seem to assure him. He did not let me go.

"Promise me you will come again."

"Yes, I will." It is at this juncture that he allowed me to bid farewell to the others. When I moved onto the celebrant, she held my hand; she was frail, almost shivering. She thanked me for coming and said in a throaty voice:

"See you when you come next time to Lima." She pressed me affectionately against her shoulder.

Miguel accompanied me down the steps and saw me off in the next *cuadra*. I enjoyed the evening with these octogenarians. They left me with the firm belief that I should come back to Peru. Perhaps I will. Perhaps I will not. But I was challenged by Oswaldo and Clarenda's belief in the future: "See you next time when you come back to Lima."

---

2 The Beti people of Cameroon.

CHAPTER 38

The Little Skinny Chola Lady

30 August 2015

I spent the whole day at home. In the evening, I had an interesting chat with Elena about racial complexes amongst the Peruvian middle class. But I only hoped it won't lead her to tears again as during my send-off party. Elena narrated to me an intriguing story.

"We belonged to a social club in Lima. It was created as a keep-fit sports club, but we carried out other activities like excursions, seminars, and even organised parties. It was mostly made up of whites, I mean Peruvian white, you understand."

I nodded. It is like she wanted me to attach a special connotation to "Peruvian white". Then she continued.

"Good. It was not a written rule. There are so many such clubs here in Peru and perhaps in many other countries with race problems. In the club, there was this woman visibly looking like a *chola* but she did everything to dye her hair, packed enough powder on her face, and other gimmicks, just to look white, like a real blonde. And she was always fond of bringing in her family history into every discussion, 'my brother who is in France, my sister in Spain, my cousin in the USA, our Father who is in Heaven, etc etc. But everyone knew all this was a complex. She became a laughingstock amongst some of the cheeky members who referred to her behind her back as la *cholitita flaquitita*."[1] It was always nice listening to Elena. She always gave a specific rendition to her stories, calling a spade a spade, adept at using typically Peruvian argot and never minding to add some tropical spices to make her stories more palatable. Frequently, I would joke with her about the fact that Peruvians were fond of using hyperboles in the same way as every word had a diminutive form, from nouns, adverbs to even verbs, prepositions, conjunctions, etc.: aquicito,

---

1   Roughly, "the little skinny chola lady"

acacito, ahoritita, arribita, diita, mismito, ratito, etc. She and some friends told me it also had to do with the influence of Quechua diminutives marked by the suffix *-chay: mamachay, papachay, wawachay, churichay, ususykicha, etc.*

Tenemos chicharon*cito* de chanch*ito* de Soqos con su pap*ita*, su mote*cito* y su pusp*ito*, mamacita. (*Criba,* Julian Perez Huarancca)[2]

"But tell me, how is it in Germany? As a black, have you ever experienced any discrimination?"

A complex question put in simple terms.

"Well, of course, I have experienced moments that I could qualify as racist. But I always think if you put it so much in your mind, you will lose your focus. But then there is always one moment that leaves its marks on you and sets you wondering who you are, where you belong, etc." I told her part of my story. "I visited Berlin some months ago where I had an appointment with someone at the Technical University of Berlin. Upon descending from the bus near the university campus, I was not sure which specific path to take to the part of the campus where my friend was waiting for me. Unfortunately, his number was not going through at that moment. I don't know why. I met two men sitting on the doorstep of a bungalow. The area looked more like a staff residential quarter. I greeted:

"Good morning." With a stranger's smile on my face. No response.

"Good morning sirs", I repeated, adjusting my smile, but slightly worried by the inattention or indifference of my putative interlocutors. No response. Perhaps, I should pose my problem head-on.

"Is this the road to the science faculty library of the University?"

Well, my voice echoed back at me. I repeated twice. I looked at them steadily, expecting even a gesture indicating they did not know the direction themselves. The writing was on the wall. It was perhaps too much on the wall for me. I could not conceive of people looking straight at me and coldly ignoring my presence. It was like they had sealed the pact of silence before my advent. Even pacts are broken when a human face is standing in front of you, waiting… I left the scene with a scarred conscience and it took me long to forget that scene. In my mind, the question posed by the master in Arguedas' *The Dream of the Serf* took a strident connotation in me: *eres gente o otra cosa? (Are you a human being*

---

2   A restaurant tender to a client: "We have chicharron, made of Soqos pork, with potatoes, corn and beans, young woman."

or something else?)"

"It is painful. And finally, how did you get there?"

"When I moved a step further I saw an old woman weeding grass in the garden in front of her apartment. I greeted her and inquired. She bade me be patient as she cleaned her hands in a nearby basin, came out and greeted me, ready to accompany me some few steps towards the direction I needed to take. I told her the description was clear enough."

"You see, women are always very humane."

Elena interjected, jokingly, provocatively, trying to score a point in our daily arguments on her feminist views. I had told her days before that she wrecked my plans of inviting her to Cameroon because of her predilection for the gizzard of a chicken which in my culture is a part meant for family heads.

"You can say so." I conceded.

"So, when I look back to the clinical rejection by the two men, the brightening face of the woman intercepts my conclusions. I have learned that there is always an *else* in every situation. That is an example with which I can summarise my experience.".

"Let me tell you another story, still about old women. In my home-town in Germany, we do a city tour, two of my colleagues and I. A German, a Ghanaian and a Cameroonian. During one of the tours, I had an interesting experience. The weather was quite fine that morning but when we began the tour at 2 P.M., it suddenly began snowing. It was damn cold. We had about ten guests of different ages and from different parts of Germany. I was explaining the life of a famous Bayreuth author Jean Paul Friedrich Richter and his strong friendship with a Jewish friend, Emmanuel Osmund, at a time when anti-Semitism was en vogue all over Europe. One of the tour participants, an old woman, on seeing me shivering as I narrated the story, she came to me, removed one of her gloves and gave me to wear against the cold. So, I had a glove on the right hand and her on the left. In other words, she and I belonged together, hands in gloves. It gave a different dimension to the tour of that day. In the cold Bavarian winter, I felt the warmth as never before. I remembered Johann Paul Friedrich Richter alias Jean Paul's *Ich und Sie, gehören zusammen, unsere Bekanntschaft ist kurz aber unsere Bekanntschaft ist ewig. (You and I belong together. Our meeting is brief but our relationship is eternal.)*

Elena wanted to learn the expression in German. After two attempts, remembering the German class with the taxi driver who took me from the airport, we came to a mutual understanding to continue the lesson some other time. Seeing that Elena was still willing to listen, I proceeded to the third story. This time, nothing to do with Germany.

"In 2012 my colleague and I were in Santa Ana, California, to carry out an interview with a Kenyan author, Ngugi wa Thiong'o. You remember my talk last last week when I mentioned the author of *No Llores, Pequeño (Weep not, Child)*?"

"Oh yes, the one who wrote the book on the *cuervo (crow)*?"

"Exactly. While in Santa Ana, my colleague and I visited a Christian church. After service, we were invited to a buffet *à l'americain*. As we served ourselves and began eating, I saw one smartly dressed old woman coming from a distance of about ten metres. She was all smiles, in spite of the network of wrinkles on her face. A true manifestation of the joy and peace of Salvation. Close to five metres from us, she tripped and fell on the bare cement floor. I hurried to raise her up. Another lady was standing close by and together we raised the old woman up even though she protested.

"Please don't bother. I just tripped. Nothing serious."

When she was up, with a slightly injured lip, she said to me.

"I was just coming to wish you good appetite and I fell. By the way, how many women have ever fallen for you in your entire life?"

The humour was impeccable and her almost cheeky style had a full impact on my colleague and me. She later confessed to me that she was seventy-eight. I hope she still lives.

"You are quite lucky with old women," Elena said, drawing my attention back to the one hour of fun I spent with her 85-year-old mom in their family home some few days back. Elena's mom looks quite strong for her age. I suffered the old woman laugh out her lungs when I joked about the fact that any name of foodstuffs in Peru has a genealogical explanation. For example, in Peru you cannot fail to have a taste of *Las papitas de Huancaya (Potatoes from Huancayna)*. Peru, they say, is the birthplace of potatoes and there you have tens of potato types.

"We hear very horrible stories from the USA and some of those European countries about the treatment of Latinos too." Elena said.

"Everyone has their story, Elena. And the experiences are mixed; it depends on how you document them in your mind and on how you remember them."

CHAPTER 39

Food for the Wretched

31 August 2015

I had a presentation at the University of San Marcos. I agreed to meet with Prof. Carlos Garcia-Bedoya in front of the statue of Cesar Vallejo, in front of the Faculty of Arts and Letters, 30 minutes before the presentation. Elena and I arrived a few minutes late because of the traffic. We spent some few minutes with Prof. Garcia-Bedoya in the staffroom. The wall of the staffroom was lined with portraits of some of the key Peruvian cultural figures that passed through the Faculty of Letters - Cesar Vallejo, Maria Arguedas, Mario Vargas Llosa and two other figures, and a linguist and a historian, whose names I cannot remember now.

"Most of them passed here as students and only about two as lecturers", Prof. Garcia-Bedoya explained to us. After about 15 minutes in the staff room, he asked us to accompany him to the classroom. It was 2 minutes to 6 A.M. Time for the presentation.

After the presentation, we took the bus back home at the bus stop opposite the university entrance. We had to drop at *Plaza San Miguel* before taking the bus across the road to Javier Prado. As we waited for the bus, one taxi driver, well dressed, came to us:

"Miraflores? Please, come let us go. Moderate fare."

We ignored him. I do not know if we looked like *pitucos*, a black guy and a Peruvian white lady. In our haste, Elena and I did not analyse why that guy thought we could be going to Miraflores.

We entered the bus to Javier Prado. Like most buses at this hour of the evening, it was jammed to capacity and we could hardly breathe. When we alighted, I reminded Elena of her promise to take me to the place where they sell food that in the centuries past was reserved exclusively for the enslaved. She suggested we go straight to the place, not far from our residence. There was a long line of *anticucho* customers. It was a delicacy. These are the intestines and liver of the cow. We bought it, S/17 per plate and shared it at the dining table when we arrived home. I was also amazed at the intricate commercial structure around the *anticucho* mobile restaurant. Lima dwellers are very creative when it comes to market strategies. I have never seen a society where shoe shining is organized on an industrial scale. When I passed at the Arenales Avenue yesterday, I saw a man dressed in suit, a bank official certainly, comfortably seated on what looked like a raised wooden platform with a tarpaulin cover. Coming closer, I discovered there was another man in squatting position, looking like a *serrano*[1] with *chino* (Chinese) eyes, polishing the "banker's" shoes with immense zeal. Forgive me for indexing the shoe shiner as serrano or chino. After spending some time here, you are likely to improve your vocabulary on facial descriptions. When I left Peru, my descriptive skills were highly enhanced for I learned to read the signs of the nose, the hair, the ears, the eyelids, the cheeks, the jawbone and the nostrils.

---

1   Someone from the mountainous region of Peru. It can also be used derogatorily to carry undertones of backwardness.

CHAPTER 40

Genesis in the End

1 September 2015

I was at home all morning, packing my things for departure. In the evening, I met up with Genesis once more at the water park, *Parque de las Aguas.* As we strolled around, all eyes were on us. Genesis confessed to me what I meant for her, something far different from the general image of blacks in her country, Venezuela.

We went to one of the most impressive of the water displays and took a joint selfie, a *dualfie.*

"At least my face has come out clearly on this photo. Not like the other day." I quipped.

We both laughed at the statement. During our first visit to the Park, it was dusk and our attempt at a joint selfie was futile. My face could not appear on the image. The Venezuelan white face smiled alone while I was invisible. She asked me questions about the experience of being black in a majority white society. I told her that as a black in many parts of the world, you always have to answer questions of race, implicitly or overtly. It is so disturbing to the point of becoming interesting. As people observe you, it permits you to cast a profound gaze at the world and to dissect your own human conscience.

As we moved out, we saw a trail of ladies following a young girl dressed in what seemed like a wedding gown.

"Doesn't she look too young for marriage, Genesis?"

"It is not a wedding occasion. It is the fifteenth birthday of the female teenager. It is a common tradition in many Latin American countries for young girls to celebrate their 15th birthday. In some countries, it is the sixteenth birthday. It is the rite of passage unto maturity. It usually ends with a sumptuous party."

"I have never heard of that. I felt like asking 'where is the lucky groom'. It could either be a young boy of her age or a lucky old fellow."

Genesis giggled at my suppositions. She told me the practice is called *el estiron*.

After touring the park, we went down towards the Lima stadium and took dinner in a Colombian restaurant. There was nice music in the background, with quasi-salsa rhythm but slightly different tempo.

"It is very popular Colombian music, with influence too in Venezuela. It is known as *bachata*." Genesis explained to me.

"Yes, I know of bachata, though am not very familiar with its rhythms."

We ordered for a Colombian delicacy, spaghetti with some chopped meat and very tasteful spices. It was very delicious. Given its quantity, we took one plate for two, with some orange juice. It was getting to 8 P.M. and Genesis had to meet up with a friend who was leaving for Cuba the following day. I went up with her to the main road where she got a taxi. It was hard separating. We hugged each other with the mutual promise to meet one day. It did not take me long to get a taxi to *Jirón Soledad*. It was relatively closer than Genesis's quarter in Lima, just S/5 as fare.

Late in the evening, I had a great discussion with Willy Guevara, one of Elena' friends, an anthropologist who specializes in Afro-Peruvian culture. He has done extensive research on Afro-Peruvian communities in Peru and shared immensely with me on the subject of Afro-Peruvian sexuality. Gustavo, Elena's friend, joined in our discussion. He is a college teacher of Afro-Peruvian music culture. When Willy left, we watched several videos of African and Afro-Peruvian music till about midnight. Since I had to travel back home the following day, I had to have enough sleep. I left Elena and Gustavo still conversing in the parlour.

As I went to bed, I was conscious this was my last night in Lima. I began to miss Lima; not only the men and women that I got to know within a relatively short time. I came to miss everything Lima, even Lima's statues. Lima is rich in history and I was greeted by this history everywhere I went through Lima's daffodils of statues. These clay figures represent a history full of twists and turns, transformations, revolutions and counter-revolutions, you could imagine the difficulty of remembering its heroes concretely and coherently on its cityscape. But somehow, as if by a streak of magic, Lima succeeds in turning its surface into a forest of giants like Miguel Gray, Caceres, Manco Capac, Túpac Amaru I, Pizarro, San Martin, Virrey Toledo, Salaverry, Manuel Prado, Pachacutec, Túpac Amaru II, Haya de la Torre, Simon Bolivar facing one another, almost threateningly, at various spots of the city. Not forgetting the Pantheon of Popes, contemporary successors of those holier ones who put their seal on the evangelization of the red Indians. Talking about the more earthen figures whose images flourish in Lima, they represent various forms of government ranging from (benevolent) dictatorship, personalist leadership, oligarchy, caudillismo, kakistocracy and democracy, not to mention the rust that runs through most governments of the world, kleptocracy. These historical icons are placed side by side in ways that some can draw their swords against their neighbours, were they to wake up through some surreal drama in the cold Lima night. But perhaps, that is also a way of remembering a history full of equivocal heroes, worshipped by some and cursed by others with equal fervour. In a way, Mama Lima accepts all her sons. If you are one of those who believe, like the historian A J P Taylor, that history gets thicker as it approaches the present, then you must invent a theory that stretches the hands of Mother Present to embrace 500-year-old sons and daughters. In other words, the history of the Peruvian melting pot was born thick from the very beginning. It has grown thicker with ingredients brought by the Mandinkas, Inkas, Japanese, Chinese, etc. You find the weight of this thickness in Peruvian creative works, in theatrical characters, in historical discourses, in public spaces and last but not the least, in Peruvian blood. *El que no tiene de inga tiene mandinga* (Who is not of Mandinka, is of Inka stock), as Peruvians themselves say.

That night, my last night in Lima, in Peru, I went to bed with a mind saddled with memories of the various encounters I had in this country, but with a heart saddened by the imminent prospects of leaving, this huayno came to my mind almost naturally.

Me voy, me voy
Mañana me voy;
Con esperanza de volver
Si no me muero...
Con la esperanza de volver,
Si no me muero.

(English translation)

I am leaving, I am leaving,
With the hope of coming back,
If I do not die,
With the hope of coming back,

If I do not die.

The piece was played by one of the bus drivers I cannot recall which of my journeys in the Andes. It came to me like one of these songs, usually melancholic that once listened to on whatever occasion, follows us like chameleon faeces and sometimes we find ourselves singing or humming it, almost unconsciously. It need not be the whole song, but a stanza, even a verse that speaks to the innermost core of our being, perhaps finding harmony with some personal and uncanny experience once lived or longed for.

CHAPTER 41

The Weeping Eye

02 September 2015

José Miguel came as early as 9:00 A.M. and we went to visit the Place of Memory, *El Oyo que Llora (The Weeping Eye)* downtown Lima. The curation of remembrance, the arrangement of space, the labyrinth, made of pebbles, each stone representing a life lost, both the perpetrators and the victims; the *Fujimoristas*, supporters of former President Alberto Fujimori, had once attacked the memorial for honouring terrorists. I went through the labyrinth, dreams buried in the stones, each stone being a soul. That stone desired for a better future, that stone had a mother, a father; that stone had children; that stone came into the world for a purpose; that stone desired to live; that stone died in known and unknown circumstances; that soul felt pain, in some cases it was slow, in others, it was a whirlwind. But pain measures time differently. Again I remembered my trip to Dachau, to Auschwitz, to the Holocaust memorial in front of the Bundestag, to Rosenfeld - Flossenbürg (which is a better-known camp). I remembered Ayacucho; I remembered the Gypsies; I remembered the Inquisition; I remembered San José in Chincha, I remembered Soweto, I remembered Namibia 1906. I remembered Rwanda, I remembered, Cameroon, I remembered Kosovo. Before leaving, we came to the pillar at the entrance. It was inscribed with

"Nunca más", "Para que la Paz prevalesca", "Never Again", "Plus jamais", "Mai piu", "manañan hayk'aspas"

After observing the systems of these languages, their renditions of this famous phrase and the therein-embedded nuances, we moved on. Miguel asked me how it would read in Limbum. I could not find an exact equivalent in my language but settled for something similar: "i fa kir koni nong moh kah!" which in English would read like "May

214

this never happen another day again".

I tried to explain to him the meaning of the statement in Limbum and its nuance. We discussed briefly with the rather upbeat watchman/cleaner of the memorial ground. He narrated to us his experience working on that memorial site. He told us that the inscription of the victims' names on the stones required the commitments of thousands of volunteers throughout the country. I took a stone from the outskirts of the hemicycle of stones that constituted the memorial and carefully kept it in my pocket. It was clear to me that in spite of the meticulous investigations by the Truth and Reconciliation Commission and the diligence of those who mounted the memorial, there would still be someone left out. There would still be someone whose name did not appear on the list, on the stones, whose whereabouts were not traced, who did not exist, who lived and died as a nobody. Forgotten.

We then went to the office of CEDET, *El Centro de Desarrollo Etnico (The Centre for Ethnic Development)*. The director gave us insight into his activities and the principles and mission of his organisation. I then bought a few books on Afro-Peruvian literature and culture. Miguel took me to a popular marketplace in downtown Lima known as canal 18. He told me this space became an iconic name in Lima popular culture. Before, it used to be full of pilferers but now it is well regulated. I bought some few films on Peruvian history and politics and we moved to the bus stop where we took the bus home to Lince.

Malambo[1]

Malambo, hearth of my blood, soul of my race,
Weary of weeping for you, for much tears we have shed,
Tears of water and brimstone, in this world of fetishized capital.

Wasteland of the degenerate worshippers of Spirit, Iron and Colour,
Malambo, land of my memories, I prefer to sing praises to your name.

Warehouse of black goods fed like pigs before market day,
Price rises and the slave merchant in pesos smiles
For each criollo and bozale[2], its (un)worth.

Waste pipe inexhaustible of pretty Lady Lima
Malambo, demarcated home of my zambo

When they turned you into abode of leprosy,
We opened our arms, for we are a race of leprosy
When they built a prison for criminals in your bosom,
We shared our chains, for our skin is but a crime from birth.

Malambo, home in foreign fields, you shall forever arise and thrive
The fecundity of your womb and the kindness of your heart shall
bring forth
The Martin de Porres, the José Olaya, and the Alejandro Villanueva of
this world,

---

1   Malambo is the name of a notorious quarter in Peru where enslaved blacks were "stored". Formerly a zone where part of Peru's indigenous population was resettled according to the colonial policy of reduction, it became a slave warehouse, where recently imported Africans were disinfected, fed and then resold to work in various parts of Peru. It was a place of transition.

2   Enslaved blacks in Peru had multiple trajectories. "Second-hand Slaves" (known as criollos) were bought from the enslaved black population in the Carribean while the rest were transported directly from the West African Coast. The latter were known as bozales. Each category had its relative advantages/disadvantages according to the stereotypes attributed to it. This and other dynamics of the slave economy affected the price ranges of each category of enslaved Africans.

Malambo!

From your scattered fields of El Carmen, El Guayabo, El Salvador,
Rimac, La Victoria, Breña, Piura, Tumbes, Lambayeque, Ancash,
Pisco, Ica, Arequipa, Yapatera,
Chiclayo, Saña, Tacna, El Ingenio, Chorillos, Cañete, Caraveli,
Chulucanas, La Lomas, La Tina, Pacaipampa...

Shall rise new Micaela Túpac, Francisco Congo, Gil de Castro, Ri-
cardo Palma, Manuel Valdés, Alberto Medina, Pancho Fierro,
Nicomedes Santa Cruz, Lucha Fuentes,
Caitro Soto, Victoria Santa Cruz, Amador Ballumbrosio,
Maria Elena, Mauro Baylón, Cheche Campos,
Jefferson Farfan,

Mamainé, Eva Ayllón, Susanna Baca...

Gil Ndi-Shang

CHAPTER 42

Don't Cry for me, Peru

We arrived back home at close to 3:30 P.M. Miguel decided to accompany me right to the airport. As he settled down in the parlour, I began clearing my room for departure. Someone rang the bell downstairs. I was not very sure who that was. I hurried down the staircase and to my surprise, it was Milli. She is an airport taxi driver and was the person to drive me to the airport.

"Welcome, Milli."

"Gil, so finally you are leaving us." Her voice sounded mournful.

"Yes, Milli, the time has finally come for me to go back home. But I will be back soon."

"You must come back! Elena told me that the trip to the airport is at 4:30 P.M., right?"

"Oh, Elena. She surely knew that you are Peruvian. And sometimes you have to play tricks to make people punctual."

"Hahaha. She does not know that I am Germano-Cameroonian too when it comes to the question of time."

We laughed as I led her upstairs. After introducing them to one another, I left Milli and José Miguel in the parlour as I went into my room to put my things together before taking my final bath. Elena came in just as we were about to leave. I was a bit worried that she had not arrived yet. I could not imagine leaving Peru without saying a special goodbye to her. She was everything to me in Lima. My landlady, my friend, my fellow sojourner, my comic partner, my camerawoman, my research assistant, etc. etc. She was a woman passionate about issues of human freedom and equality. Our sporadic arguments on her atheism and strong feminist beliefs made me admire her the more, even while remaining firm in my own convictions. I had not thought that Elena would want to come to the airport with me but she was rather enthusiastic about it. The four of us entered Milli's Toyota Corolla. Elena' daughter Naomi also wanted to come but for the constraint of space. I hugged her and promised to keep in touch on Facebook. I remembered a similar scene during my last trip to Cameroon. Due to lack of space in the car, we had to beg some close relatives to stay back. I remember the downcast face of my junior brother Etienne and his friend Mathias, casualties of the limited space in the car. Departing is not always an easy thing, especially where there is a strong family bond between the leaving and those left behind. Miguel took the front seat with the driver while Elena and I sat behind. As we drove, we kept joking about comic moments spent together. In spite of the most distressing occasions, my time in Peru was full of fun and laughter. I joked at some of what I noted as Peruvian buzzwords and catchphrases. When food is delicious, they say "Qué rico!" (What a rich meal!). Elena would say this at the beginning or the end of any meal we shared. For her, all the meals were rich in quality! In another dimension, I was leaving the land of superlative "issimo" (Peru) to that of tempered "more or less" (Germany).

At some point, Elena kept silent for a couple of minutes. She was writing something inside a book. On finishing, she handed the book to me:

"Gil, this is for you."

It was a book by José Maria Arguedas, *Nosotros Los Maestros (We, the Teachers)*. She had written a beautiful text as a dedication to me. I hugged her, full of gratitude.

"Thank you very much, Elena, for this wonderful book. More so, you did not only rent me a room, you gave me a home."

She put on a smile, a constant feature of her face. I recalled her dancing skills, the feminist debates we usually had at the dining table, I recalled her weeping like a child on Miguel's shoulders during my send-off party.

When we reached the airport, there was a long queue in the main hall. I entered with my luggage on a trolley. Since only the passengers were allowed to enter, José Miguel, Milli and Elena waited outside. The queue seemed to be still. I needed much patience. I stood there, reflecting, regretting that I was leaving Lima. Lima, this Pacific Leviathan, clay moulded by the hands of Spanish Conquistador, Francisco Pizarro, in 1535. Lima which once ruled like Rome over the entire Kingdom of New Spain. Lima, a city in constant re-making, a vast construction site with architectures of soaring heights. Lima, a re-construction site: a vast archaeological space with hordes of archaeologists constantly scavenging for remnants of pre-Inca cultures, with its entrails reaped open in an Inca post-mortem gesture. Lima, post-modern and post-mortem. With the same zeal that architects scrape the Pacific coast with impressive edifices, so do the doctors of the earth rip the crust of Lima for signs of the past. Sometimes, these archaeological craters are quite close to popular and modern junctions. These spaces intersect with one another. Lima, the city where tradition meets modernity, sometimes in a harmonious marriage, but at other times in an awkward amalgam of signs and symbols pointing to different and seemingly irreconcilable directions. Sometimes, the tradition gets massaged for touristic purpose; sometimes it is at the very core of popular customs and mores. You cannot ignore the sombrero, the poncho, the saya!!

One old man came close to the queue around where I stood. He was certainly in his late seventies. He asked me if the queue was for Air France passengers.

"Yes sir, it is."

"Ok, thank you."

Metres behind me, he located the persons he was looking for: a lady and what seemed to be her daughter. Soon he led them off and space was created for those immediately behind to fill up. Two men, directly behind me smiled reciprocally. One asked the other:

"How much is he asking for?"

"I do not know, I think it should be …" He raised four fingers. Certainly meaning S/4. I sensed something fishy. I was curious to know and decided to probe.

"Is the old man a worker here? I asked, inquisitively though he did not wear any uniform.

"He is taking money to secure a rapid check-in for customers."

"Really? He seems too old to be moving around at this time doing this kind of thing!" I exclaimed, almost with an air of naiveté.

"This is Peru." One of them responded.

The syntax is brief, laconic. Some weeks ago, on my way back from San Marcos University, our bus was caught in heavy traffic. To the anger of the impatient passengers, our bus conductor reversed, allowing a taxi driver to cross in front of our bus. Unfortunately, the driver on the next lane was not as generous. So, the taxi got stuck in front of us. The taxi could neither proceed nor reverse. Real quagmire. Meanwhile, the vehicles ahead began to move thanks to a slight de-congestion. My fellow passengers were bitter at our "Good Samaritan" bus conductor. A sharp female voice came from the back seat. *De que pais viene este conductor?*

(From which country is this bus conductor?) Serene, soft-spoken, relaxed and idiolectal. The voice came from behind but I strained in vain to identify the utterer. Amid anger, this statement caused a wave of laughter, a general détente amongst the passengers. I have met very few such affective and potent rhetorical questions. I did not think in other parts of the world there were equivalents of expressions like *C'est le Cameroun, Le Cameroun c'est le Cameroun, l'impossible n'est pas camerounais.*[1] Or the subtle and clinical German expression which I learned about not long before "Vitamine B hilft".[2] Generally, when Peruvians talk to me about corruption, I sometimes think their superlative expressions only sum up into understatements. I always think that their embezzlers are too patriotic. I have had the same feeling when talking with some Nigerian friends. Until one of them, noticing my sense of indifference went an extra mile to draw the distinctive zeros on the ground to stress his point. "I mean ten, hundred, thousand, hundred thousand, million, billion Nairas!! Just imagine my friend. Swindled by one minister, a single minister!" Of course, I then understood what he meant.

Meanwhile, I asked the two men a question that had been on my mind for some months.

"Why is the airport called Aeropuerto Jorge Chavez? Who was this guy?"

"I do not know, perhaps Victor has an idea." Said the one standing directly behind me, looking at his friend. The latter intervened.

"Jorge Chavez was a Peruvian pilot who died crossing the Alps. He was the first pilot to cross the Alps on an aircraft and he died in the attempt."

"In what year was that?" I probed further.

"I do not know exactly, but I think around 1910."

"I see. That is quite interesting." I said, showing appreciation for the explanation. I thought of the reverse adventures of the French aviator and novelist Antoine de Saint Exupéry and his maiden flights in the

---

1   "It is Cameroon." "Cameroon is Cameroon". "Nothing is impossible in Cameroon". These statements have become buzzwords in Cameroon popular culture, underlining the fact that no rules are too strong to be bent or broken nor any task too tough to be accomplished. These popular expressions underline an ambiguous "acceptance" of the corruption in the country.

2   "Vitamin B is helpful." B here means *Beziehung* – Relationship. This entails that one's connections are generally to help them even in formal situations, of course with limits.

Andes and Cordilleras, captured in *Terre des Hommes*[3] and *Vol de Nuit*[4].
Saint-Exupery, Mermoz, Guillaumet, Rivière and Fabien were pioneers
who, through their flights over the Andes and Cordilleras, transmitted
lessons of hope and courage. Man-made machines are only valuable
when they are used to enhance human relationship.

> *La grandeur d'un métier est peut-être, avant tout, d'unir les hommes: il*
> *n'est qu'un luxe véritable, et c'est celui des relations humaines. (Terre des*
> *Hommes).*[5]

Some minutes passed and the queue extended even more. The old
man who accompanied the woman and her daughter approached our
position again. He craned his neck around strenuously as if looking for
someone he could not see. But, there was always joy in the looking. The
guy who responded to my curiosity concerning airport name moved
towards the old man after briefly consulting with his companion through
eye contacts. Not before long, the two followed him, with one of them
waving me a cosy "*Adios amiguito!*" (Goodbye my dear friend). It sounded
both like a farewell amongst friends and mockery for the beautiful ones,
those patient ones who had to endure time in a fast society.

The queue snailed and snailed, but we finally reached the entrance
to the check-in desk. The controller, a lady, took my passport, some few
meters away from the check-in desk.

"I have to make a photocopy of this, ok?"

"No problem, madam," I responded.

I overheard one lady behind me, murmuring to her friend, wondering why she needed a photocopy of my passport. Perhaps she feared she
might undergo the same scrutiny.

"Certainly, he is not from Peru." opined the lady next to her.

"That is not true, I am from Peru." I intervened forcefully, to their
surprise. They smiled back. The female controller betrayed my intrigue.
Speaking this time in Spanish, she said:

"He is from Africa! But he speaks Spanish." She said looking
surprised.

---

3   Literally, Land of Men or Land of People, but translated into English as *Wind, Sand and People*.
4   *Night Flight.*
5   The greatness of any profession is, perhaps, above all, its ability to unite people: it is nothing but a real luxury, that of human relations. (*Wind, Stars and People*)

Even before taking my passport, she had intuitively assumed that I was not Spanish speaking. Our conversation was in English. When she heard me respond to the ladies in Spanish, she then switched to Spanish.

"Of course, we also speak Spanish in Africa."

"I have hardly met Spanish-speaking Africans. Apart from some few persons from Equatorial Guinea."

"Here I am."

They all laughed. Then, the colleague who had taken my passport for the photocopy brought it back to me. My turn came to proceed to the check-in desk. I went through the necessary modalities. I was supposed to pay for my second luggage, full of books that I had bought and those that were offered to me as gifts by Peruvian authors and friends. At first, the lady at the counter calculated the cost of the second luggage on her calculator. But as she was about showing the sum to me, her male colleague, seemingly her boss, asked her to register the two pieces of luggage without any extra payment. I was quite elated. I was already prepared to pay for the second luggage. Sometimes, one wakes up on a good foot, even for the airport.

When I moved out of the check-in compartment into the transit room leading up to the rolling staircase, I found José Miguel waiting for me. Miguel is an amazing guy. He showed me patience and concern at every stage of my stay in Peru.

"Elena and Milli had to go because Milli was afraid of the evening traffic." He said.

"I see, I think that was quite a wise decision. Elena sent me a text message to wish me a safe trip. Since the queue was moving too slowly. I almost called you to suggest you should not bother to wait for me. I know the traffic situation in Lima."

"No problem, my friend. I was following your movement in the hall through the window glass.

"Oh really? The glasses are made in such a way that it is easier to see someone from outside-in than inside-out. I strained my eyes but just could not see you. At some point, I was convinced you had left."

"Oh no, I could not do that!" He said, tapping me on the back.

José Miguel accompanied me upstairs. He suggested I eat something before leaving, but the boarding time was too close, 9 P.M. according to my boarding pass.

It was hard saying goodbye to José Miguel. I had intended to refund him S/20, the amount he spent on the meal and the bus tickets earlier in the day. Most of the times we went out for lunch, he was very steadfast in paying the bills while I was still scampering through my pocket for the banknotes. On a few occasions, I pre-empted his move and paid the bills, usually to his protest. Such friends are rare to find.

After a second thought, I changed my mind. That was not the right moment to do that. Giving back S/20 would be like compensating him for what he had spent for me and his goodness.

"I lack words to say thank you, José Miguel." We embraced each other affectionately.

"If there is anything you would want me to do for you while in Germany, please do not fail to let me know."

"For sure, just knowledge, my brother. Beginning with the list of some of the key African novels in Spanish that you promised me yesterday."

"Be very sure I will send the list to you."

"Do you still remember our Cameroonian way of separating?"

"*Estamos juntos.*"

"Good, but not in Spanish!"

"Miguel struggled to say it in French. I came to his rescue."

"In Limbum. 'So ku ba abi', In French 'On est ensemble' and English 'We are together'.

So ku ba abi. He struggled to respond as we parted ways.

I went through the security check right down to the passport control point. When my turn came, I stepped forth and handed in my passport to the control officer. She examined it and after scanning through the pages, took out the white flyer I just finished filling in. Shaking her head, she asked me.

"Where is the flyer you filled in the plane just before landing on Peruvian soil?"

"It is in my main luggage. Nobody told me that it would be required on my return trip."

"What I need is the original one you filled upon arrival. Not this one. In that case, you will surely have to pay," she said, in a rather lethargic tone. "Go to the next desk and talk with the officer there."

In this country too, "talking with" seemed to be very key, I thought. I moved to the lady at the cashier's desk. She was counting money and asked me to wait for a while. It was transition time and she had to put the accounts straight before handing over to the lady on night duty. After close to two minutes, she asked me to move to the next cabin. Its occupant had also just arrived for the night shift. She finished installing her accessories. I submitted my passport, boarding pass and the newly filled flyer.

"You are supposed to submit the one you filled when you arrived at the country. Since you do not have it, you have to pay." She said.

I explained to her that no one informed me about the necessity to retain the original flyer for my return trip. I told her I did not have money to pay for anything even though she had not even told me the amount I was supposed to pay. After some minutes of hesitation, she kindly ushered me to pass on, wishing me farewell, after having indicated to me the boarding gate.

I moved down the aisle and stood on the line for boarding. It was gate 15. Not before long, I moved down the transit corridor to the aircraft. Stepping on that corridor of inter-territoriality was synonymous to converting my Peruvian experience into memory. That corridor was a (non)space of transition, leaving the judicial space of Peru and stepping onto a series of territorial limbos before arriving Germany. Perhaps I was going to come back. Perhaps I would never come back, in spite of the promises. But the bridge was crossed, a family was built, a part of my dreams was fulfilled. Peru was part of me. I was part of Peru. I shared in some of its cultural codes, gestures, identities, ways of being, etc.

I began to conjecture the implications of travelling on human relationships. When we are in the air, our identities are also in the air, mixing freely, sharing common spaces with neighbours never known before, feeling their breath in ours. Some fellow passengers do not sleep on their backrest; they sleep in the arms or lean their heads on the shoulders of the ones next to them, right and left. If by some mishap, the plane crashes, the whales of the Pacific/Atlantic won't determine between white, black, Arab, Indio, Criollo, Jew, Aryan, Gypsy, Yanki, Hutu, Tutsi, Mestiza, Mulato, Zambo, Morisco, Moreno, Chino, Cholo, Rechino criollo, Torna Atras, Tente en el Aire, Salta Patras, Terceron, Quinteron, cambujo[6], etc. They won't understand our pleas for mercy, be they in Limbum, French, Spanish, English, Chinese, German, Aymara, Quechua, etc. etc. They would certainly relish the savour of flesh, the human flesh, the human meat. For a journey of twelve hours, everything that separates us reveals to us our oneness, but also our fragility.

---

6   The various nomenclatures that were attributed to subjects under the Spanish empire in Latin America depending on their racial composition and thus, their degree of "humanity". It is a difficult task of translation to find English equivalents of these terms.

On chemine longtemps côte à côte, enfermé dans son propre silence, ou bien l'on échange des mots qui ne transportent rien. Mais voici l'heure du danger. Alors on s'epaule l'un à l'autre. On decouvre qu'on appartient à la même communauté. On s'elargit par la découverte d'autres consciences. On se regarde avec un grand sourire. On est semblable à ce prisonier delivré qui s'emerveille de l'immensité de la mer.

(English translation)

Men travel side by side for years, each locked up in his own silence or exchanging those words which carry no freight–til danger comes. Then they stand shoulder to shoulder. They discover that they all belong to the same family. They wax in the discovery of their fellow beings. They look at one another and smile. They are like the prisoner set free who marvels at the immensity of the sea. (Antoine de Saint-Exupéry. Wind, Sand and Stars.)

Few metres before stepping on the aircraft, I found a newspaper stand on the left-hand side of the corridor. It is meant as a pastime for passengers. I looked through to see which ones to take as a pastime in the plane. Helas, not *El Comercio, La Republica, La Nación,* etc. Rather, *Le Figaro, Le Diplomate, Le Parisien, Le Monde,* etc. etc.

« Bonsoir et bienvenus à bord. » [7]

«Merci.»

The flight attendant looked at my boarding pass and, in French, indicated the corridor to my seat. I moved to seat 12D. I sat near a French couple to my right and a Spanish guy to my left. Twelve hours of continuous flight lay ahead of us. The captain welcomed us on board. A few minutes later, he apologized for the delay. We finally took off at 10:27 P.M., instead of 9:20 P.M. I folded my computer as requested by the flight instructions during take-off. After that, I chose to select music from the menu on my front screen. I stumbled on a concert by Dolly Parton, one of my favourite country music artists. She took me down memory lane with "Jolene", "Coat of Many colours", "Love is like a butterfly", etc. After this, I could not find any album that suited my taste. I turned on my laptop to search for African music and it was thanks to

---

7   "Good evening and welcome on board"
     "Thank you"

the rhythms of Richard Bona, Ismael Lo, Youssou Ndour and Lokua Kanza that the long transatlantic flight was rendered incredibly shorter.

Hours into the journey, I decided to peruse Alistair Cooke's *Letter from America*. My fingers again fell on the page where he talks about late 19th and early 20th-century European immigrants in the US. Unlike the Mayflower, their immigration experiences in the US presented a drama of a different nature. Some parts of Europe were plagued by poverty, hunger, wars and America was a distant land of milk and honey. Thus, the Fortune Ships that left the shores of Europe for the US contained all categories and calibres of dreamers. Some had received letters from their long-gone fiancés with testimonies of how the streets of New York and Philadelphia were paved with gold. But as it were, many of the female voyagers ended up not meeting their knight in shining armour. In a journey that took several months, they could not avoid the advances of some male fellow sojourners for long. Consequently, many got pregnant on the way and upon arrival, preferred to avoid those who had paid for their trip in the first place. Stepping foot on Ellis Island was not yet Uhuru. After an intrusive examination, some of the huddled masses were sent back to Europe on the basis of infectious diseases, fishy documents, lies as well as lice. The lucky ones entered the territory of New York with the European legal tender short-changed into US dollars by adept money dealers and with the names terribly misspelt by the customs officers. But the joy of entry was so overwhelming that they did not even realize the misspellings. This accounts for the many queer names one finds amongst the US' European immigrants today. That is how Frederick Drumpf entered New York and became Frederick Trumpf, the grandfather of Donald Trump. Many arrived in New York to discover that the streets were not only not paved with gold, but that they were not paved at all and they were expected to pave them.

For the European immigrant, the idea of return, of being sent back to the Old Continent was a nightmarish and awful eventuality. But as you would recall, this option would have sounded like an epiphany for those who came through the slave ship. In other words, it appeared as a somewhat redemptive eventuality when seen through other eyes, other times, other skins. As the ship cast sail on the shores of Luanda, Porto Novo, Port Harcourt, Badagry or Accra, they faced the Atlantic with their bodies, their spirits, their hearts. Their names were lost for good and a new name, the merchant's, was engraved and barbed into the body and mind of the commodity. Their previous life was meant to be a blank slate and no tears of separation could afford redemption. No strand of hair of a beloved one to serve as a reminder at the time of separation. No piece of cloth to hang onto, in remembrance. Perhaps, just a song in their bosom, a song hummed almost unconsciously as they looked unto the grey horizon. If by some chance it braved the Atlantic storms, the commodity could be shipped to the Caribbeans and after a series of transactions, end up in Cartagena de Indias, Rio de la Plata, Tambo de Mora, Malambo or some other processing, labelling and packaging point on the Atlantic or Pacific. If you, the enslaved African were unlucky enough to board ships such as *Le Rodeur, Salamander, Leusden, Saõ José* and many others, it meant that you would end up shipwrecked, deposited on the seabed amongst the corals of the Atlantic, forgotten for good. Otherwise, you could also be thrown into the sea by some nimble slave merchant trying to avoid customs duties or being captured by the British West African Squadron. Thus, any drop of the Atlantic and the Pacific will always be a specimen of memory, for it is mixed with the blood of the flotsam and jetsam of the earth.

For you the *fortunate* ones, the new destination was your new home, your new horizon, your new future. These thoughts reminded me of a book I had bought weeks before in a Lima bookshop. It was an anthology by a Colombian author on people of African ancestry who played important roles in political processes throughout the world. After the sections bearing names of Latin American heroes/heroines like Manuel Piar, Leonardo Infante, Prudencio Padilla, Micaela Túpac, José Olaya, Nicomedes Santa Cruz, etc., the author labelled another slot as "Diaspora" which contained figures like Kofi Annan, Leopold Sedar Senghor, Nelson Mandela, Patrice Lumumba, Amilcar Cabral, etc. I was intrigued by that apparent inversion of the positions of mainland Africa and African Diaspora. Nevertheless, it was true to me that travelling to Peru, to El Carmen, to Tambo de Mora, was a homecoming for me. For the Africans in the New World, their route became their home and they claimed it wholeheartedly.

THE END

Epilogue

I landed at the Frankfurt airport at 4 P.M the following day, on a connecting flight from Paris. I was left only with a S/20 banknote in my pocket, a little less than €5. I should have given it to Miguel, but I did not. Not out of greed but out of respect. I know I am indebted to him and many friends in Peru. S/20. No gold, no silver. I did not visit any mines, but I came back rich in heart and mind, confident that another journey, a new journey, a new exchange, was possible between continents, that a new bridge on the oceans was possible, that it was not only a possibility but an obligation. Perhaps, I will return. Perhaps not, I cannot say with certainty. But I wish to go back again. To behold once more the face of the Andean kid, Juan Sabastian de Salvador with his meek lamb and present myself to him again; to tell a grown-up Mya Zuleyka Olivero Rivadeneyra that "you are African" and see how she will react; to meet the 85-year-old Oswaldo Reynoso[1] and 86-year-old birthday celebrant Pamela Clarenda, to fulfil the promise of "coming back again"; to listen to more huayno from Ayacucho and perhaps to dance the tap-dance of El Carmen with more dexterity. I need to take part in a new cartography of the Pacific and the Atlantic: to travel along the triangle from a different angle.

---

1   On 24 May 2016, I visited a Peruvian friend in his home in Berlin where I was doing library research in the Ibero-American Institute. Just as I stepped into his living room, he said to me: "We have lost one of our country's greatest living writers today. It is so sad" "What is his name?" I probed.
"Oswaldo Reynoso." His answer fell like an axe in the deep-frozen sea of my heart.

About the Author

G il Ndi-Shang (Romance Literatures/Comparative Studies, University of Bayreuth) holds a PhD in Comparative Literature from the Bayreuth International Graduate School of African Studies (BIGSAS). He is a member of the Young Colleague Programme, Bavarian Academy of Sciences (Munich-Germany). In the recent past, he has been Research Fellow with the Fritz-Thyssen Foundation and the Alexander von Humboldt Foundation for his literary research in Congo, Peru and Colombia. He hails from the North-West region of Cameroon where he grew up before moving to Yaoundé and Bayreuth (Germany) for his university education. He is the author of *State/society: Narrating Transformations in African Novels* and co-editor of *Tracks and Traces of Violence* and *Re-writing Pasts, Imagining Futures*. He is also a contributing co-editor of the poetry volume *Emerging Voices: Anthology of Young Anglophone Cameroon Poets*.